EDITOR: WALTER A. LI

Ars Picturae

NUMBER ONE

LUDOLF DE JONGH

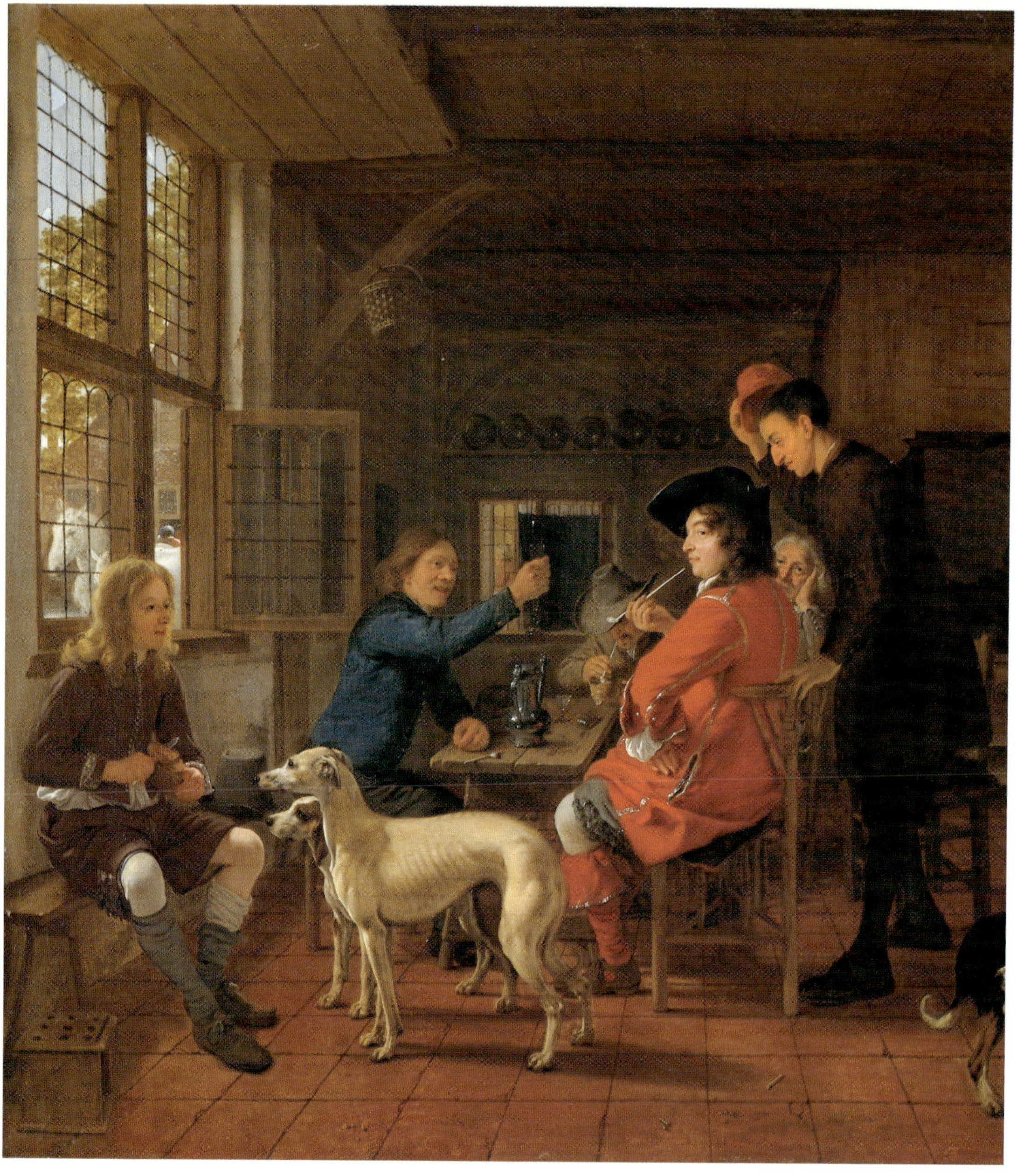

Frontispiece , Detail of Colour Plate II

ROLAND E. FLEISCHER

LUDOLF DE JONGH (1616-1679)

PAINTER OF ROTTERDAM

DAVACO

DAVACO PUBLISHERS

BEUKENLAAN 3
8085 RK DOORNSPIJK
THE NETHERLANDS

This edition is strictly limited to 600 copies

ISBN 90 70288 53 2

Printed by Giethoorn, Meppel

To Alice,

Ted and Rick

CONTENTS

FOREWORD

The present book is intended as the first in a series devoted to the "Great Minor Masters" of Dutch and Flemish art. This working title, by which the project has long been known, counts among its few virtues the suggestion of a dilemma facing scholars, *amateurs*, and others - not least, publishers - interested in the art of the Netherlands. Full-scale monographs with catalogue raisonnés cannot be expected for every artist one encounters in the galleries of Antwerp and Amsterdam, and yet dozens of painters - Gerrit Berckheyde, Pieter Claesz, and Frans Snyders, to name a few - deserve more attention than the articles (some long outdated) and scattered reproductions by which they have been represented until now.

Books in the *Ars Picturae* series will offer brief but scholarly surveys of an artist's life and work, discussions of the most salient iconographic issues, and, when appropriate, comments on patronage, social context, and the painter's reputation in his own and later times. A generous number of reproductions, having been selected with a critical eye, should make each of these volumes a valuable reference work, even for readers who, like the authors, have pored over photographs in the archives at The Hague, London, Antwerp and New York.

The role of series editor has been passed on to me by Otto Naumann, who is the true editor of the present book, and who gave great amounts of time and thought to the conception of this project and contact with contributors. The conviction that Dr. Naumann, an early Davaco alumnus, has envisioned an essential service to the study of Dutch and Flemish art enhances my gratitude to him and sense of obligation to the publisher.

Walter A. Liedtke
Metropolitan Museum of Art
New York

ACKNOWLEDGMENTS

No work of this kind is the product of a single individual. The support and resources of institutions and the generosity, knowledge, and talents of many individuals too numerous to name, have made this study possible. I should like to express my appreciation to the College of Arts and Architecture and the Institute for Arts and Humanistic Studies at the Pennsylvania State University and to the National Endowment for the Humanities for their support. While it is not possible to thank all those institutions in Europe and America that have generously made their resources available to me, I would like to pay special tribute to the staffs of the Rijksbureau voor Kunsthistorische Documentatie, the Algemeene Rijksarchief, and the Iconographisch Bureau in The Hague; the Gemeentelijke Archiefdienst, the Museum Boymans van Beuningen, and the Historisch Museum in Rotterdam; the Kunsthistorisch Instituut der Universiteit van Amsterdam; the Frans Halsmuseum in Haarlem; the Witt Library of the Courtauld Institute of Art in London; the Frick Art Reference Library in New York; and the Pattee Library of the Pennsylvania State University.

Among the many individuals who generously aided me in a variety of ways, I would like to thank especially Eugenio Battisti, Margie Christian, Rudolf E. O. Ekkart, Suzanne Heiland, Kahren Hellerstedt, Guido Jansen, Marijke C. de Kinkelder, Gerbrand Kotting, To van der Lee, Sheree Lissoos, Hessel Miedema, Joop Nieuwstraten, J. C. Okkema, Homan Potterton, Peter Schatborn, Frits Scholten, Richard Shoemaker, Peter Sutton, Willem van der Watering, Maarten Wurfbain, E. J. Zetteler, and my colleagues at Penn State: Anthony Cutler, Charles Mann, George Mauner, Inge Miller, and Jeanne Chenault Porter. I am also deeply indebted to Otto Naumann and Walter Liedtke for their careful editing of the manuscript and their many helpful suggestions.

Finally, I owe a very special debt of thanks to Stephen Reiss, whose extensive knowledge, fertility of mind, unending encouragement, and boundless generosity were both an invaluable resource and a source of inspiration for me through most of the stages of this study.

INTRODUCTION

Ludolf de Jongh was born in Overschie, near Rotterdam, in 1616, the eldest son of Leendert Leendertsz. de Jongh and Annetgen Leuven, forms of whose names were retained by Ludolf, who occasionally appears in official records as Leuff Leendertsz. de Jongh. The elder De Jongh, as Houbraken tells us, was a tanner and shoemaker, a fact verified by documentation.[1] Later, in 1647, his occupation was listed as inn keeper (herbergier).[2] The De Jongh family was, however, one of means, for in their will we find that Leendert and Annetgen were able to provide handsomely for their six children, leaving to them a number of houses as well as considerable amounts of cash.[3]

In his manner of sometimes embellishing — if not completely fabricating — his stories, Houbraken tells us that young Ludolf, trained by his father to follow in his trade as a tanner and shoemaker, was treated so harshly when his work was less than satisfactory to the elder De Jongh — even to the point of being beaten with a strap — that he determined to seek his career in another field. And so, we read, young Ludolf turned his attention to painting, and when the family moved to Rotterdam, Leendert accepted his son's inclinations and apprenticed him to Cornelis Saftleven, a talented painter and etcher of landscapes, fantasies, religious subjects, and scenes of low life genre. Although Houbraken does not indicate when De Jongh's formal training in the arts began, we can assume it was approximately 1628-1630, when he was in his early- to mid-teens and Saftleven in his early twenties. After an indetermi-

1. According to Houbraken 1718-21, vol. 2, p. 26, De Jongh was born in Overschie, the son of a shoemaker and tanner. However, Haverkorn van Rijsewijk 1896, pp. 36-37, raised doubts about both his place of birth and the occupation of his father. But the occupation of the elder De Jongh is confirmed, and Overschie as Ludolf's place of birth becomes a probability through Rotterdam archival records that support Houbraken. See Nicolaas van der Hagen, notary, 103/345a, protocol IV, which indicates the elder De Jongh was a shoemaker in Overschie in 1623. Unfortunately the pertinent baptismal records for the area do not go back to 1616, making it impossible to determine its accuracy as the year of Ludolf's birth cited by Houbraken. There is no evidence, however, to suggest that 1616 is not correct.

2. Haverkorn van Rijsewijk 1896, p. 37.

3. G. van der Hout, notary, 308/223a, 24 October 1646.

nate period of study in Rotterdam,[4] De Jongh moved to Delft to study with Anthonie Palamedesz., a painter of portraits, landscapes, elegantly clad merry companies in interiors, and scenes of soldiers quartered in barns where they gamble, drink, or listen to the pleas for mercy from the local citizenry. De Jongh, disappointed with the lack of attention he received from Palamedesz., moved on to Utrecht, where he entered the studio of Jan van Bylert. Bylert was one of the Utrecht Caravaggisti, painters who displayed in their large sculptural forms, strongly modelled with contrasts of light and dark, the influence of Caravaggio and his followers in Rome. Bylert had sojourned for several years in the Eternal City following his study under Abraham Bloemaert and had returned to Utrecht in the mid 1620s. Under Bylert, we are told, Ludolf made such rapid progress that when he returned home in 1635 he felt secure enough in his art to leave almost at once on an extended trip to France in the company of a certain nineteen year-old Frans Bacon.[5] It must be pointed out, however, that in spite of Houbraken's account, the development of De Jongh's art leaves open the possibility that his contact with Bylert may have come after rather than before his sojourn in France, for, as we shall see, the works he produced following his return from France are still strongly under the spell of Palamedesz., while it is nearer mid-century before his Utrecht experience is clearly evident.

Although he remained in France seven years, none of his works from this period is known to exist. Neither can we say for certain just where in France he lived, nor what kinds of paintings he produced. It seems likely, however, that during a sojourn of seven years he would have spent at least part of the time in Paris and that the stay would not have lasted so long had he not met with some success. Although no evidence is known to support his statement, Weyerman, writing nearly a century later, is probably correct in telling us that De Jongh's seven years in France were spent in Paris.[6] And indeed the most likely field in which a young painter would seek financial reward was in the painting of portraits.

Houbraken tells us that De Jongh's stay in France came to an end when he was summoned home because of the illness of his mother, a statement supported by his parents' will of July 4, 1643, in which his mother is described as

4. Perhaps De Jongh stayed with Saftleven until the latter's trip to Antwerp around 1632. For the fullest treatment of Cornelis Saftleven see Schulz 1978.

5. Although no known records verify Houbraken's statement that De Jongh went to France after returning to Rotterdam in 1635, a notarial record does place him in Rotterdam on October 11th of that year. See Gerrit van der Hout, notary, 288/18, protocol XXI.

6. Weyerman 1729-69, vol. 2, p. 140.

"lying sick in bed" ("sieck te bedde leggende").[7] That her illness was a long one, as Weyerman states, is confirmed by a second will, dated October 24, 1646, in which she is still described as being sick in bed.[8] She died in February of the following year, and, on the request of his father, Ludolf was named co-guardian of his younger brother, Leendert, and his three younger sisters, Ingetje, Barbara, and Maria, all of whom were still minors.[9] Another sister, Teuntge, was married to Isaak Sheppard.

On February 4, 1646, a year before the death of his mother, Ludolf married Adriana Pieters Montange of Schoonhoven,[10] whose sister Gertrui was the wife of the animal and landscape painter, Dirck Wyntrack. Houbraken tells us that the bride's father, Pieter Montagne (or Montange or Montanus) had several friends in the administrations of Rotterdam and Schoonhoven and suggests that his influence was helpful in Ludolf's later appointment in the city militia. His name, however, is not prominent in archival records,[11] and it seems likely that a painter of portraits as skillful as De Jongh who, moreover, had returned from seven years in France with a fluent command of the language,[12] would have had little difficulty making important contacts on his own and commanding respect from the patrician class of Rotterdam.

That he was a responsible and respected citizen of Rotterdam cannot be doubted. In 1651 his brother-in-law, Dirck Wyntrack, who was then living in Gouda, authorized Ludolf to collect payment for paintings Wyntrack had delivered to a dealer, and three years later Ludolf was empowered to collect for Willem Govertsz. Sinjoor, the husband of his sister Maria, the inheritance he had recently received.[13] In October 1657 Ludolf and his two brothers-in-

7. Gerrit van der Hout, notary, 271/47, protocol IV. Haverkorn van Rijsewijk 1896, p. 37, cast doubt on the accuracy of Houbraken's statement that Ludolf was summoned home in the early 1640s because of the illness of his mother at that time, but was apparently unaware of the existence of this earlier will confirming her poor health.

8. Gerrit van der Hout, notary, 308/223a, 24 October 1646.

9. Haverkorn van Rijsewijk 1896, p. 39.

10. Algemeene Rijksarchief, The Hague; Collectie Doopboeken: Schoonhoven 11 (Gerecht, Trouwboek, 1590-1794), p. 16. Earlier reference to the archival record of the marriage was made by Helbers 1955, p. 118, where the date is mistakenly given as the 6th rather than the 4th of February. The earlier date of January 28 given by Haverkorn van Rijsewijk 1896, as Helbers indicates, was really the date of the last of the customary three announcements of the forthcoming marriage.

11. Haverkorn van Rijsewijk 1896, p. 38.

12. Houbraken 1718-21, vol. 2, pp. 26-27, states that De Jongh had so forgotten the Dutch language during his years in France that upon his return to Rotterdam his parents at first had to speak with him through an interpreter. Although this is undoubtedly a colorful exaggeration, it does indicate Ludolf's fluent command of French.

13. Haverkorn van Rijsewijk 1896, p. 39.

law were named guardians of the daughter of his sister Teuntge.[14]

In addition to these indications of the respect he enjoyed within his family, De Jongh was held in great esteem by his fellow Rotterdamers. In July 1652, coerced perhaps by the rapidly deteriorating relations between the United Provinces and England, the city of Rotterdam decided to increase its municipal guard and to appoint to the position of major, "an able and qualified person who commands respect."[15] Within a month Ludolf de Jongh was named to that position. And in 1659 he became a member of the governing board of a home for the aged, a post he held for two years.[16]

De Jongh's standing among his fellow-Rotterdamers is also apparent in the personal credit that was extended to him. On January 11, 1652 he was able to borrow a thousand guilders from Andries Sourij, the burgomaster of Rotterdam, for payment on a house. Five months later, on June 12, he purchased a house on the north side of the Hoogstraat through a cash payment of one thousand guilders and loans totaling fl. 4600 from two other prominent citizens of the city.[17]

In addition to his activities as painter and as major in the civic guard, De Jongh was also a participant in at least one business venture in Rotterdam. On December 7, 1663 he was one of five partners who had a contract drawn up concerning their establishment of a sugar refinery or sugar bakery in Rotterdam.[18] He put up six thousand of the total forty thousand guilders invested by the five partners.

De Jongh's activity as a painter encompassed not only portraiture but also genre subjects, usually interior scenes, and landscapes. The landscapes, however, were never without figures and typically included the theme of the hunt, rendering them in reality a combination of landscape and genre. Moreover, on occasion his outdoor scenes included mythological or theatrical themes. This lack of specialization is in part explained by De Jongh's working in a relatively modest art center. The larger pools of patronage in the major art centers of the United Provinces, such as Amsterdam, Haarlem, Utrecht, and Leiden, made specialization possible, while the competition created by the greater concentration of painters in those towns usually made it a necessity. Rotterdam, however, in spite of its position as the second largest Dutch port, was just beginning to experience the period of artistic growth that by the end of the century would bring it more in line with the more prominent Dutch centers,

14. Haverkorn van Rijsewijk 1896, p. 39.
15. Unger 1892, vol. 1, p. 125.
16. Unger 1892, vol. 1, p. 134.
17. Haverkorn van Rijsewijk 1896, p. 39.
18. J. Delphius, notary, 411/207 1A, 7 December 1663.

and therefore the painters working there were likely to be called upon to practice their art in several areas of subject matter. Moreover, De Jongh produced not only easel paintings but in 1665 was paid for painting two banners.[19]

A review of the extant works attributable to De Jongh suggests that his painting production decreased in the late 1650s, especially in the area of landscape but also somewhat in genre. Perhaps the portrait commissions demanded as much time as he could devote to painting, for it is likely that his business activity and his duties within the city militia were quite time-consuming. While the notarial record of 11 January 1652 describes De Jongh as "painter within this city" ("schilder binnen deser stede"), the Rotterdam documents thereafter, beginning with the following year, refer to him as "majoor."[20] That the officers in the Rotterdam militia held positions that were demanding and more than honorary is indicated by the fact that they received salaries from the city.[21] And whatever the responsibilities De Jongh's position entailed, he fulfilled them with a dedication and efficiency that later, in October 1665, led to his appointment as *schout* in Hillegersberg, an administrative post that put even greater demands on his time.[22]

De Jongh's appointment as the principal administrative officer of nearby Hillegersberg required his residency in that town, and we find that in April 1666 he sold his house on Hoogstraat in Rotterdam.[23] Although the appearances of his name in Hillegersberg town records shed no light on his career as an artist, other sources confirm his continued contact with a painter working in The Hague, Joris van der Haagen, with whom he had occasionally collaborated since the late 1650s and for whose landscapes De Jongh was called upon to provide staffage.

When Ludolf de Jongh died in the summer of 1679, the Dutch republic was deprived of one of its most skillful and versatile painters and one who was for a time a leading painter of the Rotterdam area.[24] Since his death, however, his contribution to Holland's Golden Age has not received the attention it deserves.

19. Obreen 1877-90, vol. 5, p. 55.

20. A. van der Graef, notary, 339/427, protocol XX, 11 January 1652; and A. Kieboom, notary, 155/282, protocol IX, 10 February 1653.

21. Unger 1892, vol. 1, p. LX.

22. Haverkorn van Rijsewijk 1896, p. 40.

23. Haverkorn van Rijsewijk 1896, p. 40.

24. Although the exact date of De Jongh's death is not known, it is certain that he died between May 27, when he performed duties in his capacity as *schout*, and September 11, 1679, when the minutes of the meeting of the Rotterdam administrators make it clear that he had died. See Protocol van boedelinventarissen en boedelscheidingen, 1671-1685, Hillegersberg, 2060/141; and Haverkorn van Rijsewijk 1896, pp. 40-41. Haverkorn van Rijsewijk also points out that Houbraken's mention of 1697 as the year of De Jongh's death is therefore a typographical error.

The earliest publication to shed light on the art of Ludolf de Jongh was Gerard van Spaan's *Beschryvinge der Stad Rotterdam*, which first appeared in 1698 and named De Jongh as a prominent painter of portraits and genre interiors. Van Spaan further wrote that De Jongh was so skillful that he could produce a dozen paintings in twelve days and earn a hundred guilders for each.[25]

In 1719 Arnold Houbraken included De Jongh in his biographies of Dutch painters and referred not only to his many life-size portraits but also to his genre interiors, battle scenes, and hunts.[26] Houbraken's informative biography became the basis for later accounts of De Jongh in the writings of Weyerman, Immerzeel, and Kramm, who provided relatively little additional information.[27] It was not until the late nineteenth century, primarily through the assiduous archival research of Haverkorn van Rijsewijk, that significantly more was added to the known facts of De Jongh's life and art.[28]

The art of De Jongh has received praise throughout the centuries, although it has not always been correctly associated with his name. Such diverse painters as Cuyp, Metsu, De Hooch, and Van der Helst, to name just a few, have at various times been credited with paintings by De Jongh. Charles Blanc praised and illustrated De Jongh's portrait of *A Woman with Her Daughter* (Fig. 15) as a masterpiece by Van der Helst while Thoré regarded his genre-like family portrait (Fig. 30) as a work by Musscher.[29] To all writers, however, his acknowledged masterpiece was the now-destroyed civic guard portrait formerly in the Boymans Museum.

The studies of Bode in the late nineteenth century and of Hofstede de Groot and Bredius in the early twentieth century were instrumental in clarifying important aspects of De Jongh's art and correctly crediting him with works that had previously been attributed to others.[30] More recently, the perceptive eye of Eduard Plietzsch has brought the character of De Jongh's art into sharper focus.[31] In spite of a few questionable attributions, Plietzsch, perhaps more than anyone before him, has been able to recognize the specific qualities of De Jongh's style. In the area of drawing, in which De Jongh's debt to Saftleven is most apparent, the research of Peter Schatborn has provided the

25. Van Spaan 1698, p. 411.

26. Houbraken 1718-21, vol. 2, pp. 26-27.

27. Weyerman 1729-69, vol. 2, pp. 139-41; Immerzeel 1842-43 vol. 2; and Kramm 1857-64, vol.3, p. 816.

28. Haverkorn van Rijsewijk 1896.

29. Blanc 1863; and Thoré-Bürger 1858-60, vol. 2, p. 103.

30. Bode 1883, pp. 168-70; Hofstede de Groot in Thieme-Becker 1907-50, vol. 19, pp. 132-34; and Bredius 1928.

31. Plietzsch 1960, pp. 55-58.

finest study of his style and has resulted in significant attributions.[32]

Because of the great variety in De Jongh's oeuvre, I have chosen to discuss his works thematically rather than strictly chronologically. And in an effort to bring a sense of order out of that great variety, I have organized the discussion of his works into three main chapters, each dealing with a more or less homogeneous group of paintings. Within each chapter, however, a generally — although not strictly — chronological development has been followed. Here, too, it sometimes seemed advantageous to group works together by kind rather than by date.

The first chapter discusses portraits, certainly the largest category of De Jongh's work and one in which he remained very active throughout his career. The second chapter includes those paintings in which landscape plays a prominent role, even though figures may be equally important. Although most of the paintings in this chapter are hunting scenes, some include literary or historical subjects. The following chapter discusses De Jongh's development in genre painting and focuses on those works in which human figures are of primary concern. Most of the paintings in this chapter are indoor subjects, but whether indoors or outdoors the figures are in an architectural setting. Throughout the book the emphasis is on paintings; few of his drawings can be identified, and those that have been are admirably discussed in the study by Schatborn mentioned above.

32. Schatborn 1975; and Schatborn in Amsterdam/Washington 1981-82, p. 77.

CHAPTER ONE

PORTRAITURE

Although Ludolf de Jongh did not limit himself to a particular category of subject matter in painting, it was probably portraiture that provided him with more income than the other areas of his art. Of all the genres of painting in seventeenth century Holland, it was portraiture that was most in demand and that was potentially the most lucrative area for artists capable of meeting its standards. This is because a portrait, in addition to any aesthetic appeal it may possess, has the purpose of preserving the likeness of the sitter. This practical function of portraiture demands from the painter, in addition to a certain amount of observational skill, the technical ability to achieve an exacting pictorial verisimilitude, which places restrictions on him that do much to account for its conservatism relative to other categories of painting. For, whatever else the portraitist may attempt to do in his work, he must provide the sitter with a recognizable likeness. Moreover, while paintings in other areas must gain their individuality or originality through the aesthetic considerations of composition, color, texture and such, each portrait has an inherent uniqueness stemming from the individuality of the sitter. The lesser portrait painters therefore have often been able to please their patrons with stock compositions, poses, and gestures, so long as they provided the painting with a face bearing an acceptable resemblance to the sitter.

It is therefore the nature of portraiture that has made it a haven for many of the more technically skillful but less imaginative painters in the history of art and that has stiffled the creativity of many of those painters who chose to become portrait specialists. In truth, the finest portrait painters in history have been those who did not specialize in portraiture but who devoted a sizeable portion of their creative energies to other areas, carrying over into portraiture the kinds of creativity demanded by those other forms. The names of Titian, Velazquez, Rubens, Rembrandt, and Van Gogh come more readily to mind than those of Antonis Mor, Lely, Kneller, Reynolds, Gainsborough, or the late Maes. Frans Hals, essentially a specialist in portraiture, is a notable exception, but certainly Hals succeeded by expanding the traditional bounds of portraiture in both form and content through his brilliant brushwork, his innovative compositions, and his full gamut of formal and informal conceptions, frequently blurring the distinctions between portraiture and genre.

Although we are told by Houbraken that De Jongh went to France in 1635 and returned to Rotterdam seven years later in 1642, none of his known paintings can be shown to date from those years. His earliest known works date from the 1640s and the very early 1650s and reveal him as a painter still under the spell of the older generation of Dutch masters with whose works he had become familiar before traveling abroad. Such dependence on his former masters suggests that while his skill probably had increased during his absence from Holland, he had not yet developed the desire for experimentation and innovation that was soon to be expressed in his works. Echoes of the portrait style of Palamedesz. and others are particularly strong in his work until mid-century, after which they show noticeable signs of weakening under the impact of an innovative mind striving to assert itself. Indeed, during the decade following De Jongh's return from France, he gained the necessary confidence to escape the stylistic orbit of his elders and create works that are his own in conception as well as in execution.

It was probably as a portraitist that De Jongh was most active during his sojourn in France, presumably in Paris, and it was probably more to portraiture than to other forms of painting that he directed his principal efforts following his return home in 1642; the painter could find a surer market for his skills by painting likenesses, and he was able to work on commission rather than on speculation. Houbraken tells us that De Jongh produced many portraits of the most prominent citizens of Rotterdam and in doing so, made many friends.

In 1645 he painted a portait of *Jacob Jacobsz. Couwenhoven* (Fig. 1), a prominent leader of the Remonstrants in Rotterdam. Although the painting is lost, Couwenhoven's likeness from De Jongh's portrait was recorded in an eighteenth century wash drawing by Jan Stolker intended as a cartoon for a print.

The style of the Couwenhoven portrait appears again in the signed and dated *Portrait of a Man* of 1650 (Fig. 2).[1] Both portraits are of the type most frequently painted by De Jongh, a bust or half-length figure often including one or both hands, shown against a solid, usually dark background. This form of portrait, the simplest of all, had survived in The Netherlands since the fifteenth century and was still the most popular and presumably least expensive type in De Jongh's day. Certainly this type of portrait, including the

1. Sale, Brunner, Paris, 4 January 1914, no. 32.

position of the figure on the panel, the three-quarter turn of the head, and the impression of a faithful recording of the sitter's appearance, came down to De Jongh through the portrait style of this teacher, Anthonie Palamedesz., who had been taught the art by Michiel van Mierevelt. But in the studios of De Jongh and others of his generation, a broader modeling of the face and hands replaced the rather dry, linear, meticulous treatment of his predecessors. Moreover, a greater expressiveness of the face, which in this example seemingly reflects the sitter's qualities of intelligence, firmness, and humor, saves such works from being merely routine mappings of facial features.

Also signed and dated 1650 and in the same tradition are a pair of pendants, the male portrait depicting *Willem de Swaen*, Pastor at Gouda (Fig. 3). The subject of the companion portrait (Fig. 4) is uncertain since Willem de Swaen neither married nor had a sister. Possibly it is a portrait of a cousin, Maeritge Vereij, the daughter of the uncle with whom De Swaen lived.

In the majority of his portraits, De Jongh followed the prevalent tradition, traceable to the late Middle Ages, of facing adult male subjects toward the viewer's right and female subjects toward the viewer's left, resulting, in pendant portraits, in the sitters facing three-quarters toward each other with the man at his companion's right side. With the customary light from the left thus almost invariably striking the male from the side, his features are firmly modeled and the left side of his face is often strongly shadowed. His female companion, however, is struck by the light frontally, and even though she may be portrayed with unflinching realism, the direction of light results in more softly modeled and less harsh features. This practice, giving a sense of strength to the adult male subjects while gently flattering the women, was successfully used by De Jongh and others in the seventeenth century and was obviously appreciated by their patrons.

The year after painting the portait of *Willem de Swaen*, De Jongh signed and dated a much smaller version on panel and within a feigned oval (Fig. 5), probably to serve as a cartoon for a print. At the top of the panel is the sitter's family crest with three swans, while at the bottom his right hand rests on the feigned oval frame that is painted to appear as a solid form existing in the viewer's physical world. The vital presence of the sitter is enhanced by his reaching from his pictorial realm into the world of the viewer. Even the intensity of light is carefully orchestrated to heighten the illusion, for not only is the direction of light striking the oval frame consistent with that on the sitter, but his hands, partially extending beyond the frame, are more intensely illuminated than his face, which is farther back. While in the large portrait of De Swaen it is the face which is most strongly lighted, in the smaller version, it is the right hand.

Although these earliest dated portraits all reflect something of the tradition of Mierevelt and Palamedesz., the sureness of the drawing and modeling as well as the treatment of the light attest to De Jongh's personal ability and experience in portraiture by the early 1650s, and the expressiveness and sense of alertness in the subjects' faces and hands signal him as a portraitist of considerable talent and sensitivity.

The conservative nature of portraiture encouraged De Jongh's continuation throughout the 1650s and into the early 1660s of his version of the Mierevelt style of portraiture he had learned from Palamedesz. In 1656 he signed and dated his portrait of *Henriette Vroesen* of Rotterdam (Fig. 6)[2] and in 1660 he painted the beautiful signed and dated *Portrait of a Woman* in the Frans Halsmuseum in Haarlem (Fig. 7). While the broad handling and fluid modeling of the face and hands, especially evident in the Haarlem picture, reflect the portrait style of De Jongh's own generation, the meticulous treatment of the lace encircling the shoulders of the sitters provides a link with the style of the previous generation, still being practiced by Palamedesz. and others. Numerous other portraits, similar in conception to these two, exist from the hand of De Jongh.

A male portait in the same mode is the signed and dated *Portrait of a Man* (Fig. 8) in a private collection in The Hague. Although the year is no longer legible, the style of costume and hair indicates a date around 1660. The dimensions of this painting and the facial similarity of this figure to the known likenesses of Gerard ter Borch suggest that this may be the so-called portrait of Ter Borch by Ludolf de Jongh.[3]

Although De Jongh's relationship to Ter Borch is uncertain, his direct contact with the work of Frans Hals is without question. In 1652 he made a small copy in oils (Fig. 9) of a portrait of *Nicolaes Stenius* that Hals had painted two years earlier. The reason for De Jongh's copy and the circumstances under which it was painted are unknown. Stenius was the Catholic parish priest in the town of Akersloot, a few miles to the north and east of Hals' city of Haarlem. The copy is especially interesting for revealing De Jongh's ability to capture something of Hals' brushwork and fleeting impression.[4] In fact this copy probably preserves more of the Halsian flavor than the

2. Sale, F. Muller, Amsterdam, 13 April 1920, no. 24.

3. The portrait believed to be of Ter Borch was described as a panel, 71 X 63 cm.; Sale, Amsterdam 30 March 1874, no. 64; Moes 1897-1905, p. 874, no. 4; Hall 1963, p. 36, no. 11. Although painted on canvas, this *Portrait of a Man* had been adhered to a panel, which may account for the seeming discrepancy in supports.

4. Slive 1970-74, vol. 1, p. 183, has noted that, "It is fair to say that if his copy had not been fully signed, it would have been ascribed to a Haarlem artist active in Hals' circle and not to Ludolph de Jongh of Rotterdam."

original from which it apparently derived but which has over the years suffered great physical damage.[5] The freedom of Hals' brushwork which De Jongh captures in this copy is not used by him at this time in any of his original portraits, but it does appear to great effect in some of his contemporary genre pieces.[6]

Two years later, perhaps inspired by Hals' portrait of Stenius as a scholar seated at his desk, De Jongh painted a portrait of *Caspar van den Ende* (Fig. 10), a prominent Rotterdam scholar and teacher of French. Although the original painting is not known to exist, it was copied in a print by Renier van Persyn, probably shortly after it was painted. In this portrait, as in the Stenius likeness, we find the sitter surrounded by objects suggesting his scholarship — book, compasses, globe — as he rests his head on his left hand in an attitude of contemplation. In such an occupational portrait, a type traceable to the early sixteenth century in The Netherlands and having roots in Mediaeval representations of St. Jerome in his study, we are presented with a sitter in an informal attitude and in the midst of objects that have a specific relationship to him.

In another occupational portrait of a man of letters in his study, De Jongh depicted his most famous sitter, *Jacob Cats* (Fig. 11). Father Cats, as he was affectionately called, was probably the most widely read if not the most intellectually admired Dutch writer of the century, churning out advice, morals, and admonitions intended to keep his fellow-countrymen out of sin's way. His numerous, often witty verses, although never rising to the intellectual or aesthetic level of the works of Huyghens, Hooft, or Vondel, nevertheless could be found in bound volumes in countless middle class Dutch homes where they ranked second only to the Bible in guiding the human soul safely past the pitfalls of life.

The eighty-two year old Cats is shown three-quarter length, wearing a black cap and a robe and seated at his desk before a bookcase. He turns slightly toward us, his gray eyes demanding our attention as his left hand grips the chair arm and his right rests on an open book on his desk. His right index finger points ominously to a clock and reminds us of the brevity of earthly existence. This vanitas theme was probably Cats' own suggestion, for pentimenti indicate that originally the right hand did not point but supported the book from beneath, its finger tips hidden from view. Cats' concern for salvation is further indicated by inscriptions from Genesis 48:1 and 18 on the sheet

5. The original was formerly in the Bisschoppelijk Museum in Haarlem (Inv. no. 662) and is today in the Rijksmuseum "Het Catharijneconvent" in Utrecht. Concerning the original see Slive 1970-74, vol. 1, pp. 182-83 and vol. 3, p. 94.

6. See for example figures 72-74.

of paper projecting from the bookcase above the clock. The gravity of the theme is buttressed by the solemnity of Cats' facial expression and by the overall darkness of the hues; the predominant blacks hardly find relief in the grays and browns of the volumes' spines or in the dull gray-green of the chair upholstery and table covering. On the edge of the shelf immediately above the sheet bearing the Biblical passages, we read the date of the painting, 1659, and the sitter's age, and on the top shelf, above the Bible and the writings of Saints Augustine and Bernard, appears De Jongh's signature.

More successful and certainly more interesting for the present-day viewer are those portraits which follow no strict formula but which place greater demands on the artist's inventiveness and allow greater freedom to his imagination. Such a work is the *Woman Playing the Virginals* (Fig. 12), signed and dated 1651, now in the collection of the Historisch Museum in Rotterdam. The extraordinary freshness of the conception and the strong sense of characterization, coupled with the apparent ease and sureness of the drawing and the fluidity of the brushwork, alert us to the fact that we are encountering a work by more than a competent painter; we are here confronted with a creation by a highly imaginative mind and an original talent. We are not presented with a stock type predictably posed for us, but rather we come quite unexpectedly upon a seated, well-dressed young woman who looks toward us momentarily as she rests one hand on the keyboard and gently grasps the stem of a rose with the other. The total impression is one of candid relaxation. Even the traditional frontal lighting of the female face has been abandoned in favor of illumination from the side, modeling her features more strongly and convincingly presenting us with her physical presence.[7]

The treatment of the space, too, adds to the sense of immediacy. The dynamic use of perspective not only places the subject in a convincingly defined space, but the sharp convergence of the orthogonals provided by the virginal, the picture frame above it, and the chair, can only be explained by the proximity of the viewer to the picture plane. Moreover, the seemingly random cutting-off of forms at the edges of the canvas — the picture frames at upper left and upper right, the virginal, the feet of the chair as well as those of the sitter — adds to the feeling of immediacy and the viewer's own sense of personal participation in the pictorial space of the painting, all of which is

7. De Jongh's conception probably owes something to Hendrick Sorgh's *Girl at the Spinet*, signed and dated 1645. Sale, Sotheby, London, 26 February 1958, no. 46; Collection Mrs. Geoffrey Hart, Villa Millbrook, St. Lawrence (Jersey), Channel Islands, 1965. Illustrated in *Connoisseur*, vol. 159 (1965), p. 71, fig. 3; and *Oud Holland*, vol. 92 (1978), p.124, fig. 10. However, a comparison of the two paintings clearly reveals the extent of De Jongh's contribution.

enhanced by the directness of the subject's gaze as she turns toward us.

Although the sitter's hands touching the virginal and rose may merely express her interest in music and flowers, an additional meaning may be intended, for musical instruments and roses were often employed in the seventeenth century as symbols of love, especially in portraits of women and children.[8] Musical instruments can express the harmony between souls that are in tune with each other, while the beauty and sweet smell of the rose, along with the potential prick of its thorns, can remind us that love possesses both joys and sorrows. These meanings for the virginal and the rose are given additional support here by the presence of an amor or Cupid on the mirror frame on the wall behind the sitter, relating her perhaps to Venus, the goddess of love. Although these forms carry amorous overtones, they are handled with such subtlety and aptness to the painting, that they are in no way burdensome detractors from the intrinsic beauty of the work.

In depicting the sitter in more colorful clothing and engaged in a specific activity, De Jongh was reflecting the changing taste in portraiture that swept across the United Provinces at mid-century. Instead of being pictured in the mode that dominated the first three or four decades of the century, in which motionless figures were usually set against a uniformly dark background and portrayed with clothing of somber grays and blacks alleviated only by white collars and cuffs, sitters could now choose a livelier type of portrait in which a specific activity or at least an increased sense of alertness is apparent, as well as a greater variety of hues and a more spatially convincing setting. Moreover, the often meticulous linearity with which facial features and clothing were handled in the earlier part of the century, tended to give way to a broader, more plastic treatment of forms. The leading exponent of the new style was Bartholomeus van der Helst, whose influence reached out from his Amsterdam studio to affect portraiture across the land. In Rotterdam the new style can be seen in portraits by both François Verwilt and Ludolf de Jongh, although, as we will see, De Jongh seldom relied on a variety of hues but preferred instead to use an infinite variety of blacks, grays, and cool browns against which he introduced small, effective accents of a brilliant warm color, especially vermilion or scarlet.

A similar theme of love is discernible in *The Mandolin Lesson* (Fig. 13), in which the elements of the rose and music are again combined.[9] The music lesson as an expression of love appeared in emblematic literature such as

8. For the theme of music see Mirimonde 1961, Fischer 1975, and Ember 1984. The rose as a symbol of love appears in numerous emblem books beginning with Alciati 1531. See also De Jongh 1967, pp. 25-34; and Henkel, Schöne 1967, pp. 291 and 299.

9. Sale, Roos, Amsterdam, 29 March 1911, no. 1164.

Jacob Cats' *Spiegel van den Ouden ende Nieuwen Tijdt*, in which we are told that "love teaches music" (Fig. 14), and became especially popular in Dutch genre painting. The young man facing us tunes his lute to bring himself into harmony with his female companion seen in profile seated at the right.[10] His feathered beret is perhaps intended to enhance the theme of love, for Cesare Ripa's *Iconologia* tells us that "A feather on one's head indicates that one's sensitivities are as easily moved as a feather by a light breeze."[11]

Although the theme of the music lesson was especially popular in genre paintings of the period, in this work by De Jongh the size of the canvas and the nearly life-size scale of the figures, as well as their strong sense of individuality, suggest that we have a double portrait with the addition of a love theme. In fact the woman seen here in profile bears a strong resemblance to the sitter in the previous work, as is especially evident in the nose, prominent lower lip, and hair style. Also, the two canvases are so similar in their dimensions and in their apparent dates that were it not for the lack of a corresponding background in *The Mandolin Lesson*, we might accept them as pendants, with the same female subject appearing in two aspects of love.[12] Two decades later the poet Westerbaen expressed just such a theme when he wrote, "Learn to play the lute and the harpsichord. The strings have the power to steal one's heart."[13]

Certainly one of the finest portraits by De Jongh, and one which shows him to be a leading practitioner of the portrait style popularized by Van der Helst, is *A Woman with Her Daughter* (Fig. 15), a signed and dated work of 1653. De Jongh's mastery of the new style is indicated by the fact that before the discovery of his signature on the canvas in 1872, the portrait had been attributed to Van der Helst.[14] While there is no specific action conveyed in this portrait, the new style is expressed in the broad treatment of forms and the unmistakeable impression of plasticity. Much of the success of the painting stems from the feeling of strength it exudes, for De Jongh's sureness of drawing and his sculptural approach to form are happily wed here to the forcefulness of character manifest in the principal figure. Certainly De Jongh has recorded in the figure of the mother a recognizable likeness, but in the facial expression, the arrangement of the figure on the canvas, the sureness of

10. For an excellent discussion and further references on the subject see Amsterdam, *Tot Lering en Vermaak,* 1976, pp. 104-107.

11. Ripa 1644, p. 470.

12. I am indebted to Frits Scholten for bringing to my attention the similarities between these two paintings.

13. Westerbaen 1672. The lines are from "Onderwijsingh voor de Vrijsters" (Instruction for Spinsters), pp. 659-771.

14. See for example Blanc 1863, vol. I (*École Hollandaise*) which includes De Jongh's portrait as a work by Bartholomeus van der Helst.

handling, and in those magnificent hands, he has gone far beyond a mere "mapping" of a sitter and has given us in addition a presence of character that helps make this one of the most successful portraits of the seventeenth century.

Although the composition includes two figures, they are not given equal importance, for it is really the figure of the mother that dominates the canvas physically and sets the tone of the entire conception. Her small daughter, in contrast, occupies only the lower right corner. The torsos of both mother and daughter are angled to the left, toward the source of light, suggesting that this may once have been a pendant to a now unknown portrait depicting the husband, with perhaps their son or sons, adjacent to the other end of the table seen at the left in our painting.

With her right hand, the mother holds open the cover of a book which in this familial scene is probably to be understood as a Bible, adding a note of piety. The left hand of the mother engulfs the right hand of her daughter, who holds in her apron a rose, supplying a suggestion of love. The sitters may be seen then as possessing those two most desirable qualities: piety, symbolized by the Bible, and love, seen in the rose.

One of the most dashing of De Jongh's portraits is the 1656 signed and dated *Portrait of an Officer* (Fig. 16) in the Municipal Art Gallery in Johannesburg. Here the strong plasticity and clarity of form in the previous work appear to great advantage in the likeness of a military figure, probably a fellow-officer in the Rotterdam municipal guard in which De Jongh had been appointed a major three years before painting this panel.[15] Although it is tempting to see this as a possible self-portrait, the position of *vaandrig*, or company standard-bearer, was traditionally assigned to a bachelor.

De Jongh's preference for blacks, whites, and silvery grays, seen here in the costume, is relieved only by the warm hues of the face and the brilliant strip of scarlet ribbon on the sword belt adjacent to the subject's left hand. Even the banner he carries is so muted in color as to be essentially of grays and dull browns. Nevertheless the portrait is one in which the sobriety of the colors and the facial expression of the subject is alleviated by a liveliness of form and light as the brightly illuminated whites of the collar, sleeves, and cuffs play across the surface of the panel, their energetic outlines animating the two-dimensional design.

A completely charming portrait, signed and dated 1661, is the *Boy with a Dog* (Fig. 17) in the Virginia Museum, Richmond.[16] Painted a decade later

15. In the visible date on the panel the third digit is illegible. However the costume indicates that it must have been a "5" and that the year is therefore 1656.

than the *Woman Playing the Virginals*, this canvas, too, in its bright palette and emphasis on a specific activity, is in the mode of portraiture popularized by Van der Helst. The color harmony, based on the interplay of vermilion, white, and grays, is most effective, while, even more than in *Woman Playing the Virginals*, the composition has been designed to appear candid, enhancing the sense of informality. Not only is the figure of the child placed almost entirely on the left side of the canvas, but the dynamically receding orthogonals of the bench and of the stone courses of the building behind converge at a vanishing point beyond the edge of the picture, almost creating the impression that we are seeing merely a fragment of a larger composition. Such a Baroque device conveys the impression that the composition is incomplete in itself and is therefore spatially continuous with the world beyond the picture.

Here, too, as in many portraits of women and children, the rose may be intended as a symbol of love, reinforced by the dog, a frequent attribute in children's portraits and one which has been used to convey various meanings, including a reference to love. The impressiveness of the portrait was not lost on De Jongh's younger fellow-townsman, Jacob Ochtervelt, who echoed it in a family group portrait just two years later.[17]

De Jongh achieved a similarly candid and momentary quality with an emphasis on a specific activity in another signed portrait of a child (Fig. 18), painted perhaps two or three years earlier.[18] Although the dull grayish-brown background provides little suggestion of a tangible environment, the unexpected, almost startling cutting-off of the toy horse at the bottom edge of the painting, especially in view of the emphasis placed on the child's activity, creates an appearance of candid incompleteness similar to that in the Richmond portrait. Similar, too, is the preponderance of blacks, whites, and grays, relieved by well-placed accents of vermilion, here on the ribbon of the boy's hat and on the spots of the hobby horse.

The most formal portraits surviving from the hand of De Jongh are those of *Jan van Nes* (Fig. 19) and his wife, *Aletta van Ravensberg* (Fig. 20). Both works are signed, with that of Van Nes being dated 1666 and that of his wife, 1668. Van Nes, a Vice-Admiral and naval hero from a Rotterdam family of distinguished seamen, is shown three-quarter length, standing beside a balustrade that overlooks a sea on which several ships lie at anchor. His left arm is

16. The theme of a boy instructing a dog to sit up was used earlier by De Jongh's teacher, Jan van Bylert. See Hoogewerff 1965, p. 30, no. 97. Except for the similarity of subject, however, there seems little relationship between the two paintings.

17. Kuretsky 1979, p. 41, cat. no. 18, and fig. 150.

18. Galerie Sankt Lucas, Vienna, winter exhibition 1974-75, no. 13.

beneath his cape and bent at the elbow while his left hand holds his gloves. His right arm also is bent, with his right hand resting on his hip. Adding to the formality of the portrait and the aura of the subject's authority is the low point of view from which the painting has been conceived, for the admiral looks slightly down upon us from his position, suggesting that the portrait was intended to be hung with the head of Van Nes above the eye level of the viewer.

The portrait of *Aletta van Ravensberg* is a fitting counterpart to that of the admiral, for she stands majestically before a balustrade similar to that seen in her husband's portrait, giving a definite continuity to these pendant pieces. In the background of her portrait, however, we find not a seascape but rather a formal garden, reflecting her position as preserver of the home in contrast to her spouse's career on the sea.

The Van Nes portraits are masterfully painted, with no suggestion of hesitation or uncertainty. De Jongh's sureness of brushwork and feeling for the fluidity of pigment is obvious, yet such skills are not allowed to become ends in themselves, for he never loses sight of the solidity of form. The color, on the other hand, is understated, being essentially a blend of grays with only occasional accents of other hues. The vibrant colors we might expect in the portraits of a dashing naval hero and his wife are not to be found here.

In a portrait akin to that of Jan van Nes, De Jongh painted the seaman's older brother, *Lieutenant Admiral Aert van Nes* (Fig. 21). Unfortunately the painting is no longer known to exist and is known today only through an engraving made after it by Abraham Blooteling. The portrait of *Aert van Nes* was painted only one year later than that of his brother to which it bears a strong resemblance in both conception and composition. It is likely that De Jongh painted a companion portrait of Geertruida den Dubbelde, the wife of Aert van Nes, but all trace of it, too, is lost.

In 1668, the year after Aert van Nes had his portrait (and probably that of his wife) painted by De Jongh, he and his wife sat for companion likenesses by Van der Helst (Figs. 22 and 23).[19] These provide an interesting contrast to De Jongh's conceptions. While the portraits by De Jongh emphasize the stateliness and dignity of the subjects, those by Van der Helst attempt to display increased drama and animation through Baroque gestures. Aert van Nes turns from a messenger, clutches his baton of authority, and sweeps his left hand toward his head in a motion that perhaps indicates he must take leave of us to command his naval forces engaged in battle behind him in the

19. The distant backgrounds of the Van Nes portraits by Van der Helst were painted by Ludolf Bakhuysen (1631-1708). See Amsterdam, Rijksmuseum, cat. 1976, A140 and A141.

distance. The presence of the messenger, the globe, the chair and table, and the sweep of drapery — all calculated to heighten the sense of drama — could not be contained without additional canvas to the right and left of Van Nes, making the format very nearly square. Geertruida den Dubbelde, too, gestures with a sweeping motion that dominates the canvas only slightly less than that of her husband and is perhaps intended to underscore the theme of farewell and dutiful waiting suggested in the background. Instead of De Jongh's contrast of sea with land, Van der Helst opposed a storm-tossed sea behind Van Nes with a calm sea behind his wife, suggesting the traditional roles of the active male and the passive female. While Van der Helst may have felt obliged to add a sense of action to the image of a naval hero of the stature of Van Nes, the impression is more one of frozen animation than of characterization. Moreover, the facial features of Van Nes seem to be more flatteringly recorded in the portrait by Van der Helst than in that by De Jongh. All this suggests that although De Jongh's portrait style often reflects the influence of Van der Helst, his concern in the Van Nes portraits was quite different from that of the Amsterdam painter. In contrast to Van der Helst, De Jongh sought more the portrayal of the individual and less the creation of a public image.

The bravura and theatricality created by Van der Helst in his Van Nes portraits imply that he consciously strove to compete with De Jongh's versions, with which he must have been familiar. Not only do the paintings by Van der Helst bear a general similarity of conception to the three portraits by De Jongh, with each three-quarter length subject shown standing on a terrace or balcony with a dark form limiting space at one side and an airy vista at the other, but the receding masonry wall behind Geertruida den Dubbelde seemingly repeats the wall running parallel to the picture plane in De Jongh's likeness of her husband. Thus while deriving inspiration from De Jongh's portraits, Van der Helst sought to go beyond them. Rembrandt would have met the challenge with a deeper probing of character; Van der Helst, perhaps feeling himself unable to exceed De Jongh's conceptions in that direction, chose theatricality.

One of the finest of De Jongh's late portraits is that of an unidentified gentleman (Fig. 24), which had been in the Spencer-Churchill Collection at Northwick before entering the art market in 1965.[20] Although it has always been regarded as an outstanding portrait, the authorship of this unsigned and undated work long remained a mystery. It was at one time thought to be by Gerard ter Borch, an attribution that did not go unchallenged.[21] And while the

20. Sale, Christie, London, 29 October 1965, no. 76.

21. London 1952-53, no. 332 (as Gerard ter Borch). The attribution to Ter Borch was challenged by Van Gelder 1953, p. 34, no. 332 and note 1, who suggested Hanneman as the possible painter.

portrait was long recognized as the work of a Dutch painter, the barren, rolling countryside in the background was taken to be the English Downs, leading to the mistaken belief that the portrait was of an Englishman and that it was painted by a Dutch painter who had crossed the channel. But the style of the portrait is not akin to the work of any identifiable Dutch painter who had resided in England, and the authorship remained unknown until Staring pointed out that the landscape could just as easily be Dutch as English and that the style of the painting indicates quite clearly that it is a work by Ludolf de Jongh.[22]

While De Jongh's outstanding ability as a painter of animals and his special interest in greyhounds are most obvious in his hunt scenes and genre paintings, the opportunity to display this interest and skill in a portrait was apparently given to him by the gentleman portrayed. The greyhound, a prestigious hunting dog and favorite patrician attribute, is shown here nuzzling his head beneath his master's hand and looking upward toward his face. The diagonal formed by the dog's neck and head continues in the right hand and arm of the gentleman and in the gold trim running up the front of his coat to direct our attention toward his head, which is turned toward us as his eyes meet ours. A similar diagonal begins in the lower right of the painting and moves upward through the sword, white cuff of the left sleeve, and the sword belt across the chest to lead our eyes again toward the face. Although obviously subservient to his master, the dog forms an aesthetic unit with him and clearly becomes an extension of his will. Through the juxtaposition of man and dog, De Jongh has emphasized the social position of his patron and captured the essence of canine devotion.

But it is not only in the superb treatment of the greyhound that the hand of De Jongh is evident, for the modeling of the hands and face of the sitter is also characteristic of his later portraiture, especially after the late 1650s. The shadows created by the light that bathes the hands and the features of the face are treated with great subtlety, minimizing the sense of plasticity of the forms. Shadows are sometimes so restricted along the receding edges of forms as to become little more than outlines. This can be seen in the fingers of the right hand and along the edge of the nose from its tip to the right eyebrow as well as along the line of the far side of the face that separates it from the white hair behind. The same subtle modeling can be found in such signed and dated works by De Jongh as the *Portrait of a Woman* in Haarlem (Fig. 7), dated 1660, and to a greater extent in the portrait of *Aletta van Ravensberg* in Amsterdam (Fig. 20), dated 1668. While such modeling, relying almost on the

22. Staring 1954, pp. 43-46.

outlining of forms, is of course most evident in faces that are directed toward the source of light, it also appears in portraits in which this is not the case. In the portrait of *Jan van Nes* (Fig. 19), for example, dated 1666, the far side of the face, although clearly away from the source of light, is less strongly modeled than that of the woman in the portrait of 1653 in Dresden (Fig. 15), even though her head is turned slightly toward the light. And the contrast is especially evident in the strong modeling of the hands in the Dresden portrait and the gentler modeling of them in the *Portrait of a Gentleman*, the Van Nes portraits, and the Haarlem portrait. Moreover, the hands in these later works exhibit a greater elegance with their long, tapered fingers. In fact, the greater elegance and aristocratic bearing expressed in some of the late portraits by De Jongh not only reflect the general taste of Dutch patronage in the last decades of the century but suggest more specifically the influence of Van Dyck (Fig. 25).

These stylistic distinctions reflect gradual and relatively minor changes in the portrait style of De Jongh. Nevertheless, such changes, along with the more general developments in composition, color, costume, and gestures that are common to all Dutch portraiture of the seventeenth century, help us to give approximate dates to De Jongh's undated portraits and suggest that the *Portrait of a Gentleman* dates from the early 1670s.

The hand of De Jongh has also been recognized in the *Portrait of a Young Man with Dog and Musket* (Fig. 26), which is very similar to the *Portrait of a Gentleman* both in its conception as a hunting portrait and in its physical dimensions.[23] In this work the male subject is again shown three-quarter length and standing as he faces obliquely to our left with his canine companion beneath his right hand. His right elbow rests on a large rock and his left hand holds a musket at his side. De Jongh's characteristic use of vermilion accents, typically placed against a background of cool hues, is seen here at the cuffs, the lining of the coat, the ends of the coat sleeves, above the white neckpiece, and atop the hat. The young man's gray-blue coat, richly decorated with a gold floral motif, and his blond flowing wig, topped by a black hat with large white feathers, reflect the desire for elegance and sumptuousness in Dutch society at the end of the Golden Age and allow us to date this last-known portrait by De Jongh to about 1675.

The most significant and probably the most visually impressive portrait by De Jongh was the large group portrait (now destroyed) of the officers of the Rotterdam civic guard gathered before the Stadhuis. According to Van Spaan this large composition, which originally hung in the city's St. Joris Doelen

23. Sale, Dorotheum, Vienna, 14 September 1965, no. 56.

(Fig. 27), included the likeness of the painter himself, although this has not been verified.[24] When Théophile Thoré saw the painting in the Boymans Museum, to which it had been moved in 1849, he was completely captivated by it, in contrast to his indifference to De Jongh's portraits of Jan van Nes and his wife which he saw in Amsterdam during his visit to Dutch museums in the mid-nineteenth century.

> L'exécution en est large et savante; van der Helst lui-même ne faisait pas beaucoup mieux; et cette grande toile de Ludolf de Jong prendrait place, sans dommage, dans la belle série de représentations civiques que les artistes de ce temps-là ont léguée à la Hollande.[25]

It was there in the Boymans Museum that the painting perished in flames in 1864. Today the composition is known only through a colored drawing in the Atlas van Stolk Collection, Rotterdam, made after it in 1806 by G. van der Pals, and another in the following year by D. Moens (Fig. 28). In addition, the Boymans Museum has a partial copy in oils of the four principal figures. These copies confirm that the original composition was dominated by subdued, essentially cool hues only occasionally relieved by touches of brighter color as in the vermilion sash and stockings of the central officer. In the original painting the foreground figures were depicted life-size on a canvas which measured 2.65 meters in height and 2 meters in width.[26] On the basis of the costumes we can date the painting about 1655, that is, shortly after De Jongh's appointment as major. Although the painting's composition is known only through copies, a good impression of its execution, which Thoré praised, is available to us in the *Portrait of an Officer* in Johannesberg (Fig. 16), probably painted shortly after the larger work.

The group portrait, a form of painting that the Dutch made peculiarly their own and which reached its fullest expression in seventeenth century Holland, made demands on the painter far beyond a simple increase in the number of portraits included, for it required that the painter not only produce acceptable likenesses and that he arrange them in an appealing and natural manner, but

24. Van Spaan 1698, p. 402, also states that the portrait includes Johann van IJk, Dijkgraaf, as Colonel. Haverkorn van Rijsewijk 1896, p. 42, questions the accuracy of Van Spaan's statement, however, in pointing out that Van IJk did not become a colonel until 1668, three years after Ludolf de Jongh left his position in the Rotterdam guard and moved to Hillegersberg. For an account of the known facts regarding this painting and others which hung in the Doelen, see Wiersum 1915, pp. 120-125.

25. Thoré-Bürger 1858-60, vol. 2, p. 222.

26. Haverkorn van Rijsewijk 1896, p. 42. Dimensions given in the Boymans Museum catalogue before the painting was destroyed indicate that it was "Hoog 2 el, 65 d. Breed 2 el."

that he also provide each sitter with a position appropriate to his rank and importance. Moreover, the group portrait, being frequently of a semi-public nature, was often destined for a specific setting, a fact which could determine its size and shape.[27]

Outside of Amsterdam, life-size civic guard group portraits traditionally contained figures of three-quarter length. It was only later, in response to the Amsterdam tradition as practiced by Van der Helst, Rembrandt, and others, that full-length figures appeared in civic guard portraits beyond the city on the IJ.[28] Therefore, in addition to the influence of Van der Helst in his portraits of individuals, De Jongh's choice of full-length figures for this civic guard group portrait, perhaps the first such instance in Rotterdam, reflects his further awareness of developments in Amsterdam.

Perhaps the most daring feature of De Jongh's civic guard portrait is its vertical format, for traditionally Dutch seventeenth century group portraits of more than three or four figures were composed on canvases of which width exceeded height. Only occasionally do we find civic guard group portraits with a vertical format.[29] Whether originating from the demands of the wall space on which it was to hang or from De Jongh's own preference, the vertical format and the resultant composition inject a welcomed freshness and vitality into the series of Dutch civic guard group portraits.

In contrast to the usual arrangement in rows more or less parallel to the picture plane, the officers of the Rotterdam guard are united through diagonal movements that recede into the depth of the space, only to come forward again. The diagonal movement of the messenger approaching the three officers at the left, continues through the staff and diagonal body position of the first officer. The nearly vertical staff held by the second officer provides a pivotal point from which the movement turns and swings forward through that officer's angled body and extended left foot and hand. The movement reaches its forward point in the left leg and elbow of the third officer, who stands akimbo, before receding along his back toward the officers descending the Stadhuis stairs. This forward and backward movement, traveling from left to right across the composition, is generally summed up by the arrangement of the feet of the principal figures.

The stepped gables of the buildings lining the street contribute dramatical-

27. The seminal study of the Dutch group portrait is Riegl 1931.

28. In addition to De Jongh's now lost masterpiece, other civic guard group portraits with full length figures painted outside Amsterdam include those painted for Gouda companies by Wouter Crabeth (1644) and Ferdinand Bol (1652) and one in Leiden by Joris van Schooten (1650), which suffered the same unfortunate fiery end as De Jongh's.

29. Other civic guard group portraits with vertical formats include Joachim von Sandrart's *Company of Captain Cornelis Bicker* (ca. 1640) and Govert Flinck's *Company of Captain Albert Bas* (1645), both in the Rijksmuseum, Amsterdam.

ly to the dynamic space of the composition as they recede sharply, culminating at the distant tower of the Fransche Kerk. The emphatic recession of these gables provides an architectural counterpart to the angled stances of the figures as the pivotal position of the church tower echoes that of the nearly vertical staff below. Building fronts and stoops, although not unknown in civic guard group portraits, traditionally run parallel to the plane of the picture and in no other such painting provide more vitality than here.[30] In addition, the spatial depth of the view and the specificity of the location furnish us with a combination of cityscape and civic guard portrait that is unique in Dutch painting.

While De Jongh's eye for spatial effects is most obvious, his two-dimensional harmony is also worth noting. The diagonal formed by the staff at the left, for example, is continued upward through the line of gables reaching the top center of the composition, while the line of gable tops at the left descends toward the right and is continued by the sash crossing the chest of the central officer and is carried on to a lesser extent by the left forearm and sash of the officer standing akimbo. The junction of the diagonal lines thus formed is further fixed by the verticality of the church tower and the staff below, providing an area of focus that includes both distant forms (church tower) and near ones (hand and staff). This pictorial harmony of two-dimensional and three-dimensional composition on a large scale reveals De Jongh as a master of group portraiture and makes even more regretable the infrequency of his ventures into this field and the loss of this fine work.

A very different kind of group portrait by De Jongh, but one which dates from the same period, is that of *A Family Group on a Terrace* (Fig. 29), which has been previously ascribed to Anthonie Palamedesz. Here a half dozen figures have been assembled on a narrow terrace before a house and placed in a composition of classical calm; a girl, her brother, and his fishing pole define a frontal plane that runs parallel to the plane of the picture, while just behind them their parents and a nurse carrying a third child form a distinct second plane.

The blacks and whites of the costumes predominate against a background

30. See for example Frans Hals' *St. George Company* of 1639 and Hendrick Gerritsz. Pot's *St. Andrew Company* of 1630, both of which are in Haarlem and both of which gain some variety by arranging some figures on a stoop. Although the building facade behind the figures in Pot's composition recedes somewhat diagonally, it nevertheless serves as a space limiting backdrop that extends from one side of the painting to the other, while the receding architectural forms of Joachim von Sandrart's *Company of Captain Cornelis Bicker* (ca. 1640) and of Nicolaes Eliasz.' *Company of Captain Jan van Vlooswijck* (1642), both in Amsterdam, seem more like stage sets and are less compositionally and spatially effective than De Jongh's.

of dark olive-green foliage. Cool colors further prevail in the grays of the girl's dress and the boy's coat and in the light cerulean blue of the girl's overskirt. Even the roses are such pale pink as to be almost white. Against this setting of muted cool hues, De Jongh has placed his favorite accents of vermilion, seen in the bow of ribbon on the boy's hat and in the trimmings of the mother's skirt.

The six figures are nearly life-size, arranged as they are close to the picture plane on a canvas measuring six feet in height. Although still a sizeable picture, there are indications that originally it was even larger and that it has been subsequently cut down on all four sides, perhaps to fit an extant frame or a specific wall space. The shoes of the children on the frontal plane rest uncomfortably on the bottom edge of the picture while the nurse at the right is now backed up against the frame, and the group of flying cherub-like figures in the upper right, which must represent the deceased children of the family, is cut off by both the top and left edges of the canvas. Moreover, the glance of the mother toward our right suggests that a figure may have been eliminated from that side. Most telling of all is the unusual, nearly square format of the canvas, and although it was apparently cut down along all four sides, the composition indicates that it originally had a horizontal format and therefore has been most severely shortened along one or both lateral sides. It is very probably due to the unfortunate trimming of the canvas that neither a signature nor a date is visible today. Nevertheless the modeling of the figures, the handling of the pigment, and the color preferences strongly support the attribution to De Jongh, while the costumes suggest a date about 1655.[31]

A family group portrait of a very different sort was painted by de Jongh in 1673 (Fig. 30) and is therefore one of the last known works from his hand. In a middle-class interior, illuminated by a window at the left, a mother is seated slightly to the right of center with an infant on her lap and a somewhat older child at her feet. Just left of center stands her husband with a wineglass in his right hand and with what appears to be a small piece of cake or cookie in his left, which he extends toward the infant. In contrast to the formality of De Jongh's previous group portraits, we are presented here with a family portrait of such informality that the traditional distinction between group portraiture and genre subjects has been dissolved. Moreover, the modest size of the

31. The rose in the hands of the girl as well as those displayed on the balustrade at the left may be intended as symbols of family love. Similarly, the prominence given to the boy's fishing suggests that it, too, may carry an intended meaning. But although emblematic literature does sometimes equate fishing with the love between individuals, its use as a reference to familial love is problematical. For a discussion of fishing as a reference to love see Amsterdam, *Tot Lering en Vermaak,* 1976, pp. 186-189.

canvas as well as the small scale of the figures in relation to the format of the painting suggest a genre scene, while the individuality of the figures indicates that it is also a form of portraiture. Genre-like portraiture of this type, while found earlier in the works of Thomas de Keyser and others, was especially popular in the second half of the seventeenth century in the hands of such painters as Frans van Mieris and Michiel van Musscher. In fact, until Bredius discovered the date and signature on this painting, it had been attributed to the Rotterdam-born Musscher, whose work it very closely resembles.[32] Were it not for the discovery of the signature, it is highly unlikely that this canvas would ever have been associated with the name of Ludolf de Jongh. Perhaps in this instance, as with some of his late genre pieces, he felt the need to try his hand at the latest mode and prove to himself — and perhaps to his younger contemporaries — that he still had the interest and the skill to stay at the forefront of developments; only a shortage of time resulting from his official duties kept him from more active participation in the field and tended to limit him to the more traditional types of portraiture. But even so, it seems likely that many other De Jongh portraits must still be lurking under the names of several of his contemporaries.

32. Thoré-Bürger 1858-60, vol. II, p.103, as by Michiel van Musscher; Bredius 1887-88, pp. 165-166.

CHAPTER TWO

LANDSCAPE

De Jongh's interest in landscape painting expressed itself shortly after his return to Rotterdam from France, if we are correct in accepting a *Landscape with Diana and her Nymphs* (Fig. 31), dated 1644, as a work from his hand.[1] Although the full signature is no longer completely legible, perhaps having been purposely obliterated so that the work could be ascribed to a more prominent painter,[2] the first letter has been read as "L," [3] which, along with some of its stylistic qualities, supports the attribution to De Jongh. Quite apart from the several elegant greyhounds, which are all too often taken as a suggestion of De Jongh's authorship, the wagon tracks leading the viewer's eyes into the distance; the figures and trees on one side of the composition, balanced by the distant view on the other; and, above all, the silhouetting of individual leaves of the trees in the foreground into a thin, lace-like pattern across the sky, are characteristics which frequently recur in landscapes more securely by his hand. It is fitting that in this scene the landscape elements are combined with the goddess of the hunt, for De Jongh's interest in the sport of hunting, and especially its dogs, was to provide him with a favorite theme in the years ahead.[4]

To judge from this example, the major source of De Jongh's landscape style at this point in his career was the art of Cornelis Vroom of Haarlem, who was known and respected in Southern as well as Northern Holland; he contributed to the decorative program of Frederick Hendrick's country estate at Honselaarsdijk near The Hague, and one of his works was in the collection of

1. Sale, Lepke, Berlin, 27 February 1917, no. 44.

2. Bode 1887, pp. 33-34.

3. Hofstede de Groot 1904, p. 574.

4. Some other history subjects painted by De Jongh are known to us only through inventories and sales records. A Rotterdam auction of 5 April 1747, included a *Woman of Samaria* (no. 103); and another of 20 July 1768 listed a *Simeon in the Temple* (no. 88). And perhaps the painting depicting *Hagar* by 'de Jongh' in the 1687 inventory of Catharina Deyl of Amsterdam was a work by our painter. Bredius 1915-22, vol. 2, p. 544.

Constantijn Huygens.[5] Some of the qualities of Vroom's art, especially the very distinctive treatment of the foliage in the foreground, was to remain with De Jongh even after he discovered fresh sources of inspiration.

Dating from nearly a decade later than the *Landscape with Diana and her Nymphs*, and the most impressive of De Jongh's known works based on an historical or literary theme, is the painting of *Granida and Daifilo* (Fig. 32), inspired by Pieter Cornelisz. Hooft's *Granida*, the first pastoral play in the Dutch language, written about 1605. The character of Granida, as Kettering has pointed out, was associated in the mind of Hooft and his fellow countrymen with the goddess Diana.[6] The numerous editions of the play as well as its appearance in paintings and drawings bear witness to its popularity throughout the seventeenth century.[7] The scene chosen by De Jongh was the third scene of the first act, in which Granida, a Persian princess who has lost her way while hunting, asks help from Daifilo and Dorilea, a shepherd and shepherdess to whom she reveals her identity. Daifilo, who has fallen in love with Granida at first sight, offers her a drink of water. After accepting it she praises not only the water but also the peaceful simplicity of pastoral life, which she contrasts with the pressures and confusion of court life. It is perhaps the moralizing aspect of this scene, extolling the simple pleasures of rustic life at the expense of overcivilized artificiality, that made it by far the most popular moment of the play for artists and patrons.

The earliest known paintings of scenes from Hooft's *Granida* are from Utrecht, and it was probably in that city that De Jongh first developed an interest in the subject. Certainly his painting is related to an earlier one by Van Baburen (Fig. 33), for not only has De Jongh chosen the same moment from the story, but certain motifs, such as Dorilea's gesture with her forefinger and the prominent position given to Granida's horse, standing behind her with its head seen between those of the two principals, establish his reliance on the earlier work. Moreover, De Jongh's general arrangement of the three figures is similar in reverse to that of Van Baburen. But De Jongh's greater interest in landscape led him to place his figures further back in space and to surround them with exquisitely painted foliage and rocks. In neither painting, however, is there an attempt to depict the scene as it appeared on the stage; as Gudlaugsson has pointed out, only costumes and isolated motifs occasionally reflect the theatrical origins of the paintings derived from Hooft's play.[8] There

5. Keyes 1975, pp. 80, 91-94.

6. Kettering 1983, p. 105.

7. For a full discussion of the depictions of Pieter Cornelisz. Hooft's *Granida* in Dutch painting see Gudlaugsson 1948-49.

8. Gudlaugsson 1948-49, vol. 91 (1949) p. 43.

was never an attempt to give the impression of the production on the stage.

Especially striking in De Jongh's *Granida and Daifilo* is his outstanding skill in the painting of the human figure and animals, for not only are they anatomically convincing but the stances and gestures, albeit in this case somewhat theatrical, are plausible and appropriate. De Jongh apparently regarded this work as of more than average significance, for he has treated the forms of both the landscape and the figures with greater clarity, crispness, and plasticity than we find in his typical hunt scenes and genre paintings of the time. Indeed his sculptural approach to form here is closer to that found in his portraits than it is to his other works. In none of his hunt scenes and only in his genre works after 1655 do we find a comparable concern for modeled form. This strong emphasis on a sculptural quality is most clearly seen here in the kneeling Daifilo. The play of light and shadow across his shepherd's costume molds it with clarity and certainty that appeal strongly to our tactile sense. The tree behind him and the head of Granida's horse retain much the same quality, while further back, in the figure of Dorilea and in the more distant landscape, such solidity of form has been dissolved by a softer light and the intervening atmosphere.

This work by De Jongh apparently served as a source of inspiration for the young Jacob Ochtervelt, who produced a clumsy variant of it (Fig. 34), while probably giving to the fictional figures of Granida and Daifilo the portrait likenesses and dress of an actual Rotterdam couple.[9] The relationship between Ochtervelt and De Jongh evident in this painting is another example of the occasional borrowing from the older man by the younger. Still open to question is whether Ochtervelt, along with Pieter de Hooch, served an apprenticeship with de Jongh or merely found his work worthy of emulation.

A second work by De Jongh depicting the theme of the goddess Diana, but one that is stylistically closer to *Granida and Daifilo*, is that of *Diana Hunting* (Fig. 35), a painting that has until now been wrongly ascribed to Abraham

9. Galerie van Diemen, Amsterdam, 1934. The portrait-like quality of the figures was previously noted by Gudlaugsson 1948-49, vol. 91 (1949), p.40. The dependence of Ochtervelt's *Granida and Daifilo* composition on De Jongh's has previously been noted in Plietzsch 1937, p.368; in Plietzsch 1960, p. 64; and in Gudlaugsson 1948-49, vol. 91 (1949), p. 40. However, Kuretsky 1979, p. 53, argues that Ochtervelt painted his version before 1652, the date on his *Hunters and Shepherds in a Landscape* (Städtische Museen, Karl-Marx-Stadt, East Germany), which she sees as later in style. She suggests, however, a common source for the two Granida works rather than the influence of a teen-age Ochtervelt on a thirty-eight year old De Jongh. In view of other instances of Ochtervelt's borrowing from De Jongh; the apparent dependence of this Ochtervelt on De Jongh, with the inclusion of what is probably a greyhound inspired by De Jongh; and no evidence of a supposed common source for the paintings, I must agree completely with Plietzsch and Gudlaugsson that Ochtervelt's version derived from De Jongh.

Hondius. This painting, which probably dates from shortly after mid-century, depicts Diana and her companions in the left foreground, moving toward center behind a pack of dogs in pursuit of a rabbit seen at the lower right. Some trees and the dark form of a cliff dominate the middle ground at the left behind Diana and her companions and restrict movement into the distance on that side. On the right side, however, behind the rabbit and the group of dogs closest to it, a distant view includes a circular classical temple and mountain ridges on the horizon beyond, placing the scene in an unmistakably Italianate setting.

The composition, with its hill limiting the space behind the figures at the left in contrast to the distant view of mountains at the right, and the beautiful rendering of the satin dress on the most prominent figure, are reminiscent of *Granida and Daifilo*. However, the forms here of both landscape and humans are less monumental and less assertive in their plasticity. It is apparent then that De Jongh was able to change his style and conception to meet the demands of the subject, for in the *Granida and Daifilo* he was dealing with a particular moment in a well-known theatrical production in which specific figures and their interrelationships were of primary importance, whereas in this work he was treating the more general theme of the goddess of the hunt and her companions in pursuit of game.

De Jongh's interest in landscape painting, as revealed by the three works based on literary themes just discussed, reached an intensity in the late 1640s that did not abate for a decade. The landscape subjects painted in this period are not, however, solely expressions of a fascination with nature, for, in contrast to the panel of 1644, De Jongh gave equal importance to the figures, both human and animal, which populate his scenes. Landscape subjects never became for De Jongh a means of probing the changing moods and conditions of nature. He was never a combination meteorologist and artist, a blend of painter and climatologist. We feel in his works nothing of Van Goyen's gray wetness of the North Sea coastline nor the frozen brittleness of Aert van der Neer's winter nights. And although occasionally we are able to distinguish between the types of trees in his landscapes, the true botanist's concern for nature, as found in the works of Jacob van Ruisdael, held little attraction for him. To De Jongh, nature had little meaning except as an arena for man and his animal companions. While it never became a mere stage set, a backdrop, against which humans pursued their interests, it also was never allowed to intimidate and subjugate man. The balance achieved by De Jongh between the world of man and the world of nature in these paintings was a delicate one, but one which, once attained, remained consistent in his landscape compositions.

De Jongh's interest in landscape painting is nowhere better seen than in his scenes of hunting, a subject that Houbraken tells us held a special fascination for the painter.[10] Such scenes not only provided De Jongh with the opportunity to display his skill in landscape, but they allowed him to give full expression to his considerable ability as a painter of figures and animals.

Although hunting had been a popular and prestigious sport in Europe from early mediaeval times, it was certainly not a major recreational pastime for the Dutch in the seventeenth century.[11] In fact the hunting scenes painted by Paulus Potter, Philips Wouwerman, Abraham Hondius, Adriaen Beeldemaker, Ludolf de Jongh, and others, present activities and a way of life limited to a small minority of the population. Strict regulations determined that most types of game could only be pursued by the nobility and governmental officials.[12] Even this select group was restricted in the number and types of hounds to be used, the frequency of the hunts, and the quantity of game taken. In this respect the deer and fox hunts painted in seventeenth century Holland are almost as fanciful — although not nearly so dramatic — as the hunts of wolves, lions, tigers, and hippopotamuses painted in the Southern Netherlands by Rubens, Jan Fyt, and Paul de Vos. And although the participants in the hunting parties are customarily shown wearing seventeenth century Dutch dress, the imaginary nature of the scene is usually revealed in the un-Dutch character of the terrain with its rolling hills and distant mountains. Such subjects and settings belie the old conception that Dutch art holds a mirror up to nature.

Paintings of the hunt, along with the hunt portrait and still lifes of the trophies of the hunt, increased in popularity toward mid-century, reflecting the aspirations of a wealthy middle class and an increased patrician class eager to associate itself with the attributes and pastimes of the aristocracy. The pleasures and, above all, the prestige of the hunt, generally denied the middle class in reality, could be vicariously attained through paintings. It is therefore the patronage of the affluent middle class rather than that of the small aristocracy that accounts for the great upsurge in hunting themes in the second half of the century. In such paintings neither the landscape setting nor the act of the hunt itself found much basis in reality. Their exotic nature, however, provided an imaginative fulfillment for the real aspirations of the patrons. And the verisimilitude of the style with which such scenes were painted, helped make the fantasy, the visual fiction, seem a reality.

Near the mid-seventeenth century the painter Leonard Bramer recorded in

10. Houbraken 1718-21, vol. 2, p. 27.

11. Zumthor 1962, pp. 162-63.

12. For a discussion of the social implications of the hunt themes see Sullivan 1980; and Sullivan 1984, pp. 33-45.

a series of drawings the compositions of many of the paintings then in Delft collections.[13] Hofstede de Groot, in addition to demonstrating that the creator of the drawings was Bramer, was able to date them between about 1642, when several of the younger painters represented would have been about twenty years old, and 1653 or 1654, when Adam Pick, known to have been the owner of several of the paintings, left Delft for Leiden.[14] Among these drawings is one after a painting by De Jongh depicting a *Landscape with the Death of a Fox* (Fig. 36). Fortunately the original work was photographed when it appeared on the art market in 1925 (Fig. 37), although today its location is not known.[15] The presence of this painting in Delft in the mid-seventeenth century allows us to date it rather safely to about 1648-1650.

Although this and De Jongh's subsequent landscapes retain some of the Vroom-like qualities seen in the 1644 panel, they reveal still another source of stylistic inspiration, for they have an unmistakable Italianate accent, or, more properly said, are of a type popularized by many of the Dutch landscape painters after returning home from sojourns in Italy. In contrast to the "native style" of landscape with its emphasis on the character of the Dutch countryside, these so-called Italianate painters of Holland promoted a landscape created in Italy, albeit by Northerners reacting to their Italian surroundings, that has as its most salient characteristic a brilliant Mediterranean sunlight, often with a golden glow in the sky, creating strong contrasts of light and shadow and accentuating bright local color. In addition, their works often display such typically Italian and non-Netherlandish features as distant mountains and Roman ruins.

In De Jongh's renditions the sun, not seen within the picture, is low on the horizon and casts its golden rays across the scene, usually from left to right. Trees or hills typically rise behind the principal figures, as in *Granida and Daifilo* and *Diana Hunting*, and prevent them from being too strongly silhouetted against the sky, while smaller figures appear at varying distances from the picture plane and serve to convey a convincing recession of space.

While De Jongh usually chose to depict a quiet moment in his hunting scenes — most frequently a rest on the hunt — he did on occasion capture the violence of the chase as in this work from a Delft collection. In this scene, dogs, humans, and horses converge on the helpless fox, which, if not yet dead, has lost all ability to defend itself. It has become the helpless hub of an encircling wheel of attackers.

Closely related to *Landscape with the Death of a Fox* in subject, composi-

13. Moes 1895.

14. Hofstede de Groot 1895, p. 238.

15. Sale, Christie's, London, 31 July 1925, no. 155.

tion, and dimensions is the exceptionally fine painting of a *Fox Hunt* in Amsterdam (Fig. 38).[16] The white dog charging toward the kill from the right foreground of the previous work reappears in a similar position here. The rolling landscape, including the trees stepping into the distance along the right side, is found in both works, while the horseman followed by a footman in the left middle ground of the Amsterdam scene has replaced his feminine counterpart. Also in both works a footman approaches the scene in the middle ground just right of center although the rider who precedes him in the Amsterdam picture is absent from the other, while a footman racing toward the action from the right foreground in *Landscape with the Death of a Fox* is not found in the Amsterdam hunt. Another difference is that in the painting in Amsterdam the painter has provided a large tree to serve as a repoussoir along the left side of the composition.

While both works depict a kill fraught with violence, there is unfortunately a certain unintended stiffness of some of the human figures that tends to freeze the action. Dogs and horses move with convincing ease, but the three principal riders in the two paintings sit with an awkward woodeness atop their mounts while the largest figure of all, the footman in the right foreground of the *Landscape with the Death of a Fox*, seems forever in suspended animation, reminding us that although De Jongh drew animals and humans with equal skill, his attempts at setting them in motion were generally more successful with the former.

Also dating from the late 1640s is an unsigned hunt in the National Gallery in Dublin (Fig. 39). Here the figures are smaller and the landscape more barren, but perhaps most noticeable is the sense of quiet control, even though a hunt — even a kill — is in progress. In not attempting to set human figures in motion, De Jongh has avoided the sense of stiffness found in the previous two works.

It is a painting remarkable for the marvelous freshness and clarity of its forms and the apparent ease with which they are painted. Nothing is belabored or uncertain; we see here the work of a master who combined skillful draughtsmanship with a feeling for the application of pigment that makes us wonder if there might not be an element of truth in Van Spaan's assertion that De Jongh's skill enabled him to paint a dozen pictures in twelve days.

What is most remarkable about the composition of this work is the sense of

16. There has been speculation that the landscape features in this painting are the work of Joris van der Haagen. Bol 1969, p. 253, and Amsterdam, Rijksmuseum, catalogues 1921 and 1960, no. 1312. However, others have correctly rejected the suggestion of Van der Haagen's participation. Hofstede de Groot 1904, pp. 115-116, and Van der Haagen 1932, p. 48.

separateness of the figures, giving us the impression that it is not composed, at least not in the traditional sense. We feel that here we have simply come across some figures scattered but integrated into the landscape. However, this candid impression that De Jongh so skillfully gives us is yet another example of his fertile mind seeking to avoid the traditional and predictable in compositions, for in spite of the spatial intervals between the figures there is a definite compositional unity. The brilliant red jacket of the figure seated with two dogs in the lower right sings out for attention against the browns and muted greens of the landscape. His gaze is directed toward the left as is that of the woman on horseback shading her eyes and that of the figure leading a horse in the center of the panel. Further to the left an attendant restraining a dog and a rifleman behind him form a small group that continues the movement through the hunter firing a gun and the crouching dog before him. The figures are seemingly isolated from each other, but through their directed attention and their careful placement, they create a unity that carries our eye from the brilliant red jacket in the right foreground to the marksman and dog in the left middle ground and on to the golden sky beyond. A more obvious device used here is the mountain in the background sloping down to the left and aiding the movement of our gaze. All in all, this is a wonderful performance by De Jongh; the figures, in spite of their relatively small size, convey a vitality and a naturalness that is in keeping with the candid effect of the composition. We are given the impression that this painting stands apart from the general tradition of hunt scenes; De Jongh helps us see an original hunt, through the freshness of his own vision.

So important are the animal and human forms in these compositions that without them the landscape itself would have little appeal. The relative barrenness of the fields is especially noticeable in de Jongh's works of the late 1640s and early 1650s; as he moved further into the second half of the century, his landscapes became richer through the inclusion of more varied natural forms. But landscape always remained a setting for the figures and shares no more than equally with them the responsibility for the effectiveness of the painting. Nowhere is there the suggestion that an analysis of nature's changing mood or character was his dominant concern. Rather his landscapes provide beautiful idyllic settings for the interaction between mankind and those two most trusted and dependable animals — the horse and the dog. With the exception of the 1644 *Landscape with Diana and her Nymphs*, in which no horse is visible, no landscape acceptable as a work by De Jongh is without both human figures and these two creatures. Indeed the tender display of devotion between man and dog is a recurring motif in the work of De Jongh, one that frequently takes the form of an attendant bending over one of his charges.

Although the Flemish immigrants, Roelant Savery and Gillis d'Hondecoeter, created hunt scenes in the early years of the century, their otherwordly landscapes usually so dwarf the figures and animals that their example seems to have had no influence on De Jongh. Closer in time to De Jongh's paintings were the dramatic hunts painted in Antwerp by Frans Snyders and Jan Fyt. Not only is Rotterdam nearly as close to Antwerp as it is to Amsterdam, but, as Hentzen has pointed out, some definite connections can be established between the hunts of the Rotterdamer, Abraham Hondius, and those of Snyders and Fyt.[17] However, De Jongh accepted neither the theatricality and turbulence of the Antwerp hunts nor their subordination of the landscape elements to the dominating monumental forms of animals in violent motion. He remained characteristically Dutch in recessing the elements of the hunt into the landscape until a balance of interest and effectiveness was attained between them. And in this respect he is in the tradition popularized by the Haarlem-born painter, Pieter van Laer. Blankert has shown that Van Laer developed a genre of painting in the 1630s in Italy in which humans, animals, and landscape shared equally in the effectiveness of the work, and that Sandrart was correct in stating that Van Laer's paintings were so sought after that some were shipped from Italy to Holland even before his return north in the early 1640s.[18] Although few of his paintings can be identified with certainty today, his importance in the development of the Italianate landscape with figures and animals is evident not only through the series of etchings he published in Rome in the 1630s (Fig. 40) but also through the compositions of his paintings that were in the Delft collections in mid-century and that were recorded in the sketchbook of Leonard Bramer (Fig. 41). While Van Laer's influence on De Jongh is expressed in a general way through the balance between the landscape and animate forms in the compositions, his influence is more specifically indicated by the motif of an attendant bending over one of his dogs.

The type of Italianate landscape with man and animals popularized by Van Laer served as an important link between the Dutch Italianate landscape painters of the 1620s, represented by Poelenburgh and Breenbergh, and those who began their work in the 1640s, such as Berchem, Asselijn, Potter, and Wouwerman. Van Laer's conceptions also found fruitful ground in Utrecht in the hunt scenes of Dirck Stoop (Fig. 42), which in turn must have provided additional inspiration for De Jongh.[19]

17. Hentzen 1963, 33-47.

18. For Van Laer's contribution to landscape and animal painting see Blankert 1968, pp. 117-134.

19. For Van Laer's influence on Dirck Stoop see Hoogewerff 1933, p. 258; Swillens 1934, p. 134; Bredius 1939, p. 125; and Blankert 1968, p. 130.

By mid-century De Jongh's hunt themes turned away from the violent moment of the kill and toward the more relaxed theme of the rest on the hunt, a conception more clearly suited to his temperament and ability. A typical work in this vein is the *Rest on the Hunt* (Fig. 43) which appeared on the art market in 1907 as a work by J. B. Weenix.[20] The small hunting party is seen stopping near a tree at the right side, beneath which an attendant bends over two resting dogs with a marked sense of devotion that is clearly returned by his charges. From this focal point our attention moves back through the lady on horseback to the hill beyond and left through the white horse with its attendant and dismounting rider to the herd of sheep and the distant horizon. It is a simple composition but an untraditional one to the extent that all the monumental forms within the painting are concentrated in one corner.

A comparable female figure, now atop a similar white horse, appears in the signed *Hunters in the Field* (Fig. 44), which dates from a few years later. Here the landscape has become slightly richer, with more varied tree shapes, bushes, and ruins behind the riders at the left side, while in the center middle ground two beaters with a dog provide a spatial clue between the large foreground figures and the sheep and cattle beneath the tree in the center. As in many of his landscapes, De Jongh follows the convention of placing the riders before rising hills on one side of the composition and providing a distant, atmospheric view on the other.

Related to the two previously discussed works is a rather large painting with riders and a gypsy, entitled *The Cavaliers* (Fig. 45), which appeared on the art market in the 1920s and was quickly hailed by some scholars as an early work by Pieter de Hooch, seemingly confirming Houbraken's statement that De Hooch had studied under the Italianate landscape painter, Nicolaes Berchem of Haarlem, while other scholars maintained that it was a work by Ludolf de Jongh.[21] Certainly the features of the female rider and the awkwardness of her pose as well as the angular silhouette of the man before a tent in the lower left corner are strongly reminiscent of some of De Hooch's early work. Moreover, the heads of the horses, with their undersized ears and their almost human eyes, are difficult to credit to the hand of De Jongh, whose fine draughtsmanship was sometimes called upon to provide both animal and human figures for the landscapes of others.

Nevertheless, a relationship to De Jongh is unmistakable. The horses in this work are undeniably similar in stance and modeling to those in several

20. Sale, Sedelmeyer, Paris, 25 May 1907, no. 205, as J. B. Weenix.

21. For a discussion of the attributions of the painting to De Hooch and to De Jongh, see Sutton 1980, pp. 143-144.

compositions by De Jongh, including the two just discussed, while the elegant silhouette of the greyhound and the figure in the middle ground behind it are quite in keeping with similar forms in De Jongh's hunt scenes. For these reasons I suggested elsewhere that the painting was a work by the young De Hooch when he was under the influence of his fellow Rotterdamer.[22] There is, however, a tradition indicating that at one time the canvas bore a genuine Ludolf de Jongh signature that has subsequently been worn away.[23] Certainly the canvas has suffered considerable damage and is in part the victim of inferior restoration, accounting perhaps for some of the awkwardness of form and the seeming lapses in draughtsmanship. We have then a painting by De Jongh in poor condition which, to judge from the costumes of the riders and the somewhat barren landscape, probably dates about 1645-1648.

The brown horse of the male rider in *The Cavaliers* appears again, in a mirror image, in *Landscape with Riders* (Fig. 46), which also dates about mid-century and reveals in the painting of the figures some of the broad handling frequently found in De Jongh's figure pieces of the late 1640s and early 1650s.[24] The dog sniffing the ground in the lower left is also a recurring De Jongh motif as is the head peeking toward us from between the two riders, while the group of figures on the ground at the left provides a faint echo of Pieter van Laer's groups. The composition, with the massing of the major figures toward one side and a distant atmospheric view toward the other, is in keeping with other landscapes by De Jongh as we have seen, while the deep perspective view past the figures at the left parallels the dramatic perspective in some of his portrait and genre works of the same period. The foliage, however, is treated in a feathery manner that has sometimes suggested the painting as a joint effort of De Jongh and Joris van der Haagen. But no work in which the two are known to have collaborated gives such prominence to the figures or can be dated before the late 1650s.

Also we must avoid characterizing too narrowly De Jongh's style, such as his painting of foliage, for he was among the most versatile of painters, not only in the variety of his subject matter but also in his application of pigment. In the *Hunters in a Hilly Landscape* of about 1655 (Fig. 47), for example, the leaves on the foreground trees at the left are crisply delineated and dramatically silhouetted against the sky, their individuality seemingly enhanced.[25] Farther back, leaves become lost in the mass of foliage which is itself treated in a

22. Fleischer 1978, p. 49.
23. The signature, before being worn away, may have been altered to that of Pieter de Hooch. See Bredius 1928, p. 67.
24. E. de Brandere Collection, Ukkel, 1961.
25. Jhr. A. Loudon Collection, Wassenaar, 1942.

softer, more feathery manner. The foliage along the right edge of the *Hunters in a Hilly Landscape*, for example, is remarkably similar to that in *Landscape with Riders*, for in both examples the more brightly lighted leaves on the outer branches have been rapidly stippled across the solid mass of dark color beneath. While this variation in the treatment of foliage from foreground to background is common to the works of landscape painters, it is especially apparent in the landscapes of De Jongh, for he, far more than most, retains the Vroom-like custom of flattening out the leaves in the foreground and stressing their individuality by playing their star-like silhouettes against the sky. The sense of volume of foreground foliage is thus sacrificed for an almost two-dimensional lacey pattern of dark leaves against a light background, a quality that was seen in his landscapes as early as the *Landscape with Diana and her Nymphs* of 1644.

In addition to the variation in the treatment of foliage, the sense of space within the painting is also strengthened by the effective placement of forms, leading our eyes from the trees in the left foreground, through the attendant bending over one of his dogs, to the couple on horseback and on to the dogs and two attendants in the middle ground, whose movement toward the distance is paralleled by the trees that extend from the right edge of the panel on into the background. The sense of space is further enhanced by the overlapping planes and the rhythmical, nearly parallel curves formed by the arched back of the attendant in the left foreground, the upper edge of the large rock immediately behind and above him, and the rolling crest of the distant mountains.

The beauty of this Italianate landscape, with its golden glow in the sky from a sun low on the horizon, at one time made the panel's false signature of Albert Cuyp seem valid. Cuyp signatures on De Jongh paintings are not uncommon. Another example with a Cuyp signature, dating from about the same time, is the *Small Hunting Group* (Fig. 48).[26]

A picture with a landscape setting quite different from those in the paintings thus far discussed is the *Beach at Scheveningen,* dating from 1646-48 (Fig. 49). Although it is the only known beach scene attributable to De Jongh, the rendering of light and the handling of form is in keeping with his work of the late 1640s, while the treatment of the figures, especially, leaves little doubt concerning its authorship. The rather leaden-footed stance of the man in the foreground with his back to us, the small running figure in the lower left, the horse and rider, and the frolicsome dogs are all echoed in other landscape and genre scenes by De Jongh. Especially typical is the brilliant vermilion accent

26. Sale, G. Petit, Paris, 17 June 1904, no. 19, as A. Cuyp.

of the horseman's cape, forming a dramatic contrast with the cooler and more subdued hues of the remainder of the canvas. The wonderful play of light on the sand and the sureness of touch with which the boats and figures have been painted make it all the more regretable that beach scenes were not of greater interest to De Jongh.

Starting in the late 1650s De Jongh painted fewer landscapes, probably in part because of his duties in the Rotterdam civic guard and later as *schout* at Hillegersberg as well as his obligations in business ventures. What time he could devote to painting became increasingly confined to portraiture and occasional excursions into the latest developments in genre, areas which probably allowed him to work almost exclusively on commission rather than on speculation. Perhaps, also, he was less interested in the new trends in landscape painting; he obviously favored a horizontal format, for example, at a time when other painters of landscape were increasingly turning to uprights. And the emphasis on monumental vertical forms within the compositions, such as the tall, stately trees found in the works of Hackaert and others, seemingly held little interest for him.[27] But in view of the adventuresome spirit he maintained in the areas of portraiture and genre, it was probably his duties and interests outside the realm of painting that account most for the decline in his production of landscapes.

A fine example from the decade of the 1660s, however, is the Hermitage painting of *Hunters with Dogs* (Fig. 50 and Color Plate I), signed and dated 1665. In this painting our attention is focused on his favorite motif of the attendant bending over his dogs, for the standing figure on the left and the pair of white dogs slightly to the right of center as well as the approaching horse all carry our eyes to him. The crouching attendant is very similar to the one in *Hunters in a Hilly Landscape* (Fig. 47), where he assumes the same stance but is seen from a different angle. An even closer motif is found in the crouching white dog in the center foreground of the Hermitage composition and his counterpart in the center middle ground of *Hunters in a Hilly Landscape*. Also the dog slightly to the right and behind each of the crouching dogs is similar although not identical to its counterpart.

Although there was a noticeable decline in the production of de Jongh's landscapes during the 1660s, he did on occasion collaborate with The Hague landscape painter, Joris van der Haagen, painting figures into Van der Haagen's settings. In the works identifiable as their joint efforts, figures are usually small, playing a less prominent role than in the paintings entirely by

27. One of the possible exceptions to this is a hunt scene with large vertical forms on an upright panel attributed to De Jongh. Sale, Galerie Jürg Stuker, Bern, 17-30 May 1984, no. 855.

De Jongh, in which figures and landscape are celebrated equally. An example of the collaborative effort of the two painters is the square landscape panel by Van der Haagen (Fig. 51) into which De Jongh has repeated, in identical positions, the two attendants and five dogs from the foreground group of the Hermitage painting.[28] Although the treatment of foliage here does seem in keeping with De Jongh's own style, the relatively small scale of the figures suggests that De Jongh merely added them to Van der Haagen's scene.

On January 22, 1669, authorities of Schieland paid De Jongh and Joris van der Haagen for a painting which was to be placed in the new community building ("Gemeenlantshuys").[29] The painting depicted the edge of a forest with a castle near water and a distant view of mountains. Within this setting, a man and a woman on horseback, accompanied by an attendant with a dog, were shown asking directions of a shepherdess.[30] In all probability De Jongh painted the staffage and Van der Haagen the landscape background in this work which remained in the same building after it became the Boymans Museum and unfortunately perished in the fire of 1864 along with De Jongh's civic guard group portrait. It is significant that De Jongh, who was the most prestigious painter of the Rotterdam area at this time, should have shared this commission on his home ground with Joris van der Haagen, a fact which suggests his declining interest in landscape painting in the 1660s.

It was probably through his brother-in-law, Dirck Wyntrack, that De Jongh came in contact with Van der Haagen, with whom Wyntrack is known to have collaborated earlier, sometimes painting birds and animals into his landscape settings. Oddly enough, shortly after Wyntrack moved from Gouda to The Hague about 1657, his collaboration with Van der Haagen ceased and De Jongh's appears to have begun.[31] A landscape by Van der Haagen (Fig. 52) from shortly before 1660 contains staffage by De Jongh,[32] especially evident in the dog licking itself, which is identical to one in *Hunters Outside an Inn* (Fig. 85), while dating from about 1667 is another joint effort (Fig. 53) first

28. Sale, Roos, Amsterdam, 26 March 1901, no. 55, as Ludolf de Jongh. The panel was later attributed to Joris van der Haagen. See Van der Haagen 1932, p. 140, no. 439 S. In all probability the work is a joint effort. Certainly the great similarity in landscape treatment between the style of De Jongh and Van der Haagen makes it difficult to separate their contributions during the 1660s. The square format is unusual in the works of both men and suggests that this panel has been cut down, while the composition suggests that such reduction was mostly along the left side.

29. Obreen 1877-90, vol. 5, p. 55.

30. Van der Haagen 1932, p. 48.

31. For Wyntrack's collaboration with Joris van der Haagen see Van der Haagen 1932, pp. 45-46.

32. A. Schloss Collection, Paris, before 1940.

recognized by Hofstede de Groot.[33] And the painting with a false Albert Cuyp signature in Budapest (Fig. 54), in which Plietzsch and Beer perceived the hand of De Jongh, may in fact be another combined product, for the 1689 inventory of Adriana Blanckerts of Rotterdam lists, "A landscape in which a woman is milking sheep, the landscape being from Verhagen [van der Haagen] and the figures from Leuf de Jongh" ("Een Landschap alwaer een vrouw schapen melkt, sijnde het landschap van Verhagen en de beelden van Leuf de Jongh").[34]

Closely related to the hunt scenes of Ludolf de Jongh are the early works of his fellow townsman, Abraham Hondius. Hondius was born in Rotterdam about a decade after De Jongh and worked there until his move to Amsterdam in 1659. The latter part of his career was spent in London, where he died sometime after 1690.[35]

Generally speaking, Hondius favored the more violent moments of the hunt, when dogs and their prey — deer, bears, wild boars — are locked in a ferocious struggle to the death. In this respect his art, as Hentzen has shown, owes something of its monumentality and drama to the school of Rubens, especially to Frans Snyders and Jan Fyt.[36] Often, however, in what appear to be among his earliest works, dating mostly before about 1655 and certainly before his move to Amsterdam, Hondius chose to depict those quieter moments before or after the hunt. So close are some of these to the conceptions of De Jongh that they have not infrequently been wrongly attributed to the older painter.[37]

The signed and dated *After the Hunt* of 1653 (Fig. 55)[38] is so close to the contemporary scenes of De Jongh, and so counter to the natural inclinations of Hondius, that a direct influence is certain. The general restfulness of the scene and the relatively modest size of the figures in relation to the picture surface are foreign to his personal tendency toward more monumental figures in greater tension. But even at rest the figures in Hondius' scenes reflect a certain tension and uneasiness through the caricatured faces and mannered attitudes of the humans, the aggressiveness of the dogs, and the frequently wildly rolling eyes of horses and dogs alike. Moreover, there is usually greater

33. Hofstede de Groot in Thieme-Becker 1907-50, vol. 19, p.133.

34. Van der Haagen 1932, pp. 48 and 144n.

35. While the year of his death is given by Walpole 1765, vol. 3, p. 14. as 1695, other sources, including Vertue Note Book A. c., p. 123, cite it as 1691.

36. Hentzen 1963, pp. 35ff.

37. See, for example, Kuretsky 1979, in which figure 7 seems clearly a work by Hondius attributed to De Jongh, just as figure 6 appears equally clearly to be a painting by Hondius in spite of its J. B. Weenix signature. See also Hentzen 1963, p. 48, cat. no. 6.

38. Sale, Sotheby, London, 29 November 1950, no. 124.

variety to his color and a more hard-surfaced and less supple quality to his forms than in De Jongh's works. In this painting, for example, a study of details confirms the validity of the signature and the date. Not only the snarling dogs at the right, with their lips curled beyond all physical possibility, but the presence of exaggerated reflected light in some of the shadows, seen here for example lighting the underbelly of the spotted white dog near the lower right, is a frequent Hondius mannerism that gives the surfaces of animals a wooden or metallic quality. Moreover, the slitted sleeves of the man's costume is a recurring fashion in Hondius that is not found in any hunt acceptable as by De Jongh.

A large and impressive painting by Hondius dated 1654 (Fig. 56) is so reflective of De Jongh's work of the same period that it has sometimes been attributed to the older painter in spite of the full Hondius signature.[39] The white spotted dog of the previous example appears here at the lower right edge. And not only the type of female figure, but the dogs especially, with their nervous contours and gnarled ears, attest to the signature's validity, as does the overstated highlight of the horse's eye, to cite only a few telling traits.

Another signed painting by Hondius of a kindred theme, a *Rest on the Hunt* (Fig. 57), must also have been painted about 1654.[40] It contains a female figure remarkably similar to her counterpart in the previous example, even down to the same elongated, pointed slippers, while the wildly rolling eyes of the dogs behind her add a note portending the violence that will reach a peak in his later work.

While the degree of emotional restraint as well as the themes seen in these early works by Hondius reflect the influence of De Jongh and have even led to some of them being wrongly attributed to the older painter, Hondius was also influenced by the school of Utrecht, and it is probably from the example of Dirck Stoop that he appropriated in some of these early paintings the favorite motif of the trumpeting horseman, a form unknown in the acceptable works of De Jongh.

A painting clearly reflecting the influence of De Jongh and traditionally ascribed to his younger Rotterdam contemporary, Jacob Ochtervelt, is the *Halt on the Chase* (Fig. 58).[41] The striking similarity of such motifs as the white horse, the dog sniffing in the lower left, and the dog licking itself at the right, to their counterparts in the work of De Jongh has been pointed out

39. Formerly Figdor Collection, Vienna. See Hentzen 1963, p. 42 and p. 48, cat. no. 6.

40. Sale, Sotheby, London, 4 April 1984, no. 70.

41. Sale, L. Spik, Berlin, 11-12 February 1943, no. 296; later, Munich Collecting Point, no. 3666.

elsewhere.[42] However, what has not been previously recognized is the strong relationship of this work to the early works of Hondius, especially the signed *Rest on the Hunt*. The trumpeters on horseback and the well-dressed couples are similar in the two works as are the white greyhounds relieving themselves in the lower right corners. Furthermore, both works are on panels of nearly identical dimensions. And the snarling dogs in this work as well as the exaggerated reflected light, seen especially on the dog licking itself, are typical traits of Hondius. The whereabouts of the panel is unknown, and the examination of old photographs does not support the presence of a signature reportedly seen on it by Hofstede de Groot in 1900.[43] The authorship of this painting, consideration of which now favors Hondius, must therefore remain in doubt. But it seems clear that it is either another early work by Hondius, painted about 1655 and reflecting the influence of De Jongh, or a youthful effort by Ochtervelt, combining motifs and traits of his fellow-Rotterdamers, De Jongh and Hondius.

Although De Jongh's influence on the early work of Hondius and Ochtervelt is readily apparent, fainter echoes of his outdoor scenes also appear in the art of other painters of the younger generation who spent time in the Rotterdam area. This is especially seen in the borrowing from De Jongh of animal forms. Compare, for example, the seated greyhound in Adam Pynacker's *Landscape with Sportsmen and Game* in the Dulwich Picture Gallery (Fig. 59), painted in the early 1660s, with its counterpart in De Jongh's *Small Hunting Group* (Fig. 48), which dates from the previous decade.

42. Fleischer 1978, pp. 51-53.
43. Kuretsky 1979, p. 53.

CHAPTER THREE

GENRE

Probably the most interesting, although certainly not the largest, category of Ludolf de Jongh's oeuvre is that of genre. Scenes of everyday life apparently appeared early in his career, for a now untraceable painting of fighting cavaliers on the art market in 1914 was dated 1633, two years before he began his sojourn in France.[1] Unfortunately few of De Jongh's genre paintings bear such dates, making the development of his work in this category very difficult to determine. The evolutions in costume and in the style and subject matter common to seventeenth century genre painting in general, are of some help as guidelines to De Jongh's chronological changes, as is also the concurrent development of his portrait style, which is based more securely on dated examples.

One of the earliest known genre scenes by De Jongh is the *Soldiers with a Kneeling Prisoner* (Fig. 60), formerly in the Palmer Collection in London. Although we understand from Houbraken that De Jongh received so little attention from his second teacher, Anthonie Palamedesz., that he left his studio in Delft to study with Bylert at Utrecht, the effect of his stay with Palamedesz. is certainly evident in this work. In fact, were it not for the signature, this work would almost certainly have been attributed to Palamedesz. The officer in light clothing, as well as the bundled straw in the corner, appears in several works by Palamedesz. (Fig. 61); even the motif of the kneeling prisoner derives from the Delft painter's work.

In addition to the soldier scenes painted under the influence of Palamedesz., De Jongh also produced early interiors with elegant gatherings of music making ladies and gentlemen, which likewise reflect the tutelage of Palamedesz. One of the earliest such scenes by De Jongh is a *House Concert* (Fig. 62) that was at one time in possession of Catherine the Great of Russia and later entered the Hermitage Museum. There has been no trace of it since its appear-

1. Sale, Delaroff, Paris, 23, 24, 27 April and 2 May 1914, no. 177.

ance on the art market in 1931.[2] The panel is signed on the rear wall and, although it bears no date, it must have been painted in the early 1640s.

In a dimly lit room a group of richly clad men and women, seen full-length, converse and make music around a table. The rear wall, on which the artist has signed his name, is parallel to the picture plane and close behind the figures, limiting their space and giving them a stage-like arena in which to act out their roles. A door at the left edge of the panel and a large cupboard or kast at the right halt the lateral movement. A dog in the lower left and a boy entering through the door balance the chair and cloak in the lower right.

Such merry company scenes, related to the work of Dirck Hals in Haarlem and Pieter Codde and Willem Duyster in Amsterdam, were popular with Palamedesz. throughout his career and frequently contain the same elements we see in De Jongh's painting. The *Musical Gathering* (Fig. 63), probably painted in the previous decade, is a typical Palamedesz. of the sort that served as a model for De Jongh and one that even makes similar use of a kast at the right side behind a conversing couple.[3] De Jongh, however, even in such early works, shows himself to be a superior painter of figures. He never adopts Palamedesz.'s frequent use of voluminously clothed pear-shaped seated female figures with under-sized heads and badly-placed knees, who seem to be in a semi-squat in front of their chairs instead of being comfortably seated upon them.

Another signed painting by De Jongh in the same vein is the *Musical Company* (Fig. 64), also dating from the early 1640s and painted under the spell of Palamedesz.[4] Here, too, De Jongh's superior skill as a figure painter is evident, for the seated woman just left of center provides a telling contrast to those in a similarly conceived work by his former Delft master (Fig. 65).[5]

A third such elegant interior is the *Gathering at a Table* in Leipzig (Fig. 66). This work, signed with a monogram on the chair back, is more advanced than the previous two and probably dates a few years later. Here the enclosed space is more clearly defined, the handling of light is more effective with its source included, and the overall tonality is somewhat lighter. The figures break with their prototypes in the work of Palamedesz. in appearing more as individuals and less as types. Moreover, they have assumed more natural

2. Sale, Schwarz, Lempertz, Cologne, 10-11 June 1931, no. 113.

3. Sale, A. Holtzman e. a., Amsterdam, 31 October 1905, no. 87, as A. Palamedesz.; Collection of J. V. Novak, Prague, 1906. The painting bears the false signature of D. Hals.

4. Sale, Ernst Museum, Budapest, 29 April 1929, no. 207.

5. Sale, Lange, Berlin, 5 April 1940, no. 52. Two of the figures in this painting reappear with only slight changes in a signed and dated work of 1634 by the same artist. Philadelphia 1984, p. 293, fig. 2.

poses and their grouping has become more spontaneous and seemingly less contrived; there is more informality and less formula. And yet there is still present the influence of Palamedesz. and lingerings from the earlier works. The female figure seen from the rear, with the middle of her back occupying the exact center of the composition, echoes some of the elegant figures in merry company scenes of Palamedesz. as does the page standing at the left, while the features of the male figure with hat in hand just left of center, correspond quite closely to those of the officer holding a piece of paper just left of center in De Jongh's earlier *Soldiers with a Kneeling Prisoner* (Fig. 60).

In the sketchbook by Bramer which recorded paintings from collections in Delft, there is a second drawing after a work by De Jongh (Fig. 67), this one depicting a merry company in an interior. In this instance, unfortunately, there is no trace of the original painting.[6] However, some years after Bramer made his sketch, the composition by De Jongh caught the eye of Jan Verkolje, who recorded it in a more detailed drawing of pen and brown ink with a gray wash (Fig. 68). Six figures, two men and four women are the focus of attention and share the foreground with a covered table topped with a bowl of fruit. Seated at the left edge of the table are a man playing the violin and a woman who raises her voice in song as her right hand moves rhythmically with the music. At the front edge of the table a richly clad woman stands and plays the lute as her body faces to the right while over her shoulder she looks toward the viewer. A young man seated at the right of the table holds one woman on his knee and raises his wine glass toward another woman for filling. A seventh figure enters the room through a half-open door in the left background.

Several elements taken in combination point to this being a bordello scene: the low-cut necklines of the two seated women,[7] the emphasis on wine and music, the girl seated on the young man's lap, and the prominence of the canopied bed in the right middle ground. Moreover, the higher neckline and the turbaned head of the woman pouring suggest a figure considerably older than the others, probably in the traditional role of the procuress. That the theme relates more specifically to the Prodigal Son dissipating his inheritance among the whores is suggested by the finery of the young man at the right as well as the attention paid to him. The trio of figures of which he is the center is enframed by the canopy of the bed behind them while the standing female lute player serenades him as she looks meaningfully toward us. Moreover, although they are not exclusively attributes of Prodigal Son scenes, the feather-

6. A clumsily painted variant was in the Suminski Collection in Tharandt. Mentioned by Hofstede de Groot in Thieme-Becker 1907-1950, vol. 19 (1926), p. 133.

7. Slive 1970-74, vol. 1, pp. 92-94.

ed hat and the table laden with fruit are traditionally found in illustrations of that story.[8]

The theme of the Prodigal Son was a favorite one in both the theater and the visual arts of sixteenth and seventeenth century Holland, encouraged in part by its role as a warning against the excesses of worldliness and by the lesson of contrition and forgiveness exemplified in the son's return to his father. While there are essentially five episodes in the story of the Prodigal Son — his taking of his inheritance and his departure for a foreign land; the dissipation of his inheritance through gambling, drinking, and carousing with whores; his expulsion from the brothel when his funds are gone; his being forced to live among the swine for survival; and his repentance of his sinful ways and his reunification with his forgiving father — his riotous life among the harlots, although not specifically mentioned in the Bible, is by far the most frequently depicted chapter in his eventful life. Sixteenth century portrayals of the Prodigal Son squandering his inheritance were usually clearly recognizable. In the seventeenth century, however, they were frequently treated with such subtlety that they metamorphosed almost imperceptably into the kind of scene more generally identified today as merry company or musical party but which were undoubtedly intended to remind the seventeenth century onlooker of the evils inherent in a life given over to the pleasures of the senses.[9] But whether Prodigal Son or Merry Company, the usual visual attractiveness of the scenes seems hardly capable of dissuading the viewer from an evening of wine, women, and song. An ostensible warning served, in effect, as a justification for such scenes of merriment.

Several features of this painting relate to Palamedesz. or to other works De Jongh produced in his style. The kast at the right side of Verkolje's drawing, although not included in Bramer's less detailed version, must have been in the now lost painting, for it frequently appears at the sides of Palamedesz.'s Merry Company scenes and was adopted as a compositional device by De Jongh. Moreover, the figure entering through the door at the left rear in the *Prodigal Son* also appears on the side opposite such pieces of furniture in De Jongh's Palamedesz.-like *House Concert* (Fig. 62) and *Gathering at a Table* (Fig. 66). Also, the seated musician at the left side of the table and the singing woman behind it in the *Prodigal Son* are foreshadowed by similar figures in De Jongh's *House Concert*. And the wine cooler atop the stand in the lower right of the *Prodigal Son* has a square shape that is unusual in such Merry

8. For discussions of the iconography of the Prodigal Son theme see Vetter 1955; Bergström 1966; Renger 1970; Leppert 1974, pp. 80-91; and Slim 1976.

9. For the merging and ambiguity of such themes see Stechow 1972.

Company scenes but that can be found in the work of Palamedesz.

In addition to its kinship with Palamedesz., the composition relates generally to an engraving published on the title page of Willem Dircksz. Hooft's play, *Heden-daeghsche Verlooren Soon* (Contemporary Prodigal Son) (Fig. 69), which was first performed at the Amsterdam Academy on February 3, 1630. In both the engraving and De Jongh's composition the son is the center of a trio of figures at the right side, the other two being a harlot and a procuress, while at the left, two women and a man are engaged in music-making. Also in both works a large wine and water cooler is positioned in the lower right corner.

However, the *Prodigal Son* by De Jongh also reflects his study in Utrecht, for its animated spirit more than its details is close to works of the same theme by his third teacher, Jan van Bylert (Fig. 70). Bylert's conceptions also suggest an awareness of the title page of Hooft's play, as we find in his inclusion of a serving woman tallying expenses and the peacock pastry on the table.[10] The plumed headdresses of Bylert's Prodigal Son and female lute player, which are not found in the engraving, may have served as models for De Jongh. A second *Prodigal Son* by Bylert (Fig. 71), probably dating close to De Jongh's, also relates to the engraving in its seated viola player at the left edge of the table, while the leg positions of the Prodigal Son himself and his female companion may have been known to De Jongh, who reversed their places by seating the woman on the man's lap.[11]

De Jongh gave his elegant Palamedesz.-like genre scene an outdoor setting in the *Departure for the Country* in the Castello Sforzesco in Milan (Fig. 72).[12] Here a richly clad group of ladies and gentlemen are gathered beside a horse drawn carriage that waits before a large baroque palace. Farewells are being said as some figures stand beside the carriage while others come down the stairs and approach it in a unifying flow of movement. Two of the figures, the page in the lower right corner and the woman in yellow silk dress near him, make eye-contact with the viewer. The running posture of the page as well as his placement on the panel is reminiscent of the youthful attendant in the *Landscape with the Death of a Fox* (Fig. 37), suggesting that the two derived from the same figure drawing.

This panel and the *Gathering at a Table* in Leipzig (Fig. 66), which dates

10. Sale, Muller, Amsterdam, 15 April 1947, no. 540. For the significance of the peacock in the Prodigal Son theme see Emmens 1968, pp. 166-167; and Bergström 1966, pp. 157-159.

11. E. H. Abt Collection, Zollikon, 1957. Sale, Sotheby, London, 9 April 1986, no. 99, signed, ill.

12. De Jongh's signature was at one time visible on the back of the carriage. Rosa 1966, p. 110, n. 7. During a recent examination, however, it could not be seen.

from the same time, indicate that in genre as well as in landscape and portraiture De Jongh's earliest works already express his preference for an overall muted coloration against which he could skillfully play striking accents of brilliant, highly saturated hues, as in the red jacket of the gentleman and the yellow dress of the lady in the right foreground of the Milan panel and in the red upholstery of the stools and undercloth of the table and the yellow dresses of the women in the Leipzig work.

Another slightly later outdoor scene with figures is the signed *Canal Boat Station* in the National Gallery of Ireland (Fig. 73). In this work as in his hunt scene of *A Shooting Party* (Fig. 39), which dates from the same period and is in the same collection, De Jongh seems to be experimenting with composition and avoiding traditional solutions. The result in this instance is one of his least successful and at the same time most interesting paintings. The individual parts of the canvas, figures as well as setting, are painted with the technical skill we have come to expect in De Jongh's works; the pigment is handled with the same broadness and boldness found in the *Gathering at a Table* in Leipzig and in the tavern scenes painted near the end of the decade. On the other hand, there is a lack of unity, a sense of forms not belonging together, that prevents this from being one of his finer efforts. We are presented not with figures belonging to a setting, but rather we are confronted with figures that seem to have been almost arbitrarily placed within the setting and that bear little or no relationship to it or to each other. They seem to be visitors from several other places who have been chosen for the moment to populate this scene. They are actors on a stage, frozen in a *tableau vivant*.

The two men at the left side of the painting, with their right hands clasped, form a unit that bears little relationship to the rest of the work and one that would probably be at least equally at home in numerous other situations. The two figures derive, as Schatborn has shown,[13] from an extant drawing by De Jongh, but we have the impression that the drawing was not made with this painting in mind but rather that De Jongh searched through his reservoir of drawings to find figures that could be used to animate the left side of the painting. The same appears true of the gentleman with the plumed hat astride a rearing horse at the right side of the composition. He seems even more unrelated to the surroundings and the other figures than the pair at the left. We might expect him to appear in another painting by De Jongh, perhaps one for which he was originally created. The woman slightly left of the rearing horse and carrying baskets suspended from a yoke across her shoulders is certainly more comfortable within the composition than most of the other figures, while

13. Schatborn 1975, p. 82.

the greyhound running behind her seems as isolated in both form and action as the leaping horse.

This attempt to break away from a sense of conscious composition gave De Jongh considerable problems, as pentimenti indicate. Just left of center in the composition was a dog that later was painted over, probably by De Jongh himself. Its presence, of course, gave greater meaning to the position of the greyhound dashing toward it. And extensive changes were made along the right side in the area of the shed and adjacent structures.

The attempt to escape established compositional solutions in the *Canal Boat Station* is paralleled by De Jongh's effort to people the setting with figures in more natural attitudes, as comparison with the previous work indicates. The graceful but self-consciously elegant poses of some of the figures in the *Departure for the Country* have all but disappeared from the *Canal Boat Station* of only a few years later. De Jongh seems in this painting to have consciously cast off the influence of his former teachers, especially Palamedesz., and to have turned more to the world around him, perhaps relying less on preconceived forms inspired by the works of other painters and more on drawings from his own hand made from life.

Concurrent with his progress in the mode of fashionable middle class interiors, with its growing concern for lighter tonality and more clearly defined space, De Jongh continued to develop the murky tonalistic scenes of soldiers and peasants in the darker, more modest interiors of stables and taverns. He apparently moved back and forth as easily between the two forms of genre as did several of his talented contemporaries, including Quirijn van Brekelenkam in Leiden and his fellow-Rotterdamer, Hendrik Sorgh. Even his less imaginative teacher, Anthonie Palamedesz., painted colorful Merry Companies and dark tonalistic soldier scenes throughout his career. There were challenges in each mode; there was no need for an aesthetic sense as restless as De Jongh's to be confined to only one path.

In his tavern and stable interiors painted near mid-century, De Jongh tended to use fewer and larger figures, as in *The Reprimand* (Fig. 74), signed but undated, while still retaining the dark tonality seen in the soldier paintings he produced under the spell of Palamedesz.[14] The principal figures now, larger and more prominent in the format of the painting, tend to be more strongly modeled in light and dark, affording them a more sculptural tangibility. This interest in more sculpturally modeled form even extends to the broken and almost animated pieces of straw on the floor, which not only cast distinct shadows but are themselves modeled in light and dark with carefully placed

14. Sale, Charpentier, Paris, 24 March 1952, no. 50.

highlights. Also evident is De Jongh's growing interest in a more dynamically receding space, as we have already noted in some of his portraits, seen here in his placement of the vanishing point near the left edge of the composition and his use of rapidly converging orthogonals. A noticeable shortcoming of this painting, however, is the weak drawing of the standing woman, a rarity in such a prominent figure by De Jongh and one that may be the result of later overpainting by another hand.

Here, too, we have a genre subject with such strong anecdotal quality that we suspect we may be witnessing an event from a story or theatrical production that would have been recognizable to many of De Jongh's contemporaries, but that today is seen merely as the depiction of the commonplace. The storytelling character of the panel is strengthened not only by the standing mother who admonishes her young son but also by the animated reactions of the male figures.

A similar young man and his older companion appear in *A Public House* (Fig. 75).[15] The pervasive dark tonality of the painting is relieved by the light which comes from the left and selectively plays on the two principal figures and on the triangular stool and rumpled cloth at the lower right. In the background are the less prominent figures of a seated woman and a standing man before a fireplace. The fireplace wall at the rear runs parallel to the picture plane and limits the space, with the vanishing point in the center of the composition, in a more conventional way than in the previous painting. But here, too, the forms in the lighted area are modeled with a definiteness that is clearly seen not only in the figures themselves but also in the fold of the tablecloth and even in the three-dimensionality of the lacing that dangles from the left knee of the youth's trousers. And yet this plasticity does not result in a trivial compilation of details, for De Jongh is a talented visual editor, emphasizing the principal features of a painting through light, clarity, and strong modeling, while subordinating the less important parts by minimizing their modeling, softening their edges, and engulfing them in darkness.

The major protagonists are even more animated here than in the previous example, and what is most interesting is that the seated young man, whose head is very near the center of the composition, laughs and seeks eye-contact with the viewer. His older companion looks at him with a smile while he places his right hand over his heart and his left on a flagon.

Perhaps the same pair of figures reappears in *Hunters in an Inn* (Fig. 76), a painting that dates from the same period and gently suggests the art of Sorgh. Although the older man in the scene is now seated and apparently shares his

15. Private collection, Brighton, 1929.

food with a greyhound, the figure of the young man assumes a position very similar to his counterpart in the previous painting.[16] Rather than facing us he now turns his head to the side, and the position of his left arm has changed as his hand now rests on his hip. Otherwise the two figures bear a remarkable resemblance to each other, especially in their clothing and leg positions, suggesting that they were derived from the same drawing. Even the flagon on the table is the same type as in *A Public House* and occupies a like position on the table. It is now the standing woman instead of the youth who makes eye-contact with the viewer as she extends toward us a flagon of the same design as the one on the table. And the sculptural modeling of the strongest lighted forms is most noticeable here in the two flagons, the youth, especially his left arm, and the white greyhound, including the dog's lead held by his master's left hand. The elderly man and the standing woman, although presumably struck by light as strongly as that which plays on the younger man and his dog, are on a plane slightly further back in the pictorial space and are less crisply modeled, adding a sense of atmosphere and increasing the feeling of distance.

Although the figures are stationary, the space recedes dramatically as a result of the painting's being conceived — and intended to be viewed — from a point very near the frontal plane of the picture. This is apparent in the swift convergence of orthogonals created by the rapid diminution of forms receding in space, and especially evident in the contrasts in dimensions between the near and far ends of the window opening, its shutter overhead, and the planked area of the ceiling. De Jongh's interest in dramatically receding space appeared also at this time in his portraiture, as we have seen.

In color these rather early genre paintings by De Jongh, depicting lower middle class subjects in rustic inns or barns, are dominated by overall dark browns and grays relieved only here and there with small areas of bright color. This taste for tonalist painting, in which forms are defined more through differences in light and dark than through differences in hues, prevailed in Holland during the second quarter of the seventeenth century and suggests that such works by De Jongh were probably produced in the 1640s and not later than the mid 1650s. The subjects, too, with their emphasis on a less than genteel rural and rustic life are in keeping with Dutch taste of that same period.

In his dark, tonalist genre paintings of the 1640s and the early 1650s, De Jongh dealt not only with lower middle class subjects but also with scenes of off-duty soldiers, a theme equally popular with the Dutch during the second

16. A slightly smaller variant of this painting, with a "Maas" signature, was sold at Christies, London, 20 October 1972, no. 88. In it the woman's right hand gestures toward the viewer but holds no flagon, and the dark greyhound at the right has been painted out.

quarter of the century, but one which lost much of its appeal after the signing of the Treaty of Munster in 1648, bringing an end to the Thirty Years War. In his *Tavern Scene* in the National Gallery in Prague (Fig. 77), a painting long thought to be an early work of Pieter de Hooch, De Jongh has chosen characters and a setting similar to those in *Hunters in an Inn*, but now his drinkers, seen here in a tavern scarcely more well-furnished than a stable, are soldiers rather than hunters or peasants. The two men are seen facing each other across a triangular stool which serves as a modest table, just beyond which stands a serving girl whose body faces toward one soldier as she turns her head toward the other. The three figures are in the left half of the painting, toward the source of light which is out of the composition.

As in his other genre paintings of this time, the single source of light models the figures with a solidity and exactitude that appeals strongly to our tactile sense. The folds of the white hooded shoulder cape worn by the serving girl are rendered with such visual clarity that they invite imaginative translation into a sculptural material. Likewise the stem of the clay pipe atop the triangular stool, the fragments of straw on the earthen floor, and even the edge of tunic lying across the right thigh of the soldier facing toward the light are given tangibility through carefully placed lights and shadows. Still, this skillful modeling of form is not to be confused with the style of the "fijnschilders" of Leiden whose emphasis on exactitude was expressed in an extensive compilation and minute rendering of details. The editing and simplification characteristic of sculpture is not to be found in their work to the extent that we see it in the art of De Jongh. For example, the left sleeve and skirt of the tunic worn by the soldier holding the glass, while presented with palpable clarity, are nevertheless simplified or abstracted in a manner not usually associated with the art of Dou, Van Mieris, or Schalcken.

A similar painting, also formerly considered an early work by Pieter de Hooch, is *Soldiers at Reveille* in the North Carolina Museum of Art in Raleigh (Fig. 78). Obviously from the same hand as the *Tavern Scene* in Prague, this painting is traceable to two eighteenth century sales in which it appeared as a work by De Jongh.[17] The sculptural treatment of form, especially evident in the seated soldier at the left and in the shadows and highlights of the crumpled straw on the floor, as well as in the animated expressions of the figures, confirms the eighteenth-century evidence that it is a work by De Jongh.

While the theme of sleeping soldiers being awakened to duty was a popular

17. Sale, J. Pompe van Meerdervoort, Soeterwoude (near Leiden), 19 May 1780, no. 45; and Sale, Joh. Engelman, Haarlem, 16 July 1782, no. 12.

one around mid-century,[18] De Jongh's use of it here may have been inspired by a work of Jacob Duck of Utrecht. De Jongh's use of large figures on the left balancing the prone waking warrior on the right, with other soldiers visible through an open door at the rear, is reminiscent of Duck's *Soldiers Arming Themselves* (Fig. 79), of the mid-1630s, suggesting a possible direct influence. Moreover, Duck's frequent use of a figure making eye-contact with the viewer is reflected here in the standing woman — remarkably similar to the serving girl in the *Tavern Scene* in Prague — who laughs and points to the waking soldier.

Another figure with a laughing expression who looks toward the viewer with squinting eyes is seated in the lower right corner of *Paying the Hostess* (Fig. 80), a beautifully painted stable scene in a private collection. The signature of "Pr. d. Hooch," which appears on the triangular stool, is either a later addition or an alteration of "L. de Jongh."[19] The modeling of the principal figures, the treatment of the pieces of straw on the floor, and the skillful painting of the horse being led from the stable combine to establish the authorship of De Jongh and to make this one of his most attractive works. This may be the painting by "de Jongh," of "An Officer Paying his Landlady," which appeared in a sale in 1751.[20] A few years after De Jongh painted this panel Pieter de Hooch did paint the same subject (Fig. 81), obviously influenced by this work, and turned to the theme at least one additional time later in his career.[21]

The anecdotal character of the scene is suggested not only by the interplay of the standing officer and the hostess but also by the seated figure in the lower right who looks toward the viewer as he places his right index finger to his cheek just below his eye. This gesture indicates to the viewer that something happening or being said is not to be taken at face value. Most likely, in this instance, we are to understand that the officer is attempting to mislead the hostess or vice versa.[22] The gesture appears in the oeuvre of Jan Steen and is used in a work by Karel Dujardin (Fig. 82) in a way that is remarkably similar to that of De Jongh.

Although this panel is today in a vertical format, it was originally horizontal, for a section of approximately fifteen centimeters has been added to the

18. For a discussion of the theme of the sleeping soldier see Kuretsky 1979, p. 58.

19. Fleischer 1978, p. 63; and Sutton 1980, p. 141.

20. Sale, Dr. Bragge, Prestage, London, 19-21 March 1751, no. 41. Neither the artist's first name or initials nor the painting's support or dimensions appear in the catalogue of the sale.

21. Fleischer 1978, p. 64 n. 17; and Sutton 1980, p. 81.

22. See Sutton in Philadelphia 1983, p. 34; and Christopher Brown in Philadelphia 1984, p. 195.

top. Its original dimensions therefore corresponded very closely to those of the previous painting with which it is also closely allied in style, suggesting the possibility that originally the two were pendants or part of a series illustrating a story that is no longer recognized.[23]

The progress toward the recording of interior space and light noted in De Jongh's earlier *Gathering at a Table* (Fig. 66), is even more evident in *The Message* in the Mittelrheinisches Landesmuseum in Mainz (Fig. 83). Signed and dated 1657, this work displays an interior with a more clearly defined space than we have noted up to now. This increased sense of clarity and order is achieved through a lighter tonality that illuminates the geometrical arrangement of architectural forms in the background. These qualities foreshadow the still more clearly articulated spatial settings in his paintings of the following years. In this transitional work, with its emphasis on geometric forms and pervading light, the volume of enclosed space is beginning to assume a volumetric definition that had long been characteristic of the figures.

The four figures are united in a compact arrangement. The arched back of the elderly listener at the left rear has a counterpart in the curved form of the girl at the right who bends over the shoulder of the seated man with a beard, while the diagonal of the messenger's trumpet joins the figure behind him to another diagonal formed by the extended left leg of the bearded man, his left hand and forearm, and the left forearm of the girl behind him. The diagonal and curvilinear forms of the figures play very effectively against the verticals and horizontals of the chairs and the back wall.

But even more than the compositional arrangement, the figures are united by the concentration and intensity with which they listen to the news in the message. The mood is one of a serious stillness broken only by the voice of the messenger as he reads the contents of a document that will perhaps affect their lives. How different this is from the light-hearted atmosphere of De Jongh's earlier genre! Adding to the effect is the appearance here of four very distinct and plausible individuals in contrast to the anonymous figures in his very early Palamedesz.-like works or even the somewhat caricatured figures in his slightly later tavern and stable scenes. The anecdotal element in *The Message* is treated with restraint and tenderness.

The subject of a message being delivered orally is certainly not unique to this painting, but it was usually presented as a written order being read to a soldier, such as a call back to duty requiring him to leave the company of his

23. Sutton 1980, p. 141, has pointed out that approximately 15 cm. were added to the top of this panel at an early date, changing it from a horizontal to a vertical format, and that its original dimensions were comparable to those of the painting in Raleigh.

female companion.[24] But there are no military figures in De Jongh's painting, leaving us to puzzle, for now at least, over the exact nature of this message. But regardless of the specific meaning, De Jongh has produced a situation involving believable individuals that is fraught with subtle emotional depth and pathos.

The following year De Jongh returned to one of his earlier themes when he painted *Hunters in an Inn* (Fig. 84 and Color Plate II), signed and dated 1658. Although he has revived in this work the festive mood he felt appropriate to such scenes, he has retained the concern for more clearly defined interior space that was evident in *The Message*. Moreover, the orderliness and cleanliness of the interior as well as the dress of some of the patrons reflect a more prosperous milieu than found in his previous tavern interiors. The earthen floor strewn with straw, so characteristic of his earlier works, is here replaced by a floor of neatly laid tiles. The increased intensity of the daylight seen through the windows at the left as well as its effectiveness in flooding the interior is more apparent here than in his past works and is in keeping with the general developments in Dutch genre painting. The head and knees of the youth seated at the left, the dogs he is preparing to feed, and even the wall at the right side with the serving girl entering through a door show the effects of the increased luminosity. Another change that reflects the general taste in Dutch painting of the time is the increased variety and intensity of hues. Although De Jongh tends in all his work to prefer subdued coloration, relieved only here and there with accents of brighter hues, the increased luminosity of this example does result in a more colorful overall effect that reaches its apex, as we might expect, in an area of brilliant vermilion, seen in the jacket of the hunter seated in the center of the composition.

One of the most beautiful of De Jongh's paintings of hunters and their dogs at rest is the Geneva scene of *Hunters Outside an Inn* (Fig. 85), painted in the mid-1650s and at various times believed to have been the work of Pieter de Hooch or Albert Cuyp. Here De Jongh's interest in creating a dramatic perspective near one edge of his composition — usually at the left — which we have already noted in several of his other works, is combined with the distant atmospheric view and further enhanced by the convergence of the architectural lines on both the right and left, and by the diagonal shadow of the building and trees at the right.

In spite of the unusual composition in which a tree near the center of the canvas provides a strong vertical divider between the mass of human and

24. Gudlaugsson 1959-60, vol. 1, pp. 92-93, discusses Ter Borch's use of the motif and its apparent influence on others.

animal forms concentrated on the right and the distant view on the left, the painting does not fall into two halves but is held together by the dynamic thrusts of the diagonals moving toward the horizon. Crossing these thrusts and providing a sense of classical stability is the arrangement of the humans and animals into three more or less clearly defined planes running parallel to the surface of the painting. The first plane is defined by the youth sitting at the right edge of the painting and the figure of the horse whose reins he holds. The second is formed by the servant girl and the standing hunter with his back toward us, and the third by the figure seated beneath the tree and the line of dogs arranged across the road as well as by the shadowy figures between the tree and the door to the inn. The prominently placed white dog in the center foreground, obviously derived from the same drawing — but here reversed — as the dog in the lower right corner of the previous work, extends the frontal plane formed by the horse and his seated groom, and is perhaps an afterthought resulting from a felt need to unite more strongly the two halves of the composition. The prominent position given to his seemingly abrupt but unjustified action adds the only discordant note to this masterful work.

The dynamic perspective and the spatial determinants used by De Jongh in *Hunters Outside an Inn* reappear in essentially the same form but in a very different setting in his *Scene in a Courtyard* (Fig. 86) of only a few years later. In this work in the Metropolitan Museum of Art, dating from approximately 1660 and nearly identical in its dimensions to the previous painting, the vanishing point again appears near the left edge of the canvas and the space is laterally enclosed by the broadly presented wall of a building at the right and a sharply receding one at the left, while once more the animated forms are arranged parallel to the plane of the picture. In place of the wagon tracks leading to the distant vanishing point, De Jongh here uses the diminishing pattern of the pavement bricks to thrust space through a series of arches. While relying on a nearly identical treatment of space, De Jongh has produced a very different painting.

Although it is unsigned, the *Scene in a Courtyard* was for many years regarded as a painting by De Hooch[25] before being attributed to Hendrick van der Burch[26] and finally being recognized as a work by De Jongh.[27] A scene by De Hooch to which it obviously relates is *A Woman and Maid in a Courtyard* in the National Gallery in London (Fig. 87), which dates from the early

25. Smith 1829-42, vol. 9, suppl., p. 568, no. 16; Havard 1879-81 III, p. 101; Hofstede de Groot 1907-28, vol. 1, Pieter de Hooch no. 304; and Brière-Misme 1927, pp. 261-262.

26. Valentiner 1929, no. 252; and Hartford 1950-51, no.25.

27. Attributed to Ludolf de Jongh (verbally) by J. van Gelder, S. J. Gudlaugsson, and A. B. de Vries. Curatorial files, Metropolitan Museum of Art.

1660s.[28] Although the dimensions of the two paintings are similar, the De Hooch is a vertical while the De Jongh is a horizontal. In each case a mistress is shown giving instructions to her maid who prepares fish on a circular platter. The painting by De Hooch, like that by De Jongh, has at the right side a modest brick structure, against the wall of which is a pump, while in the right background is the steeply-pitched roof of a taller building. Also in both works the deep space near the left side moves through the courtyard gateway to reveal the small figure of an approaching man. Moreover, the mistresses as well as the servant girls are similarly dressed in the two paintings. Absent from the version by De Hooch is the building bordering the courtyard at the left.

It is the treatment of space that links De Jongh's *Hunters Outside an Inn*, his *Scene in a Courtyard*, and De Hooch's *A Woman and Maid in a Courtyard* in London. What seems apparent in this relationship is that it is De Jongh's New York canvas that occupies the central position in the development, for through its unmistakable affinity to the others, it provides a linkage between his earlier *Hunters Outside an Inn* and De Hooch's *A Woman and Maid in a Courtyard* that is not otherwise obvious. Therefore, in contrast to the general assumption that De Jongh's courtyard scene derived from De Hooch's, it would seem that again the younger man received inspiration from the older. But what seems equally true is that De Jongh's venture into such Delft School domestic courtyard views was prompted in turn by courtyard scenes De Hooch had painted as early as 1658.

The relationship between the works of De Jongh and De Hooch is a clear indication that they remained in contact even after the younger man's departure from his native city of Rotterdam and that by at least the 1660s the general flow of influence from De Jongh to De Hooch had stabilized into a mutual give and take. By at least 1660 De Jongh's productivity in the field of genre had declined, although not quite to the extent noticeable in his landscape scenes. As with the *Scene in a Courtyard*, some of the genre paintings he produced during the last two decades of his life give the impression that he re-entered the field to try his hand at the latest trends and developments. Nevertheless, as is also evident in the *Scene in a Courtyard*, he never became a mere follower; his creations always remain his own.

De Jongh's interest in precisely defined interior space flooded with daylight is nowhere more clearly seen than in his *Woman Receiving a Letter*, from the Rothschild Collection in Ascott House, now part of the National Trust

28. De Hooch's painting is dated 166(?), the last digit being illegible. Sutton 1980, p. 89, suggests that it probably dates 1660-61 or 1663, when De Hooch is known to have been in Delft.

(Fig. 88). This work, painted about 1663-65 to judge from the costumes, is yet another of the genre scenes by Ludolf de Jongh which, in spite of his signature on the painting above the door, was for many years assigned to the oeuvre of Pieter de Hooch.[29] The long confusion of this work with the style of De Hooch is certainly understandable in view of the parallels that exist between it and some of the works of the younger man. The general theme of the lady of the house receiving a letter from a male messenger in the entrance hall or voorhuis was treated by De Hooch in a painting dated 1670 (Fig. 89) and in another (Fig. 90) of about the same time.[30] Moreover, the seated woman seen sewing in the De Jongh composition may have inspired a De Hooch figure in a similar setting (Fig. 91), painted about 1668. But while there are similarities in theme and even somewhat in the architectural forms, there are clear differences between the works of the two men, not only in the figure types and their construction — compare, for example, the right hands of the two ladies receiving letters in the De Jongh and in the De Hooch painting in Hamburg — but especially in the intensity of light streaming in from the outdoors. While the light in the De Hooch paintings remains relatively soft and subtle, in the De Jongh its force all but obliterates some of the mullions in the windows and the modeling of the right side of the mistress's face, neck, and shoulder, much as an overexposed photograph obscures the modulation of form. Indoor light of this intensity and contrast, which first appeared in De Jongh's œuvre in *Hunters in an Inn* of 1658 (Fig. 84 and Color Plate II), is nowhere to be found in the indoor scenes of De Hooch. Such strong contrasts that do exist in De Hooch's interior, result from shadows being deepened rather than light being intensified. And, of course, the skillful painting and animation of thc playful dogs, including a greyhound, is a familiar feature in many of De Jongh's works and has no true counterpart in the art of De Hooch.

Although specific paintings by De Hooch apparently bear a direct relationship to De Jongh's *Lady Receiving a Letter*, they again seem to be later in time. Thus, while it is likely that the "Delft School" quality of De Jongh's *Lady Receiving a Letter* again reflects a general De Hoochian influence, the circumstances leading to the more specific relationship noted between this

29. It appears as a Pieter de Hooch in Smith 1829-42, vol. 4, no. 32; and in Hofstede de Groot 1907-28, vol. 1, no. 230. It was first recognized as by Ludolf de Jongh in the Royal Academy Exhibition, London, 1938, no. 248.

30. Genre scenes set in the entrance hall of a Dutch house were especially popular with still another native Rotterdamer, Jacob Ochtervelt. See Kuretsky 1979, pp. 34-39. As Scholten 1985, p. 26, has pointed out, the forerunner of this type was Nicolaes Maes, who, in the late 1650s, produced a number of genre scenes in which milkmaids or musicians are placed before a house, while it was perhaps Quirin van Brekelenkam in Leiden who first moved the activity into the voorhuis.

painting and two or three by De Hooch cannot be determined. The distances between Rotterdam, Delft, and Amsterdam are not great, even by seventeenth century standards, making it likely that the relationship between the two men remained close and that both profited from a mutual stimulation, periodically renewed.

The painting above the doorway in De Jongh's scene depicts the story of Diana and Acteon, which, Kuretsky has suggested, may represent a witty mythological parallel to the scene below in which a male intrudes into a world of women.[31] More recently Scholten has interpreted the letter in the hands of the young woman as a message of love, with the theme of the painting over the doorway serving as a warning to its amorous writer, whose messenger has just delivered it. He has further shown that the painting of *Diana and Acteon* derives from a composition by Antonio Tempesta.[32]

De Jongh's interests in the effects of strong sunlight, in clearly defined and limited space, and in genre subjects, especially those including animals, are all combined in two canvases of similar size, dating from the mid- or late 1660s. The *Hunting Party in the Courtyard of a Country House* (Fig. 92), in the Detroit Institute of Arts, depicts a varied group of people with dogs and horses in the clearly limited confines of a courtyard of an elegant country villa such as the Dutch patrician class built along the Amstel and Vecht rivers. The composite pilasters as well as the prominent use of stone reflect the architectural style that came into vogue in Holland in the middle decades of the century.

Most of the figures in the scene are preparing to participate in the hunt. A well-dressed lady and gentleman are on horseback and an attendant bends over to ready the dogs, a favorite motif of De Jongh. A young man with a firearm approaches the group from the right while another attendant, accompanied by two dogs, walks toward the portal at the left. In the right foreground a servant girl, seemingly deep in her own thoughts, crosses the courtyard toward a wheelbarrow in the left foreground, and the heads of two other figures, whose relationship to the principal activities is unclear, are seen above the servant attending the dogs. The hour is quite early, for the morning light strikes the attendant at the portal, as well as the lady on horseback, from a nearly horizontal direction as it casts elongated shadows on the floor of the courtyard. All else in the courtyard is illuminated by the diffused light from above.

In spite of De Jongh's great skill in drawing human figures, his limited

31. Kuretsky 1979, p. 34.
32. Scholten 1985.

ability to set them in motion, as we noted earlier in his hunt scenes, is nowhere more clearly evident than in this work. The servant girl and the attendant with a firearm in the right foreground and the attendant approaching the portal at the left are all in striding positions, yet they seem motionless. Probably the drawings from which these figures derive were made from live models who posed motionless for De Jongh in balanced stances that could be maintained for long periods. The visual imbalance of genuinely striding figures, compensated for by their forward motion, is not found here. The result is one of frozen animation.

A similar work, also on canvas and very close in size to the Detroit painting, is *Figures with Coach in a Courtyard* (Fig. 93). The location of this painting, which last appeared on the art market in 1963, is unfortunately not known.[33] In an earlier sale it was regarded as a work by Jacob Ochtervelt,[34] and somewhat later it was attributed to Hendrick van der Burch,[35] and still later to Pieter de Hooch[36] based on what was regarded as a signature on the back of the carriage. Plietzsch has assigned it correctly to the oeuvre of De Jongh.[37] Its kinship with the painting in Detroit is found not only in their dimensions but also in their architectural forms and their very similar treatment of space. And even though the sun is higher in the sky in this scene, the play of strong sunlight on some of the figures, contrasting with the diffused light on others, is entirely in keeping with the painting in Detroit. In view of these striking similarities, it is possible that the two works were intended as pendants, depicting the commonplace events at a grand country house. But whether the setting is that of a specific house or not, it is really the activities of the figures that are featured rather than an accurate portrayal of a particular structure.[38]

Another scene of fashionable life in the surroundings of a grand country house was recorded by De Jongh in *Women in a Garden* (Fig. 94), a work in the Count Labia Collection in Capetown. The painting was considered to be by De Hooch until 1923, when Hofstede de Groot discovered that his signature on it had been formed by altering that of Ludolf de Jongh.[39] Based on the costumes of the figures and the taste reflected in the painting, the date it

33. P. de Boer, Amsterdam, 1963.

34. Sale, C. T. D. Crews, London, 2 July 1915, no. 55.

35. Valentiner 1929, no. 253.

36. Sale, Dr. Edward Beith, Christie's, London, 8 April 1938, no. 24; van Thienen 1945, p. 51; and Paris 1967, no. 51.

37. Plietzsch 1960, p. 57.

38. Robinson has noted that pentimenti appearing in some areas of the architecture reflect changes of details that suggest the setting was not derived from an actual building. St. Petersburg/Atlanta 1975, p. 32.

39. Hofstede de Groot in Thieme-Becker 1907-50, vol. 19 (1926), p. 133; and Bredius 1928, pp. 66-67. See also White 1982, p. 66, no. 94.

bears of 1676 is probably genuine, making this the artist's last known dated work, executed just three years before his death. Certainly the two ladies in the foreground, with their fine clothing and elongated proportions, recall the rather mannered and elegant style that characterized the figures in much Dutch painting of the 1670s. These refined ladies provide an interesting contrast to the gardener kneeling behind them at the right and the woman with a basket at the left side of the composition, who not only are more in keeping with De Jongh's earlier figures but who also represent a distinctly different social class.

The perspective and treatment of space in this work is strongly reminiscent of those same elements in the *Scene in a Courtyard* (Fig. 86) in New York and the *Hunting Party in the Courtyard of a Country House* (Fig. 92) in Detroit. In all three works the vanishing point is near the left side of the composition, and the enclosed space is visually bordered at the left side by a sharply foreshortened form, at the rear by a form parallel to the picture plane, and at the right side by a structure running parallel to the form at the left but receding more gently into the distance. Moreover, two of the paintings have a small figure near the vanishing point in the left distance to furnish us with a spatial reference. And in both the Capetown and Detroit paintings a wheelbarrow in the foreground points its handles toward the vanishing point, while a strong shaft of light from a sun low on the horizon breaks through the left side of the enclosure, boldly illuminating figures at the opening and casting long shadows across the middle ground.

Clearly related to the Capetown *Women in a Garden* is *A Formal Garden* in the Queen's collection at Windsor Castle (Fig. 95), which may represent the same garden from a more rearward position, if indeed the views are not imaginary. The tall hedge at the left, and rear and the building at the right again enclose the space, although in this work the vanishing point has been moved slightly more toward the center. The lady sniffing a flower in the Capetown painting and the two fashionable women in the foreground bear a striking resemblance, in costume, hair style, and figure type, to the three women at the left side of the Windsor Castle scene.

Although it bears no signature, the painting in Windsor Castle had been attributed to Pieter de Hooch until the genuine signature of De Jongh was discovered on the Capetown canvas. While the difference in sizes precludes the possibility that the two paintings are pendants, they nevertheless date from the same period and are clearly by the same hand.[40]

40. A larger version of the Windsor Castle painting was sold at Christie's, London, 3 May 1974, no. 75, as by a follower of De Hooch.

A large painting in Vienna depicts the *Kneuterdijk in The Hague* (Fig. 96) and presents us with a most impressive cityscape by De Jongh. The expansiveness of the scene is stressed as the gently sloping ground spreads out before us and gabled houses on either side diminish rapidly in size, along with the stately trees before them, to lead our eyes toward the distance. Various forms are strategically placed across the square not only to serve as spatial guide posts but also to underscore the vastness of the scene. From the small group of figures clustered around the knife-grinder's wheel in the left foreground we can move, via the hunter and his dog, to the fountain in the middle distance near the center of the canvas. Other forms, notably the carriage with white horses in the left middle ground and strolling figures on the right, further clarify and accentuate spatial distances.

The painting has created a particularly difficult problem of attribution. In 1880 it was sold as a work by Jan Vermeer, presumably because of a similarity to that painter's renowned *View of Delft*, but by 1907 Hofstede de Groot had rejected the attribution.[41] Similarities between the treatment of the trees in the Vienna painting and in some of the works of Joris van der Haagen, coupled with the fact that he is known to have lived in The Hague from 1640 to 1669, resulted in the work being attributed to him, certainly a more likely possibility. The recognition, however, that the figures were not the work of Van der Haagen, led to the belief that they were added by Ludolf de Jongh, with whom, as we have seen, Van der Haagen occasionally collaborated.[42] A later suggestion retained the attribution of the setting to Van der Haagen but credited the figures to Adriaen van de Velde.[43] More recently Plietzsch has attributed not only the figures but the entire canvas to De Jongh, finding no justification for assigning any portion of it to Joris van der Haagen.[44]

Plietzsch's attribution seems correct. There is no reason to assume that this painting is a joint effort: certainly the figures are by De Jongh, and the landscape portions of the canvas are perfectly in keeping with his style and not entirely typical of the work of Van der Haagen.[45] The sun, low in the sky, casts long shadows across the ground and creates patterns of light and dark against

41. Sale, Demidoff, Palais de San Donato, 15-17 March 1880, no. 1128 (as Vermeer). Hofstede de Groot 1907-28, vol. 1 (1907), p. 609, no. 54.

42. Hofstede de Groot in Thieme-Becker 1907-50, vol. 19 (1926) p. 133; and Van der Haagen 1932, no. 62 and fig. IX.

43. Glück 1935, pp. 174-78.

44. Plietzsch 1960, p. 56.

45. Glück 1935, pp. 175-76, while regarding the background as the work of Van der Haagen, recognized its exceptional quality for his oeuvre: "..man muss es wohl als sein Meisterwerk betrachten, wie es fast jeder von den kleineren holländischen Malern mindestens einmal im Leben geschaffen hat."

the facades on the right in a manner reminiscent of the *Hunting Party in the Courtyard of a Country House* (Fig. 92) in Detroit, and *Women in a Garden* (Fig. 94) in Capetown. The figures, too, are close to those in the Detroit painting, especially the group in the foreground struck by the strong horizontal light, while the old man with the walking stick has the characteristic plodding gait found so often in De Jongh's work, such as the striding figures in the Detroit painting. While the greyhound in the lower left of the Vienna painting is similar in a general way to several dogs in other works of De Jongh, the horsedrawn carriage in the left middle ground closely corresponds to those in the *Departure for the Country* in Milan (Fig. 72) and *Figures with Coach in a Courtyard* (Fig. 93). Also the cringing dog seen from the rear in the lower left corner appeared earlier in the foreground of the signed *Fox Hunt* in the Rijksmuseum (Fig. 38).

The four principal figures grouped around the knife-grinder's wheel were used again by De Jongh in a small oil study on paper in the British Museum (Fig. 97) that was formerly attributed to Adriaen van de Velde.[46] The painting, which also depicts a town square, also includes the running greyhound, seen now in a reverse image, and a coach drawn by white horses, seen now from the front. Light falls across the town square in a way similar to that in the Kneuterdijk view, although the tall gabled houses bordering the square are here arranged parallel to the picture plane, and the left foreground includes a marketing group that has no counterpart in the previous painting. The general conception, however, is reminiscent of marketing scenes by other Rotterdam painters, especially those of Hendrick Sorgh (Fig. 98). The purpose of this small sketch is not known; it may have been intended to serve as a modello, but no larger painting based on this composition has come to light, and no other oil study on paper by De Jongh is known.

The general coloration is in keeping with De Jongh's preference for grays and muted browns relieved only occasionally but very effectively by masterfully placed accents of brighter hues, seen here for example in the vermilion cap of the knife-grinder and the skirt of the woman with her back to us at the lower left.

The sureness and deftness of De Jongh's hand is nowhere better seen than

46. Hind 1931, vol. 4, p. 75, no. 4, attributed the oil sketch to Adriaen van de Velde. Glück 1935 accepted Hind's attribution. Lugt 1931, vol. 2, p. 42, no. 789, attributed a small ink drawing to Adriaen van de Velde on the basis of its generally similar theme to the British Museum oil sketch: a town square with a knife grinder and a carriage drawn by two horses. The composition, however, bears little similarity either to the British Museum oil sketch or to the *Kneuterdijk in The Hague*. Both the oil sketch and the *Kneuterdijk* were correctly attributed to De Jongh by Plietzsch 1960, p. 56.

in the economy of means with which he is able to suggest forms. Only a few touches of the brush were needed to render effectively the play of light on the faces of the three figures near the right side of the composition. The right forearm and wrist of the woman and especially the hands of the old man with a walking stick and small flask are painted with such an easy simplicity that we wish more sketches like this by De Jongh were known.

He was a principal painter in Rotterdam for nearly two decades following his seven year absence, and he became a leading and respected official, first as *stadsmajoor* in Rotterdam and later as *schout* in Hillegersberg. De Jongh therefore presented a model of success to young painters of the area. His influence on genre painters of the next generation appeared shortly after mid-century in the early works of both Pieter de Hooch and Jacob Ochtervelt.

Genre painters of lesser renown also reflect in their works the influence of De Jongh. Jan Natus (act. ca. 1658-1662) produced genre paintings around 1660 (Fig. 99)[47] that are strongly reminiscent of De Jongh's tavern scenes of a few years earlier. His use of light to enhance the plasticity of the slightly simplified figures as well as his facial types suggest the influence of the older painter.[48] Although the scant facts known of Natus' life identify him only with Middelburg, in 1658 he copied a painting of 1652 by the Rotterdammer Hendrick Sorgh, with whom, it has been suggested, he may have studied.[49]

At the same time, Jacob Andries Schaeck, active in the third quarter of the century and of a Rotterdam family of painters, created genre subjects equally inspired by De Jongh. His *Interior with Peasants* (Fig. 100) is signed and dated 166(?).[50] Although here the forms are somewhat less firmly modeled than we are accustomed to meeting in a work by De Jongh, the male figures are strongly reminiscent of his types and relate closely to his painting of 1658 in Groningen (Fig. 84 and Color Plate II). The peasant playing cards in Schaeck's composition bears a striking resemblance to his counterpart in De Jongh's painting, seated at the table with his glass raised, while the standing males in each work are only slightly less similar. Moreover, at the left side of each composition is a seated male, with feet together and knees apart.

A shadowy figure, Jan van der Meer of Utrecht (ca. 1630?- after June

47. Sale, Sotheby, London, 12 July 1978, no. 29.

48. The similarity in style between Natus and De Jongh of the 1650s has resulted in an interior genre scene being wrongly suggested as a work by De Jongh. See Brière-Misme 1954, p. 80, fig. 14. The work is clearly closer to the style of Natus. Compare it, for example, to Natus' *Peasants Singing*, signed and dated 1660. Sale, Maak van Waay, Amsterdam, 26 April 1976, no. 40; and later, Sotheby, Park Bernet, 11 June 1981, no. 106 (illus.).

49. Schneeman 1982, p. 123 and figs. 20 and 140.

50. Formerly on the art market in Vienna, 1960.

1692), apparently produced a few genre paintings that bear a definite relationship to the art of De Jongh (Fig. 101). According to Houbraken he was born in Schoonhoven, the town of De Jongh's in-laws, and traveled to Italy in the company of Lieve Verschuer of Rotterdam before finally settling in Utrecht. He was married in Utrecht in 1662, and was listed in records as being from Rotterdam.[51] Three paintings, similar in style, composition, and subject — each depicts a seated hunter resting before a tavern and attended by a standing serving girl — link him closely with the style of De Jongh. Were it not for a signature on the version in Paris, which bears a date of 1653, and another on the one in Hamburg, all three would certainly be attributed to De Jongh.[52] Because of the signatures on two of the paintings, the version which appeared on the art market in 1921 has also been attributed to Van der Meer of Utrecht.[53]

51. E. Tautscholdt in Thieme-Becker 1907-1915, vol. 34, p. 275.

52. Paris, Louvre, cat. 1979, no. 1452; Hamburg, Kunsthalle, cat. 1966, no. 291.

53. Sale, Major Dermot McCalmont, e.a., Christie's, London, 26 November 1920, no. 7, as Ludolf de Jongh; The Pall Mall Studio, London, 1921, as Jan van der Meer of Utrecht

CHAPTER FOUR

CONCLUSION

The development of the style of Ludolf de Jongh mirrors his study in Rotterdam, Delft, and Utrecht, as well as the general development of painting in The Netherlands during his career. While his debt to Cornelis Saftleven is best seen in his few known drawings, his simple bust-length portraits reflect his study in Delft under Palamedesz. His training under Palamedesz. is also apparent in his earliest known soldier paintings and middle class interiors, dating from the early and mid 1640s. Toward the later 1640s the influence of his stay in Utrecht is felt in the genre scenes that bear echoes of Jan van Bylert and Jacob Duck, while his hunt scenes owe a debt to Dirck Stoop, who, like De Jongh, was sometimes inspired by the work of Pieter van Laer.

In addition to his simple bust-length likenesses, De Jongh, beginning about mid-century, painted livelier compositions of the sort popularized by Van der Helst. His acknowledged masterpiece and his most ambitious work in this vein was the large group portrait of the Rotterdam civic guard, which was unfortunately destroyed by fire. Although De Jongh's portraits did tend to lighten in their tonality after mid-century, they did not become so colorful as those of his contemporaries; his preference for muted hues serving as a foil for a few carefully placed areas of brilliant color remained with him throughout his career. Even his genre scenes of the 1650s, which gradually express concern for more clearly defined space and more brilliant light, do not become so colorful as those of the majority of his contemporaries. Nevertheless, his development in genre painting in Rotterdam ran parallel to that of Ter Borch, Van Zyl, Van Loo, and Eeckhout in the centers to the north, placing him among the pioneers of the new style.

Although his production of hunt scenes noticeably declined toward 1660, he continued to be active in portraiture and genre. His portraits of the 1670s display an increased elegance that reflects the general taste of the time and is perhaps more specifically inspired by the conceptions of Van Dyck, while his genre scenes occasionally bear an affinity to the art of Pieter de Hooch and the School of Delft.

The position of De Jongh in the Golden Age of Dutch painting has unfortunately been obscured by the frequent attribution of his works to artists of greater renown. Paintings by De Jongh have been ascribed — often with false signatures — to Metsu, Van der Helst, Ter Borch, De Hooch, Palamedesz., and others. While numerous mistaken attributions are to be expected in the case of "followers," they are unusual in the work of a master of De Jongh's ability and inventiveness. Only in his known works of the early to mid-1640s, when he was clearly under the spell of Palamedesz., can he be regarded as a follower. His subsequent efforts, while often displaying an awareness of recent developments, were the products of an original artist. And although he was an influence on several younger painters, his work was seldom closely imitated.

The frequent confusion of De Jongh's paintings with the works of several better known painters has been possible because of a combination of factors. In the first place, his art is much more varied than that of most Dutch painters from the major artistic centers. The Rotterdam area in which he painted had not yet developed into a leading art center with competition among painters, which is partly the cause of specialization within a specific pictorial category or subject-matter. De Jongh's art therefore never developed into an easily identifiable mode. Moreover, it is likely that De Jongh had sufficient income from his investments and from his positions first as an officer in the civic guard and later as the principal administrative officer of Hillegersberg, allowing him greater freedom than the majority of his fellow painters. He was not forced in his art to rely on a limited but marketable repertoire. This is especially true in his portrait and genre paintings, which are of such variety that they seem to reflect his efforts to try his hand at the latest artistic developments.

But the variety of De Jongh's work, resulting in an unclear conception of his individual style, is not the only reason he has so often been confused with his better-known contemporaries. Were it not for the high quality of his paintings, they would not have been attributed so readily to other painters of more prestigious reputations. The false signatures that have appeared so frequently on his paintings would not have been so convincing on works of lesser merit.

In spite of the subsequent confusion of his art with the work of others, De Jongh was very much his own man. His search for fresh solutions to compositional problems, his frequent dramatic use of space, and his obvious desire to try his hand at new conceptions of genre and portraiture, reflect an inquisitive mind and an original talent. His civic guard group portrait was one of the freshest and boldest works of its type, while his signed *Woman Receiving a Letter* (Fig. 88) of the early or mid-1660s, which had been thought to be by De Hooch, certainly bears a relationship to contemporary developments in Delft and Amsterdam but is in no way imitative of the work of anyone. Indeed the paintings by De Hooch to which it can be most closely compared, are apparently later in date.

De Jongh's influence on the younger painters of his day has not been fully appreciated. Of particular importance in this respect was his work of the 1650s, when he was most active and perhaps the most highly respected painter of the Rotterdam area. While his work in genre was especially significant for the early development of Pieter de Hooch, echoes of his art are also apparent in the paintings of Ochtervelt and lesser masters of everyday scenes. His hunt scenes of the early 1650s were instrumental in the development of Hondius' early style, and his skill as a figure and animal painter was called upon to provide staffage for the landscapes of Joris van der Haagen.

Younger painters obviously admired De Jongh as an animal painter as well as a landscapist, portraitist, and genre painter. De Jongh's influence was probably as diverse as his many sources, which implies that his work will take time, and further research, to earn the reputation that it clearly deserves.

BIBLIOGRAPHY

Alciati, Andrea. *Emblematum Liber*. Augsburg, 1531.

Amsterdam, Rijksmuseum. *Tot Lering en Vermaak*. September 16-December 5, 1976. Catalogue by E. de Jongh et al.

Amsterdam, Rijksmuseum. *All the Paintings of the Rijksmuseum in Amsterdam*. 1976. Catalogue by Pieter van Thiel et al.

Amsterdam, Rijksmuseum, Rijksprentenkabinet. *Dutch Figure Drawings from the Seventeenth Century*. December 19, 1981-February 21, 1982; and Washington, D.C., National Gallery of Art, April 11-June 13, 1982. Catalogue by Peter Schatborn.

Bangel, Rudolf. "Zur holländischen Porträtmalerei des 17. Jahrhunderts," *Monatshefte für Kunstwissenschaft*, 8 (1915), pp. 17-21.

Bartsch, Adam von. *The Illustrated Bartsch*. vols. 1-. New York,1978-.

Bax, D. *Hollandse en Vlaamse Schilderkunst in Zuid-Afrika*. Amsterdam, 1952.

Bergström, Ingvar. "Rembrandt's Double-Portrait of Himself and Saskia at the Dresden Gallery: A Tradition Transformed." *Nederlands kunsthistorisch Jaarboek*, vol. 17 (1966), pp. 143-69.

Bernt, Walther. *The Netherlandish Painters of the Seventeenth Century*, 3 vols. London, 1970.

Blanc, Charles. *Histoire des peintres de toutes les écoles*, 9 vols. in 12, Paris, 1861-76.

Blankert, Albert. "Over Pieter van Laer als dier- en landschapschilder." *Oud Holland*, vol. 83 (1968), pp. 117-34.

_________. *Nederlandse 17e eeuwse Italianiserende landschapschilders*. Soest, 1978.

Bode, Wilhelm von. "Die Ausstellungen alter Gemälde...in Düsseldorf und Brussels 1886." *Repertorium für Kunstwissenschaft*, vol. 10 (1887), pp. 30-50.

Bol, Laurens. *Holländische Maler des 17. Jahrhunderts nahe den grossen Meistern*. Braunschweig, 1969.

Bredius, Abraham. *Die Meisterwerke des Rijksmuseum zu Amsterdam*. Munich, 1887.

_________. "Drie Delftsche Schilders: Evert van Aelst, Pieter Jansz. van Asch, en Adam Pick," *Oud-Holland,* vol. 6 (1888), pp. 289-98.

_________. "Het Schildersregister van Jan Sysmus, Stads-Doctor voor Amsterdam," Parts 1-3. *Oud-Holland,* vol. 8 (1890), pp. 1-17, 217-34, 297-313; Part 4. vol. 9 (1891), pp. 137-49; Part 5. vol. 12 (1894), pp. 160-71; Part 6. vol. 13 (1895), pp. 112-20.

_________. *Künstler-Inventare: Urkunden zur Geschichte der holländischen Kunst des XVIten, XVIIten, und XVIIIten Jahrhunderts*. 8 vols. The Hague, 1915-22.

_________. "Pieter de Hooch und Ludolph de Jongh," *Kunstchronik und Kunstliteratur*, vol. 62, no. 6 (September 1928), pp. 65-67.

Brière-Misme, Clotilde. "Tableaux inédits ou peu connus de Pieter de Hooch." Parts 1-3. *Gazette des Beaux-Arts*, 5th ser., vol. 15 (1927), pp. 361-80; vol. 16 (1927), pp. 51-79, 258-86.

_________. "Un 'Intimiste' hollandais, Esaias Boursse, 1631-1672." Part 2. *Oud-Holland*, vol. 69 (1954), pp. 72-91.

Budapest, Szépmüvészeti Muzeum. *Katalog der Galerie Alter Meister*. 2 vols. 1968. Catalogue by A. Pigler.

Cats, Jacob. *Spiegel van den Ouden ende Nieuwen Tijdt.* The Hague,1632.

Dresden, Staatliche Kunstsammlungen. *Gemäldegalerie Alte Meister Dresden: Katalog der ausgestellten Werke.* 2nd ed. Dresden, 1982.

Dublin, National Gallery of Ireland. *Illustrated Summary Catalogue of Paintings.* 1981.

Ember, Ildiko. *Music in Painting.* Budapest, 1984.

Errera, Isabella. *Répertoire des Peintures Datées.* 2 vols. Brussels, 1913.

Fischer, Pieter. *Music in Paintings of the Low Countries in the 16th and 17th Centuries.* Amsterdam, 1975.

Fleischer, R.E. "Ludolf de Jongh and the Early Work of Pieter de Hooch." *Oud Holland*, vol. 92 (1978), pp. 49-67.

Gelder, Jan Jacob de. *Bartholomeus van der Helst.* Rotterdam,1921.

Gelder, J.G. van. "Editorial: Dutch Pictures at the Royal Academy," *Burlington Magazine*, vol. 95 (1953), pp. 33-34.

Geyl, Pieter. *The Netherlands in the Seventeenth Century.* 2 vols. London, 1961-64.

Glück, Gustav. "Eine Haager Stadtansicht von Joris van der Hagen und Adriaen van de Velde," *Oud-Holland*, vol. 52 (1935), pp. 174-78.

Gudlaugsson, S.J. "Representations of Granida in Dutch Seventeenth Century Painting." Parts 1-3. *Burlington Magazine*, vol. 90 (1948), pp. 226-30, 348-51; and vol. 91 (1949), pp. 39-43.

__________. *Gerard ter Borch.* 2 vols. The Hague, 1959-60.

Haagen, J.K. van der. *De Schilders van der Haagen en hun Werk.* Voorburg, 1932.

Hall, H. van. *Portretten van Nederlandse Beeldende Kunstenaars.* Amsterdam. 1963.

Hamburg. *Katalog der alten Meister der Hamburger Kunsthalle*. Hamburg, 1966.

Hartford, Wadsworth Athenaeum. *Life in Seventeenth Century Holland.* 1950-51. Introduction by C. C. Cunningham.

Haverkorn van Rijsewijk, P. "Ludolf (Leuff) de Jongh." *Oud-Holland,* vol. 14 (1896), pp. 36-46.

Hazewinkel, H.C. *Geschiedenis van Rotterdam.* 4 vols. Zaltbommel, 1974-75.

Helbers, G.C. "Archiefsprokkelingen." *Oud-Holland*, vol. 70 (1955), p. 118.

Henkel, Arthur and Albrecht Schöne. *Emblemata: Handbuch zur Sinnbildkunst des XVI. und XVII. Jahrhunderts*. Stuttgart, 1976.

Hentzen, Alfred. "Abraham Hondius," *Jahrbuch der Hamburger Kunstsammlungen*, vol. 8 (1963), pp. 33-56.

Hind, Arthur M. *Catalogue of Drawings by Dutch and Flemish Artists preserved in the Department of Prints and Drawings in the British Museum.* 5 vols. London, 1915-32.

Hoet, Gerard. *Catalogus of Naamlyst van schilderyen*. 3 vols. in 2. The Hague, 1752-70. Reprint. Soest, 1976.

Hofstede de Groot, Cornelis. "Nogmaals: Een merkwaardige verzameling Teekeningen," *Oud-Holland*, vol. 13 (1895), pp. 238-40.

__________. "Kritische Opmerkingen Omtrent Oud-Hollandsche Schilderijen in Onze Musea," *Oud-Holland*, vol. 22 (1904), pp.111-20.

__________. "Zu Kritik einiger holländischer Bilder," *Repertorium für Kunstwissenschaft*, vol. 27 (1904), pp. 573-78.

__________. *Beschreibendes und kritisches Verzeichnis der Werke der hervorragendsten holländischen Maler des XVII. Jahrhunderts.* 10 vols. Esslingen and Paris, 1907-28.

Hollstein, F.W.H. *Dutch and Flemish Etchings, Engravings, and Woodcuts.* Vols. 1-. Amsterdam, 1949-.

Hoogewerff, G.J. "Pieter van Laer en zijn vrienden," Part 4. *Oud-Holland*, vol. 50 (1933), pp. 250-62.

__________. "Jan van Bijlert, Schilder van Utrecht (1598-1671)," *Oud Holland*, vol. 80 (1965), pp. 2-33.

Houbraken, Arnold. *De Groote Schouburgh der Nederlantsche Konstschilders en Schilderessen*. 3 vols. Amsterdam, 1718-21. Reprint. Maastricht, 1943-53.

Immerzeel, J. *De levens en werken der Hollandsche en Vlaamsche kunstschilders, beeldhouwers, graveurs en bouwmeesters*. 3 vols. Amsterdam, 1842-43.

Jongh, E. de. *Zinne- en minnebeelden in de schilderkunst van de zeventiende eeuw*. Amsterdam, 1967.

Kettering, Alison McNeil. *The Dutch Arcadia: Pastoral Art and Its Audience in the Golden Age*. Montclair, N.J., 1983.

Keyes, George. *Cornelis Vroom: Marine and Landscape Artist*. 2 vols. Alphen aan den Rijn, 1975.

Klinge-Gross, Margret. "Herman Saftleven als Zeichner und Maler bauerlicher Interieurs," *Wallraf-Richartz Jahrbuch*, 38 (1976), pp. 68-91.

Kramm, Christiaan. *De Levens en Werken der Hollandsche en Vlaamsche Kunstschilders, Beeldhouwers, Graveurs en Bouwmeesters*. 7 vols. Amsterdam, 1857-64.

Kuretsky, Susan Donahue. *The Paintings of Jacob Ochtervelt (1634-1682)*. Montclair, N.J., 1979.

Lawrence, The Spencer Museum of Art. *Dutch Prints of Daily Life*. Lawrence, Kansas, 1983. Catalogue by Linda A. Stone-Ferrier.

Leningrad, Hermitage Museum. *Peinture de l'Europe Occidentale*. Catalogue 2. Leningrad, 1981.

Lilienfeld, Karl. "Wiedergefundene Gemälde des Pieter de Hooch," *Zeitschrift für Bildende Kunst*, 58 (1924-25), pp. 185-88.

London, Royal Academy of Arts. *Catalogue of the Exhibition of Seventeenth Century Art in Europe*. London, 1938.

London, Royal Academy of Arts. *Catalogue of the Exhibition of the King's Pictures...at the Royal Academy of Arts*. 1946-47. London,1946. Introduction by A. F. Blunt.

London, Royal Academy of Arts, Winter Exhibition, 1952-53. *Dutch Pictures, 1450-1750*. London, 1952. Catalogue by David Thomas and Richard T. James.

London. The National Gallery Catalogues: *The Dutch School*. London, 1960. Catalogue by Neil MacLaren.

Lugt, F. *Musée du Louvre. Inventaire général des dessins des écoles du Nord*. vol. 2. Paris, 1931

Martin, W. *De Hollandsche schilderkunst in de zeventiende eeuw*. 2 vols. Amsterdam, 1935-36.

Mirimonde, A. P. de. "Les Sujets Musicaux Chez Vermeer de Delft," *Gazette des Beaux-Arts*, 6th ser., vol. 57 (1961), pp. 29-52.

Moes, E.W. "Een merkwaardige verzameling Teekeningen," *Oud-Holland*, vol. 13 (1895), pp. 182-92.

__________. *Iconographia Batava*, 2 vols. Amsterdam. 1897-1905.

Montias, J. M. *Artists and Artisans in Delft in the Seventeenth Century*. Princeton, 1982.

Muller, Gustav. "Die Bildersammlungen Anhalts," *Zeitschrift für Bildende Kunst*, vol. 14 (1879), pp. 387-92.

Nieuwstraten, J. "Netherlandish Italianising Landscape Painters at Utrecht," *Burlington Magazine*, vol. 107 (1965), pp. 271-75.

Obreen, F.D.O. *Archief voor Nederlandsche Kunstgeschiedenis*. 7 vols. Rotterdam, 1877-1890. Reprint. Soest, 1976.

Paris, Musée des Arts Décoratifs. *La vie en Hollande au XVIIe siècle*. Paris, 1967. Introduction by Paul Zumthor.

Paris, Musée du Louvre. *Écoles flamande et hollandaise*. Vol. 1 of *Catalogue sommaire illustré des peintures du Musée du Louvre*. Paris, 1979. Catalogue by Arnauld Brejon de Lavergnée, Jacques Foucard, and Nicole Reynaud.
Philadelphia, Philadelphia Museum of Art. *Jan Steen: Comedy and Admonition*. Philadelphia, 1983. Catalogue by Peter C. Sutton with appendix by Marigene H. Butler.

Philadelphia, Philadelphia Museum of Art; Berlin, Gemäldegalerie, Staatliche Museen Preussischer Kulturbesitz; and London, Royal Academy of Arts. *Masters of Seventeenth-Century Dutch Genre Painting*. Philadelphia, 1984. Catalogue by Peter C. Sutton et. al.

Piles, Roger de. *Abrégé de la Vie des Peintres*. 2nd. ed. Paris, 1715.

Plietzsch, Eduard. "Jacob Ochtervelt," *Pantheon*, vol. 20 (1937), pp. 364-72.

__________."Ausstellung Holländischer Gemälde in der Londoner Akademie," *Kunstchronik*, vol. 6 (1953), pp. 121-32.

__________. *Holländische und flämische Maler des 17. Jahrhunderts*. Leipzig, 1960.

Prague, Národni Galerie. *Sbírka Starého Um ̃ eni*. Prague, 1971.

Rapp, Bertil. "Abraham Hondius," *Oud-Holland*, vol. 64 (1949), pp. 65-70.

Renger, Konrad. *Lockere Gesellschaft: Zur Ikonographie des verlorenen Sohnes und von Wirtshausszenen in der niederländischen Malerei*. Berlin, 1970.

Riegl, Alois. *Das Holländische Gruppenporträt*. Vienna,1931.

Ripa, Cesare. *Iconologia of Uytbeeldinghe des Verstands*. Translated by D. P. Pers. Amsterdam, 1644. Reprint. Soest, 1971.

Rosa, Gilda, "La Raccolta Greppi," *Arte Lombarda*, vol. 11 (1966), pp.105-10.

Rosenberg, J., S. Slive, and E.H. ter Kuile. *Dutch Art and Architecture, 1600-1800*. Harmondsworth and Baltimore, 1966.

Rotterdam, Museum Boymans. *Beschrijving der Schilderijen enz. in het Museum te Rotterdam*. Rotterdam, 1862.

Rotterdam, Archief der Gemeente. *Catalogus van de Portretverzameling*. Rotterdam, 1917. Catalogue by H.C.H. Moquette.

Rotterdam, Museum Boymans. *Vermeer. oorsprong en invloed. Fabritius, de Hooch, de Witte*. Rotterdam, 1935. Catalogue by D. Hannema.

Saint Petersburg, Florida, Museum of Fine Arts, and High Museum of Art, Atlanta. *Dutch Life in the Golden Century*. Saint Petersburg, 1975. Catalogue by Franklin W. Robinson.

Schatborn, Peter. "Figuurstudies van Ludolf de Jongh," *Oud Holland*, vol. 89 (1975), pp. 79-85.

Scheffer, J.H. and F.D.O. Obreen, eds. *Rotterdamsche Historiebladen*, vol. 2. Rotterdam, 1880.

Schneeman, Liane T. "Hendrick Sorgh: A Painter of Rotterdam." Diss., The Pennsylvania State University, 1982.

Scholten, Frits. "...dat menighen onbedachten Actaeon van zijn eyghen lusten wort ghevanghen...," *AKT*, vol.26 (1985), pp. 26-32.

Schulz, Wolfgang. *Cornelis Saftleven, 1609-1685*. Berlin and New York, 1978.

Slatkes, Leonard J. *Dirck van Baburen*. Utrecht, 1965.

Slim, H. Colin. *The Prodigal Son at the Whores; Music, Art and Drama*. Irvine, California, 1976.

Slive, Seymour. *Frans Hals*. 3 vols. London and New York, 1970-74.

Smith, John A. *A Catalogue Raisonné of the Works of the Most Eminent Dutch, Flemish, and French Painters*. 9 vols. London,1829-42.

Spaan, Gerard van. *Beschrijvinge der Stad Rotterdam*. Rotterdam, 1698, Reprint. Antwerp, 1943.

Staring, A. "Een portret door Ludolf de Jongh," *Oud-Holland*, vol.69 (1954), pp. 43-46.

Stechow, Wolfgang. *Dutch Landscape Painting of the Seventeenth Century*. London and New York, 1966.

__________. "Lusus Laetitiaeque Modus," *Art Quarterly*, vol. 35 (1972), pp. 165-73.

Sullivan, Scott A. "Rembrandt's Self-Portrait with a Dead Bittern," *The Art Bulletin*, vol. 62 (1980), pp. 236-243.

__________. *The Dutch Gamepiece*. Montclair, N. J. and Woodbridge, Suffolk, 1984.

Sutton, Peter C. *Pieter de Hooch*. New York, 1980.

Swillens, P.T.A. "Dirck en Maerten Stoop," *Oud-Holland*, vol. 51 (1934), pp. 116-35, 175-81.

Terwesten, Pieter. *Catalogus of Naamlyst van Schilderyen*. The Hague, 1770. Reprint. The Hague, 1976.

Thieme, U., and F. Becker. *Allgemeines Lexikon der bildenden Künstler von der Antike bis zur Gegenwart*. 37 vols. Leipzig, 1907-50.

Thienen, F.W.S. van. *The Great Age of Holland, 1600-60. Costume of the Western World*. Translated by F. G. Renier and A. Cliff. London, 1951.

Thode, M. "Die Ausstellung von Gemälden aus Mainzer Privatbesitz in Mainz im Mai 1887," *Repertorium für Kunstwissenschaft*, vol. 10 (1887), pp. 408-415.

Thoré, T.E.J. [W. Bürger]. *Trésors d'Art exposés à Manchester en 1857*. Paris, 1857.

_________. *Musées de la Hollande*, 2 vols. Paris, 1858-60.

Unger, J.H.W. (ed.) *Bronnen voor de Geschiedenis van Rotterdam. 2* vols., Rotterdam, 1892.

Utrecht, Centraal Museum. *Nederlandse 17e eeuwse Italianiserende landschapschilders*. 1965. Catalogue by Albert Blankert.

Valentiner, W.R. *Handzeichnungen Altholländischer Genremaler*. Berlin, 1907.

__________. "Pieter de Hooch." Parts 1 and 2. *Art in America*, vol. 15, no. 1 (December 1926), pp. 45-64; vol. 15, no. 2 (February 1927), pp. 67-77.

_________. *Pieter de Hooch*. Klassiker der Kunst. Stuttgart, 1929.

"Vertue Note Book A.c.," *The Walpole Society*, vol. 20 (1932), pp. 94-158.

Walpole, Horace. *Anecdotes of Painting in England*. 2nd. ed. 4 vols. Strawberry Hill, 1765-71.

Westerbaen, Jacob. *Gedichte II*. The Hague, 1672.

Weyerman, J. C. *De Levens-Beschryvingen der Nederlandsche Konstschilders en Konstschilderessen*. 4 vols. The Hague, 1729-69.

White, Christopher. *The Dutch Pictures in the Collection of Her Majesty the Queen*. Cambridge, 1982.

Wiersum, E. "Verdwenen Rotterdamsche Schilderijen," *Oud-Holland*, vol. 33 (1915), pp. 120-125.

__________.*Archieven der notarissen, die op het tegenwoordig grondgebied der Gemeente Rotterdam gefungeerd hebben, 1585-1811*. The Hague, 1920.

__________. "De Van Nes-portretten in het Rijksmuseum te Amsterdam," *Oud-Holland*, vol. 51 (1934), pp. 231-36.

Winternitz, Emanuel. *Musical Instruments and Their Symbolism in Western Art*. New York, 1967.

Wurzbach, A. von. *Niederländisches Künstler-Lexikon*. 3 vols. Vienna and Leipzig, 1906-11. Reprint. Amsterdam, 1974.

Zumthor, Paul. *Daily Life in Rembrandt's Holland*. Translated by S.W. Taylor. London, 1962.

GENERAL INDEX

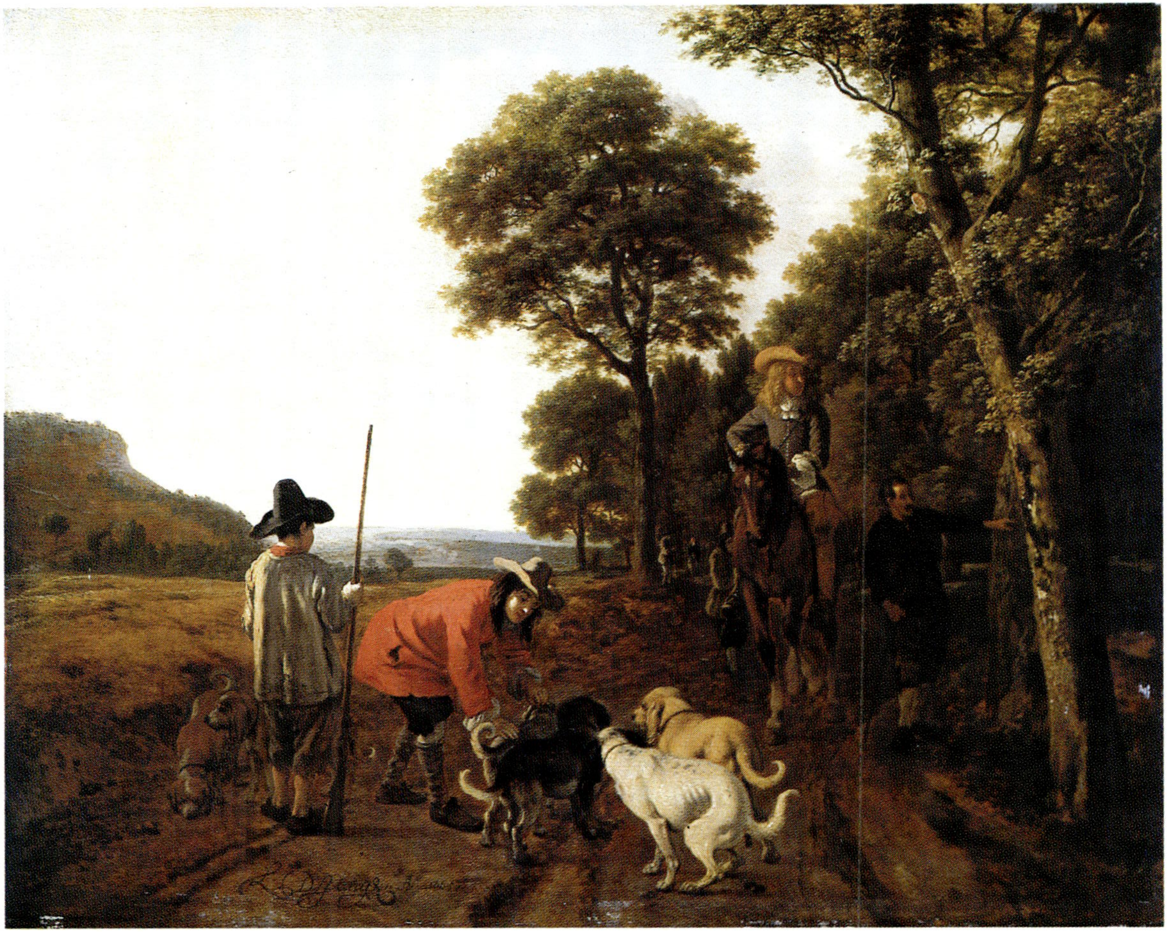

I *Hunters with Dogs*, signed and dated 1665. Panel, 39 · 5 x 49 · 5 cm. Leningrad, Hermitage Museum

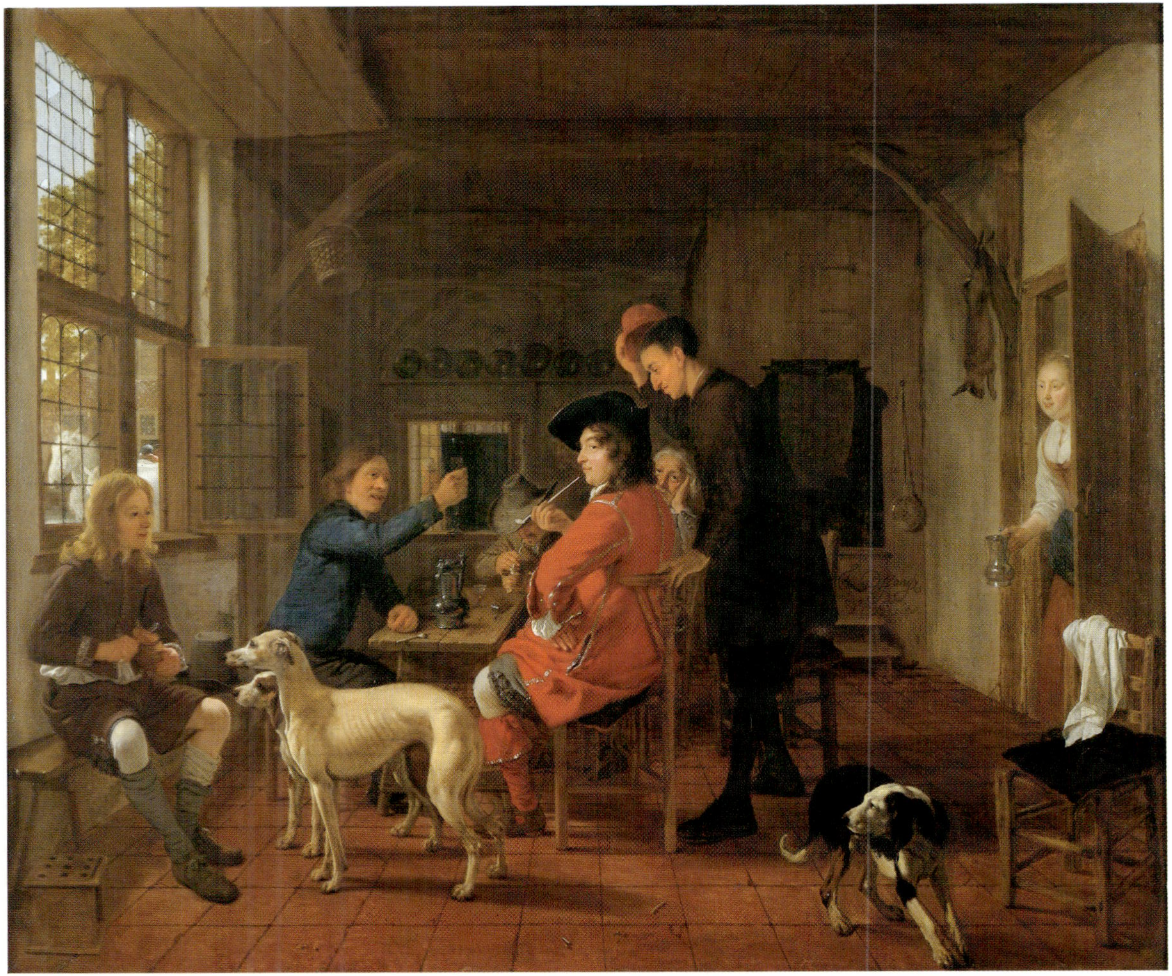

II *Hunters in an Inn,* signed and dated 1658. Canvas, 67 x 81 cm. Groningen, Museum van Oudheden

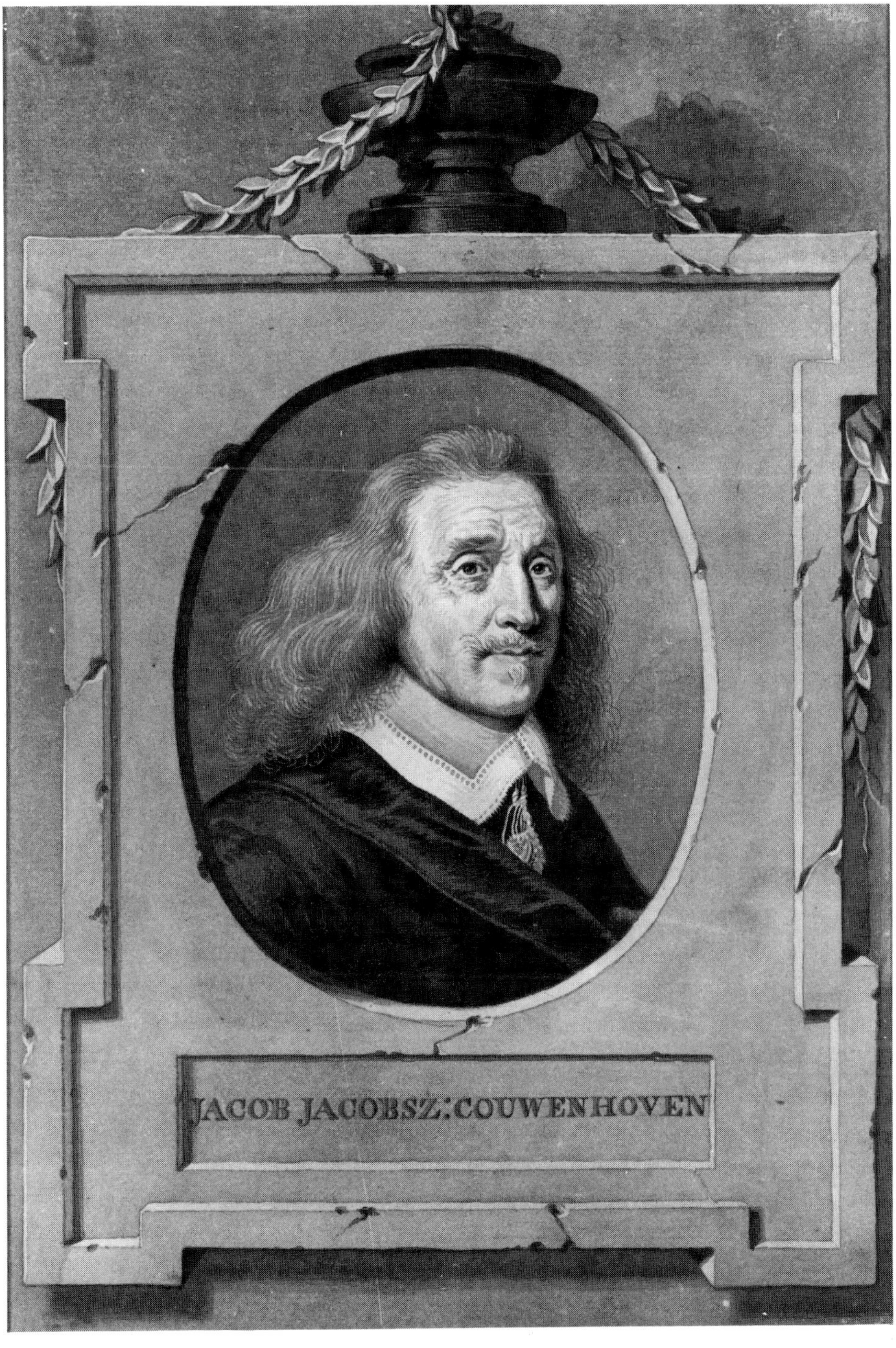

1. Jan Stolker, *Jacob Jacobsz. van Couwenhoven* , India ink wash on paper, 27 x 18 cm. After a painting of 1645 by Ludolf de Jongh. Rotterdam, Gemeentelijke Archiefdienst

2. *Portrait of a Man,* signed and dated 1650. Panel, 72 x 62 cm. Present location unknown. Photograph, Courtauld Institute of Art, London

3. *Willem de Swaen,* signed and dated 1650. Panel, 72 x 62 cm.Voorhout, Dre. R. O. J. M. Baron van Hövell tot Westerflier, 1954. Photograph, Iconographisch Bureau, The Hague

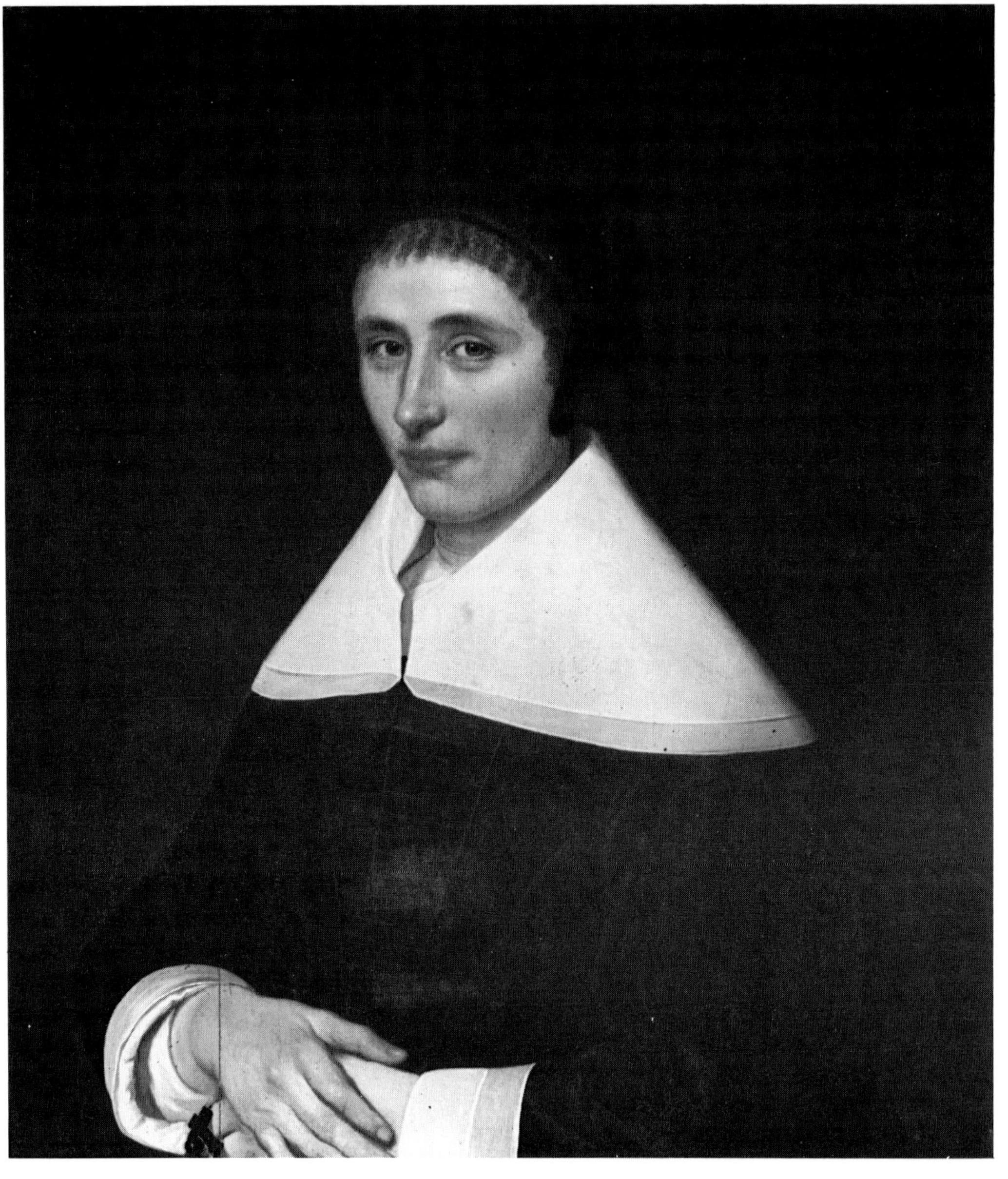

4. *Maeritge Vereij* (?), signed and dated 1650. Panel, 72 x 61 cm. Voorhout, Dre. R. O. J. M. Baron van Hövell tot Westerflier, 1954. Photograph, Iconographisch Bureau, The Hague

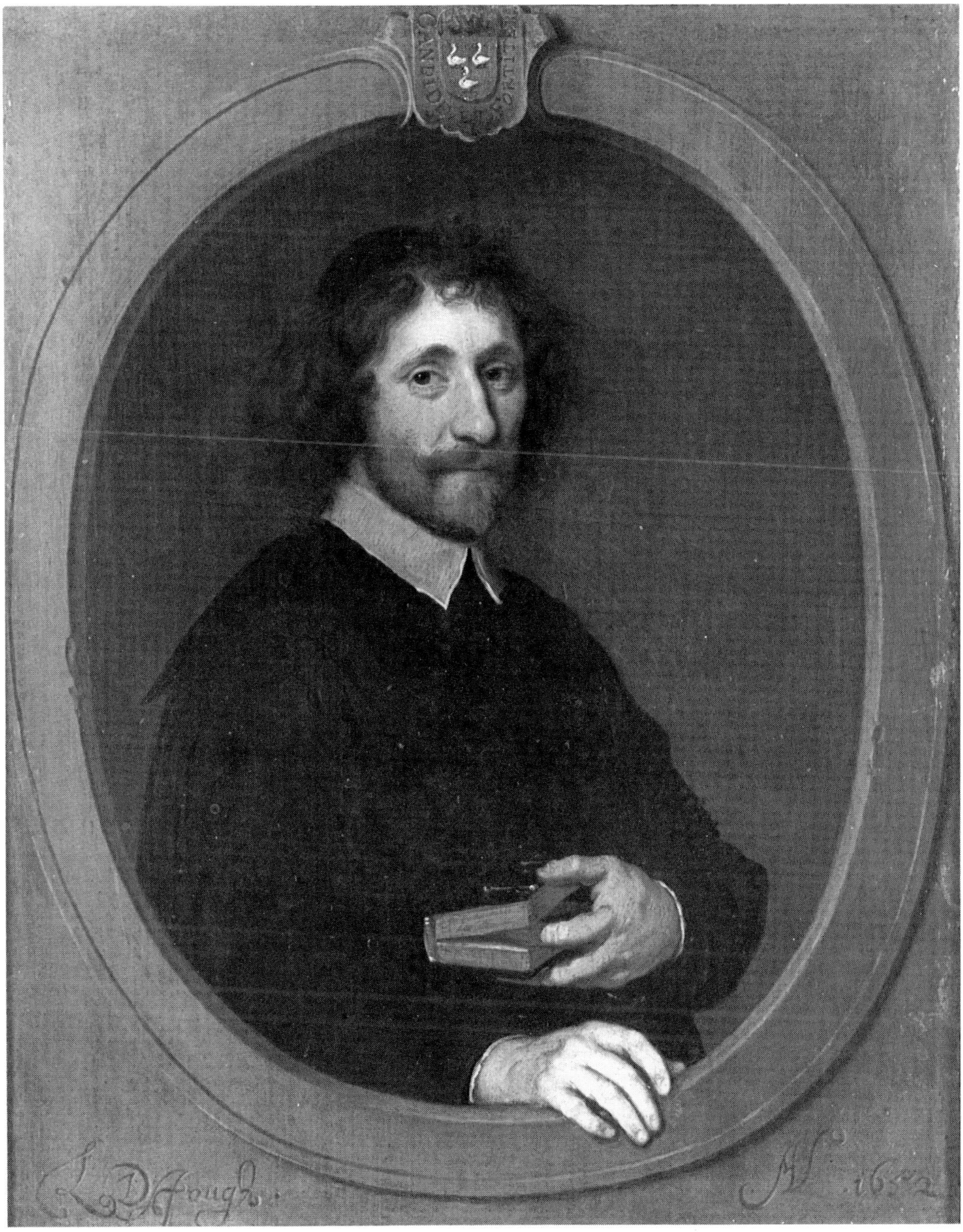

5. *Willem de Swaen*, signed and dated 1652. Panel, 34 · 3 x 26 · 7 cm. Rotterdam, Historisch Museum

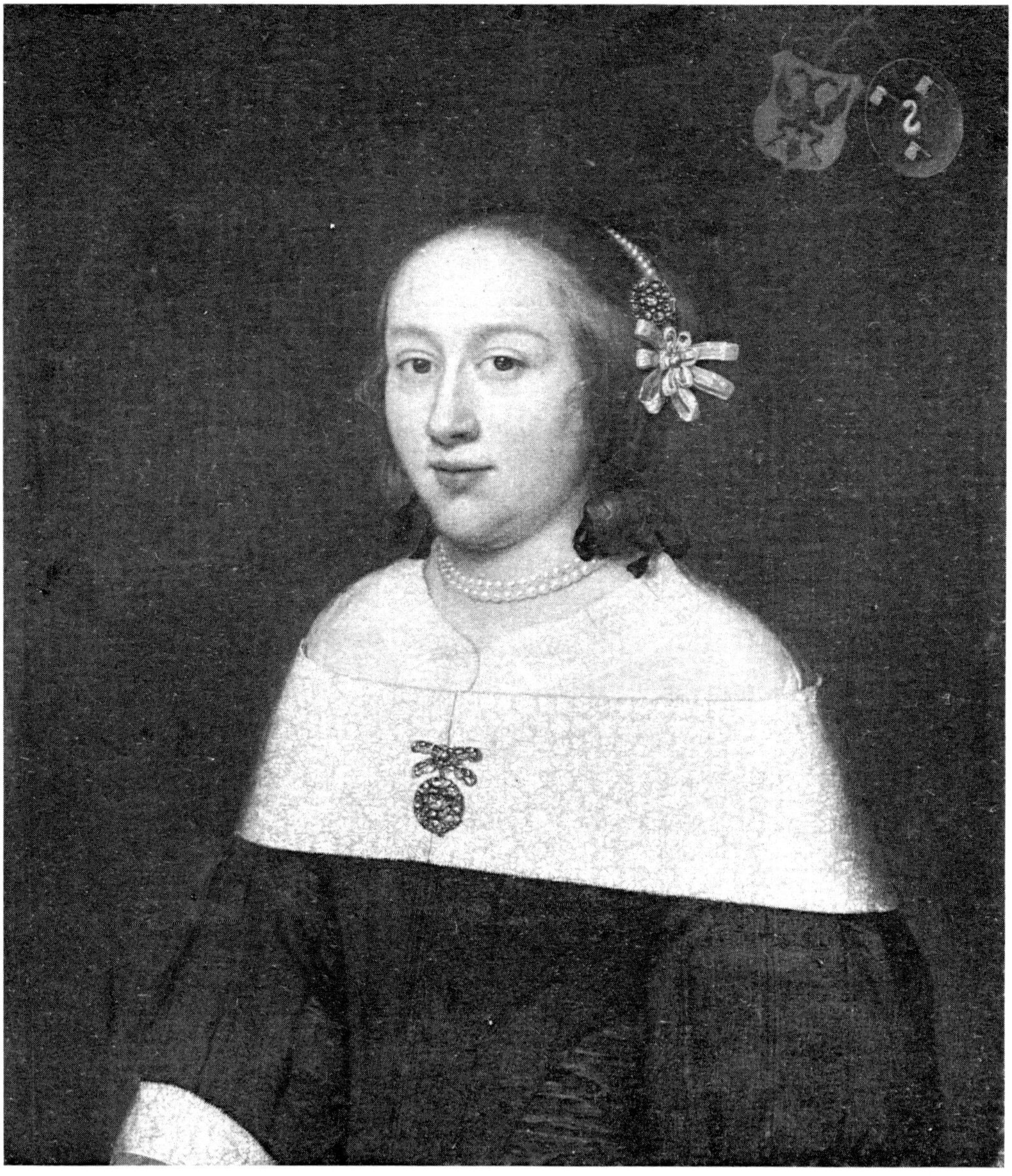

6. *Henriette Vroesen,* signed and dated 1656. Panel, 74 · 5 x 61 cm. Present location unknown. Photograph, Courtauld Institute of Art, London

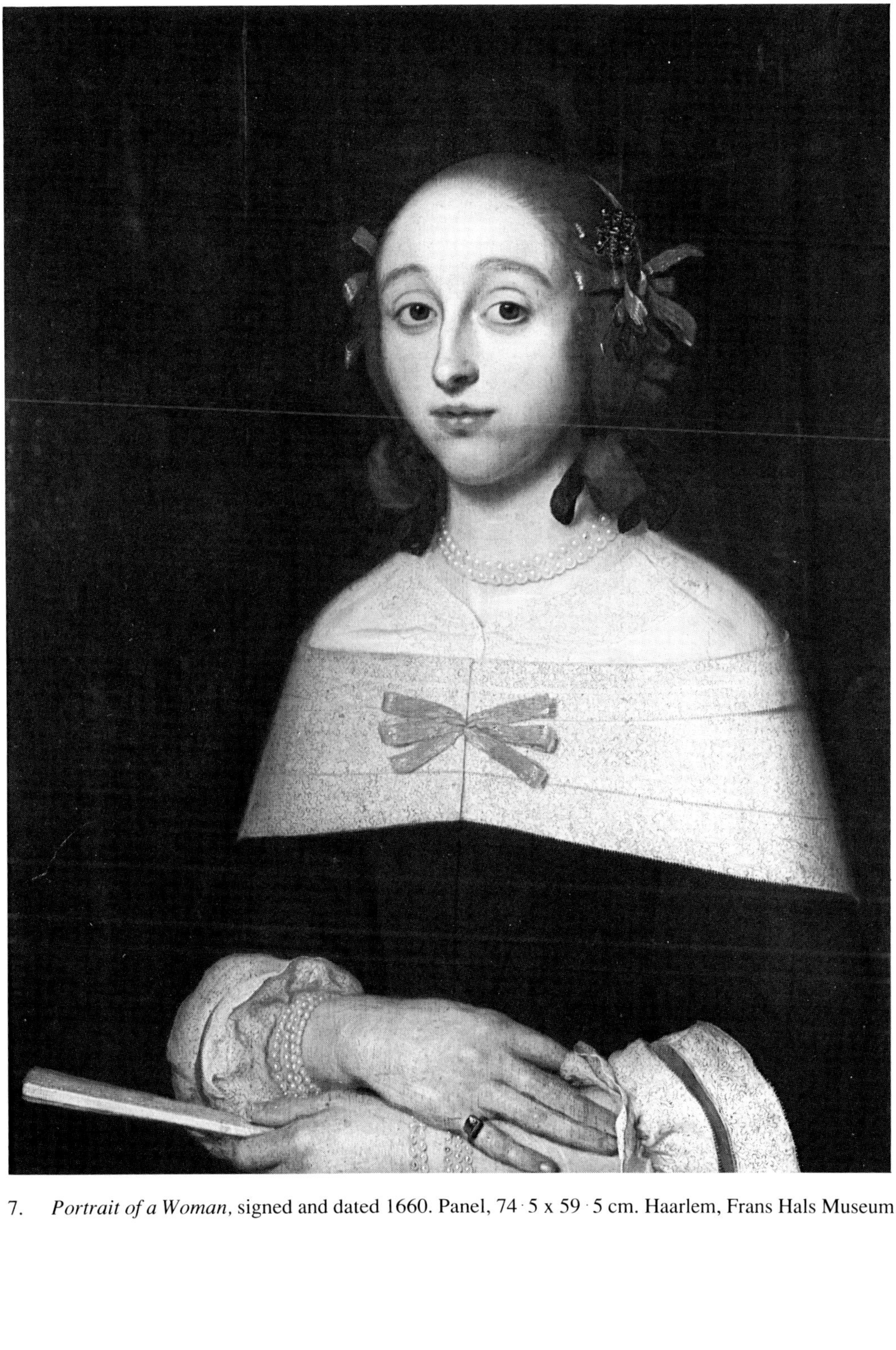

7. *Portrait of a Woman,* signed and dated 1660. Panel, 74·5 x 59·5 cm. Haarlem, Frans Hals Museum

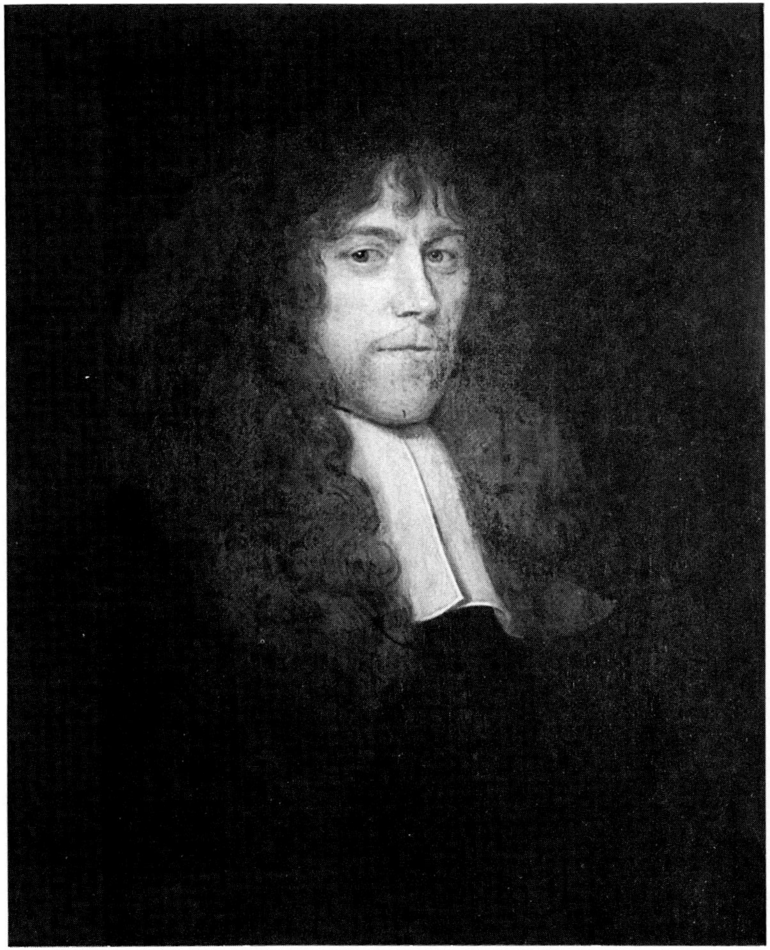

8. *Portrait of a Man*, signed and dated (date illegible). Canvas on panel, 70 · 5 x 59 cm. The Hague, E. Baron Speyart van Woerden

9. *Pastor Nicolaes Stenius* (after Frans Hals), signed and dated 1652. Gnadental, private collection. Photograph courtesy of the Rijksbureau voor Kunsthistorische Documentatie, The Hague

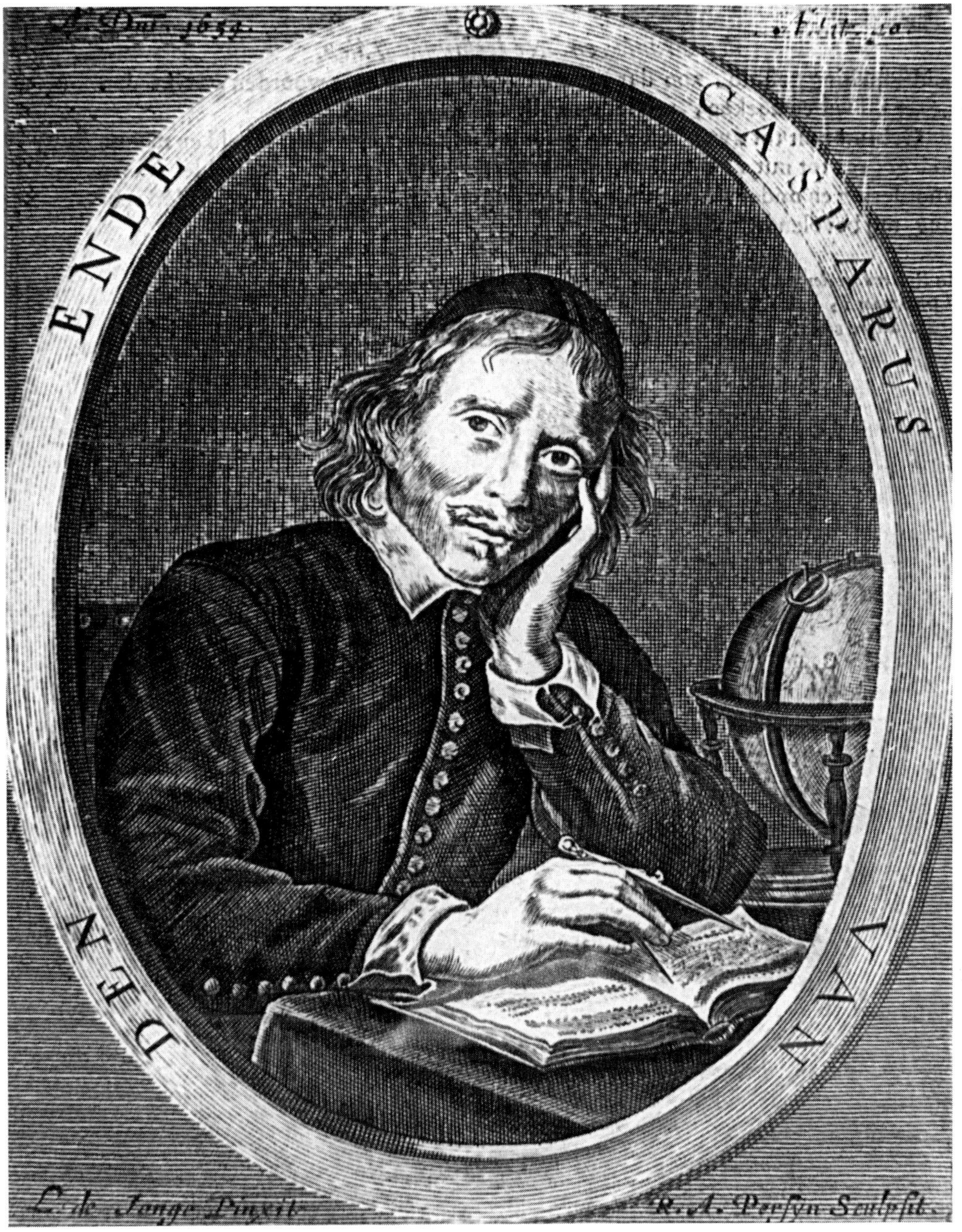

10. R. A. Persyn, *Caspar van den Ende*, dated 1654. Print after a painting by Ludolf de Jongh. Photograph courtesy of the Rijksbureau voor Kunsthistorische Documentatie, The Hague

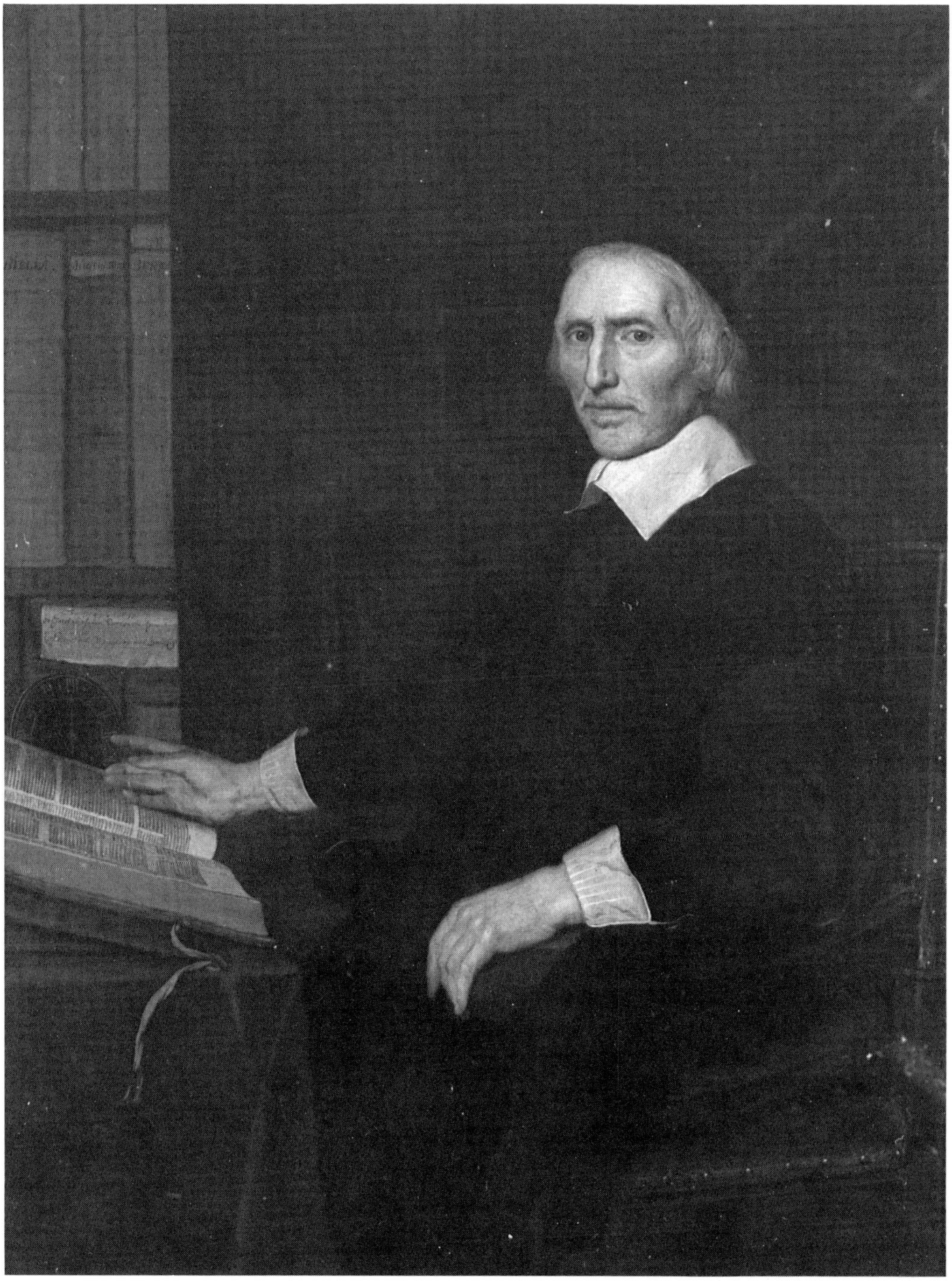

11. *Jacob Cats*, signed and dated 1659. Canvas, 121 x 89 cm. The Hague, Gemeentemuseum

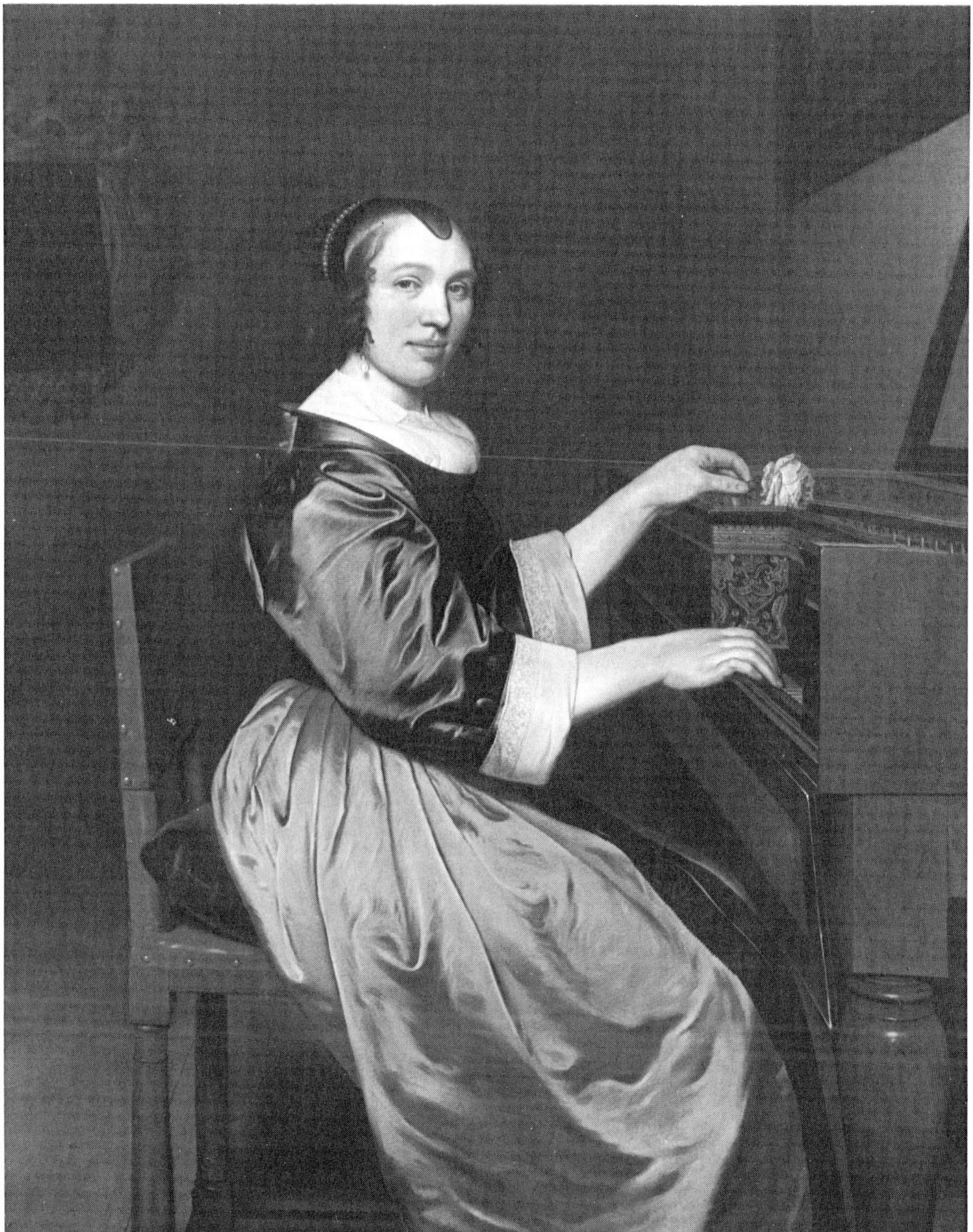

12. *Woman Playing the Virginals,* signed and dated 1651. Canvas, 133 x 103 cm.
Rotterdam, Historisch Museum

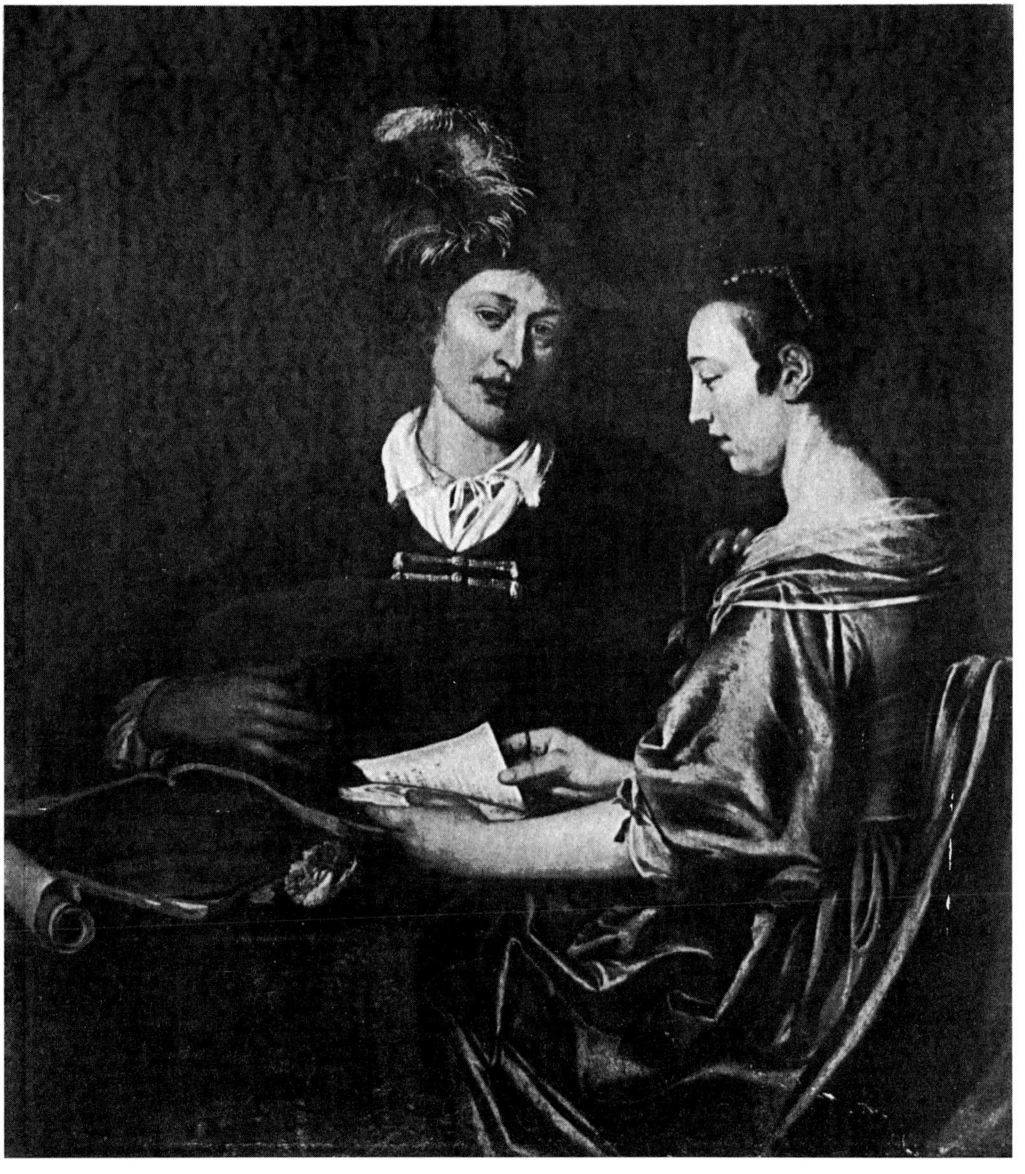

13. *The Mandolin Lesson,* c. 1650. Canvas, 125x 105 cm. Present location unknown. Photograph courtesy of the Rijksbureau voor Kunsthistorische Documentatie, The Hague

Amor docet Musicam.

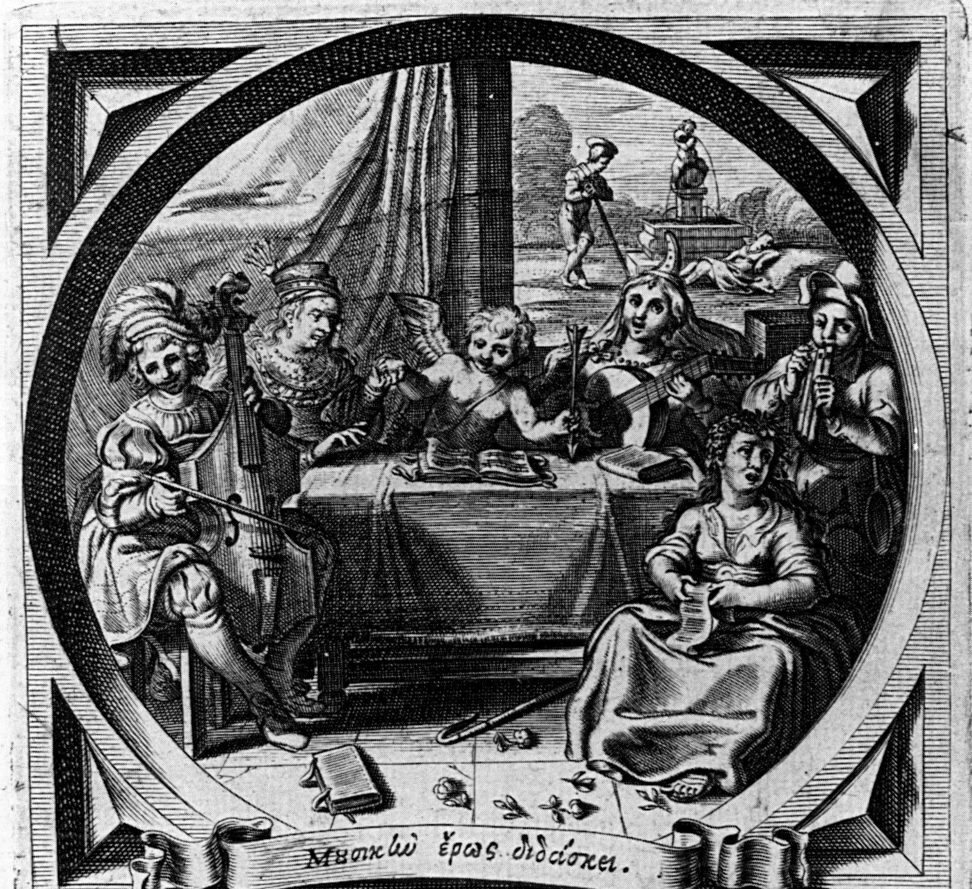

Eerlicke Vryagie

GHy, die op dese prente siet,
Maer weet daer van de meyning niet,
En vraegt wat dese kleyne Guyt,
Wat Venus Iongen hier beduyt;
Ick bidde staet een weynigh stil,
En hoort eens wattet seggen wil.

14. *"Amor docet Musicam"*. Emblem from Jacob Cats, Spiegel van den Ouden ende Nieuwen Tijd, The Hague, 1632

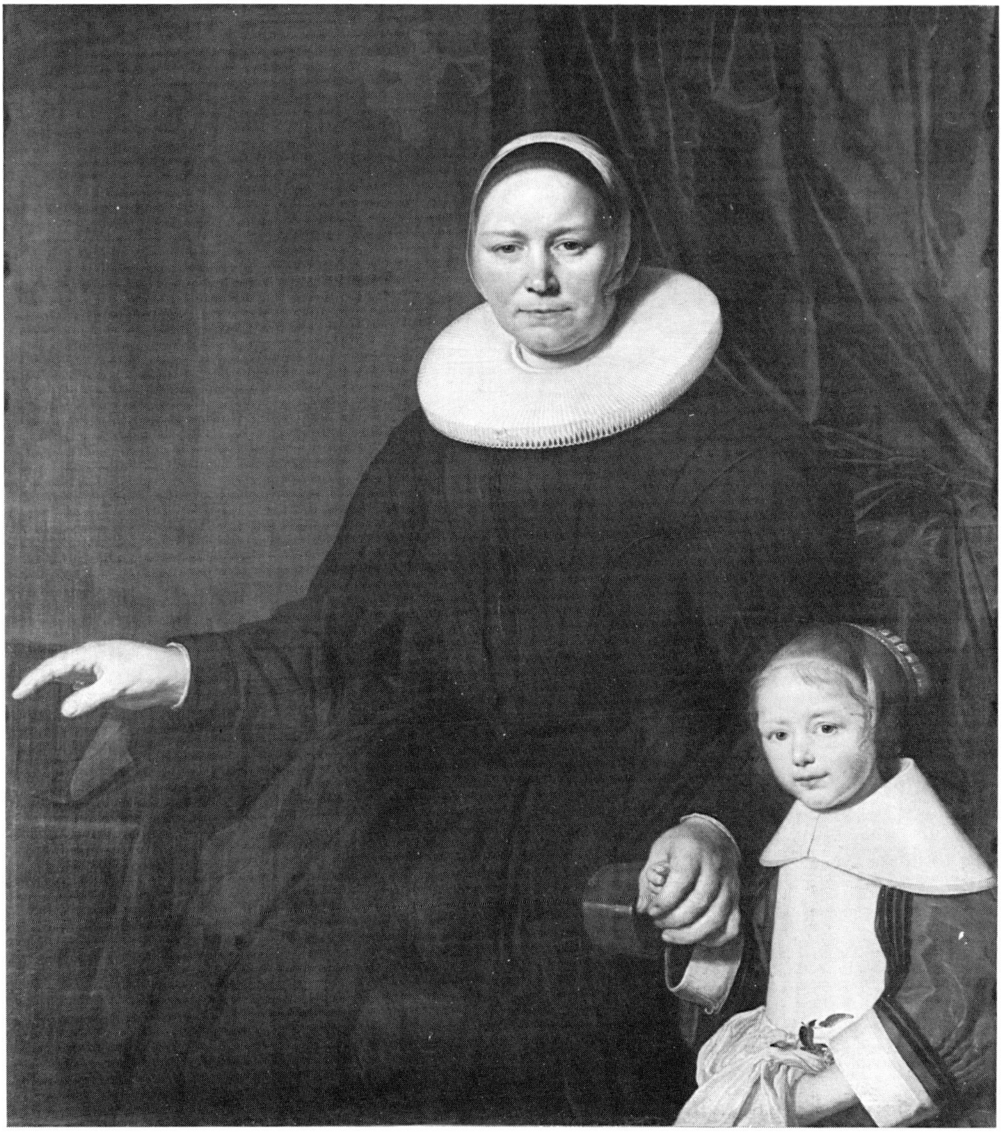

15. *A Woman with Her Daughter*, signed and dated 1653. Canvas, 110 x 97 cm. Dresden, Gemälde Galerie

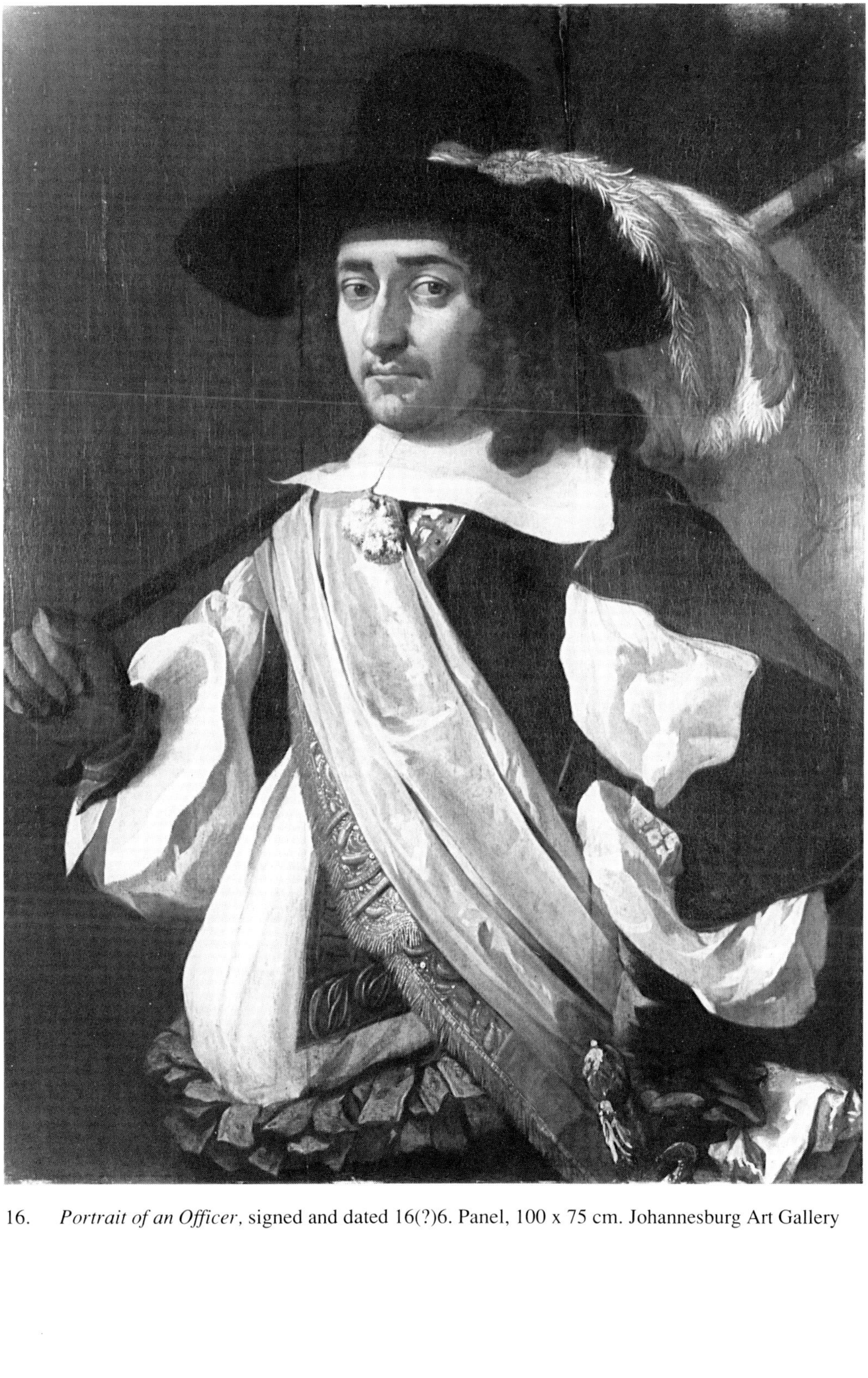

16. *Portrait of an Officer*, signed and dated 16(?)6. Panel, 100 x 75 cm. Johannesburg Art Gallery

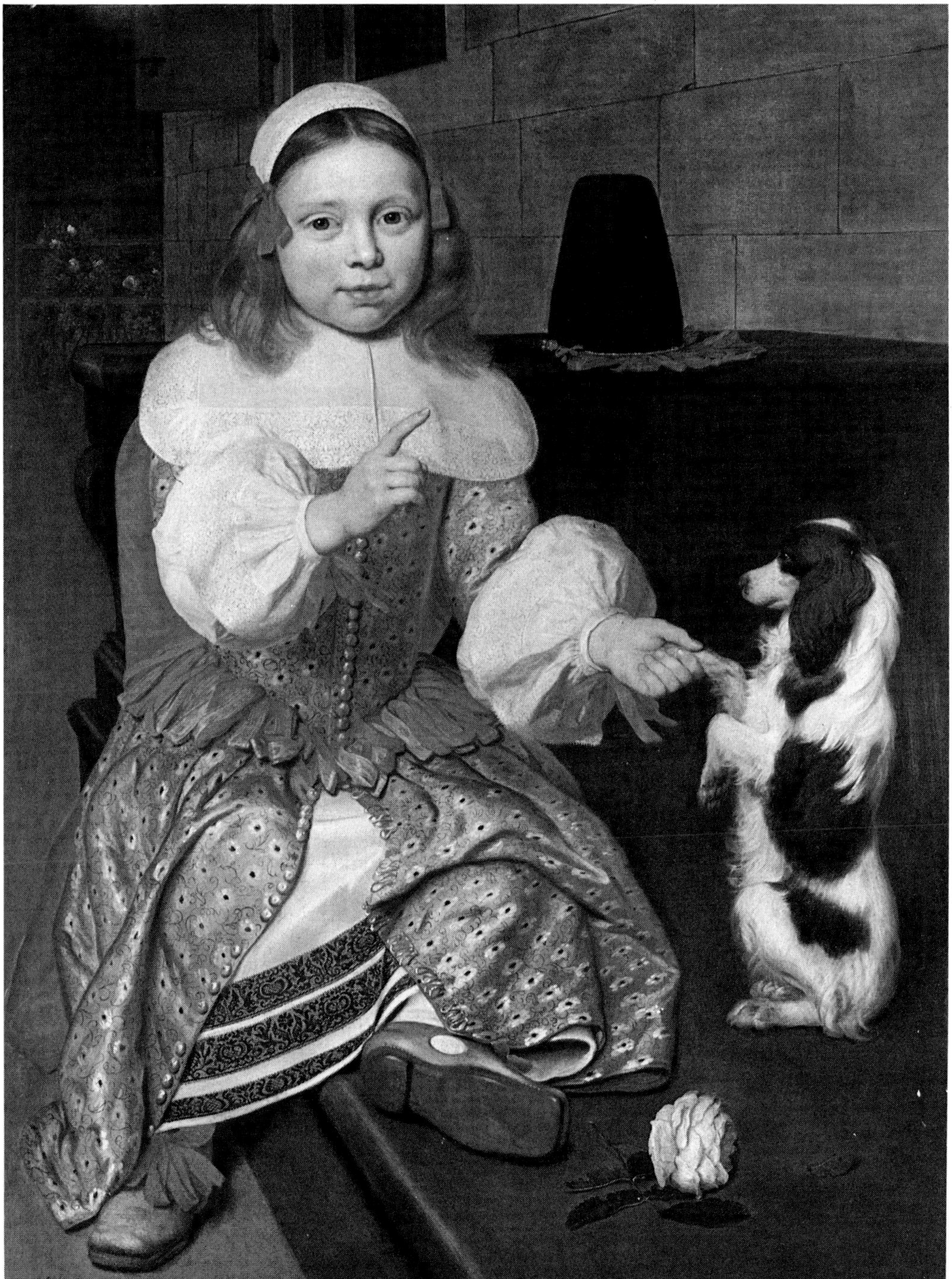

17. *A Boy with a Dog,* signed and dated 1661. Canvas, 98 x 72 cm.
Richmond, Virginia Museum of Fine Arts

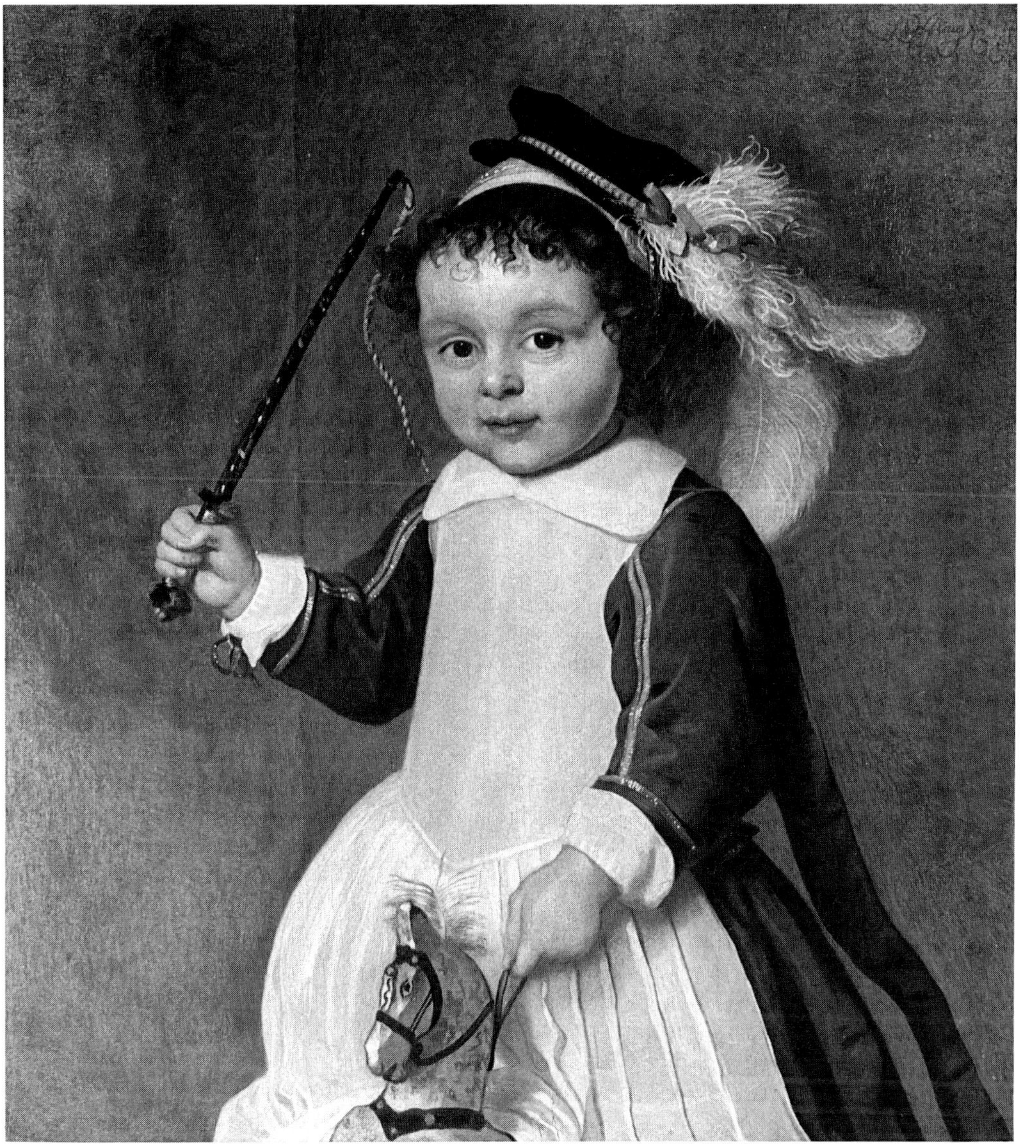

18. *Young Child on a Hobby Horse,* signed. Canvas, 68 · 5 x 60 cm. Present location unknown. Photograph courtesy of the Rijksbureau voor Kunsthistorische Documentatie, The Hague

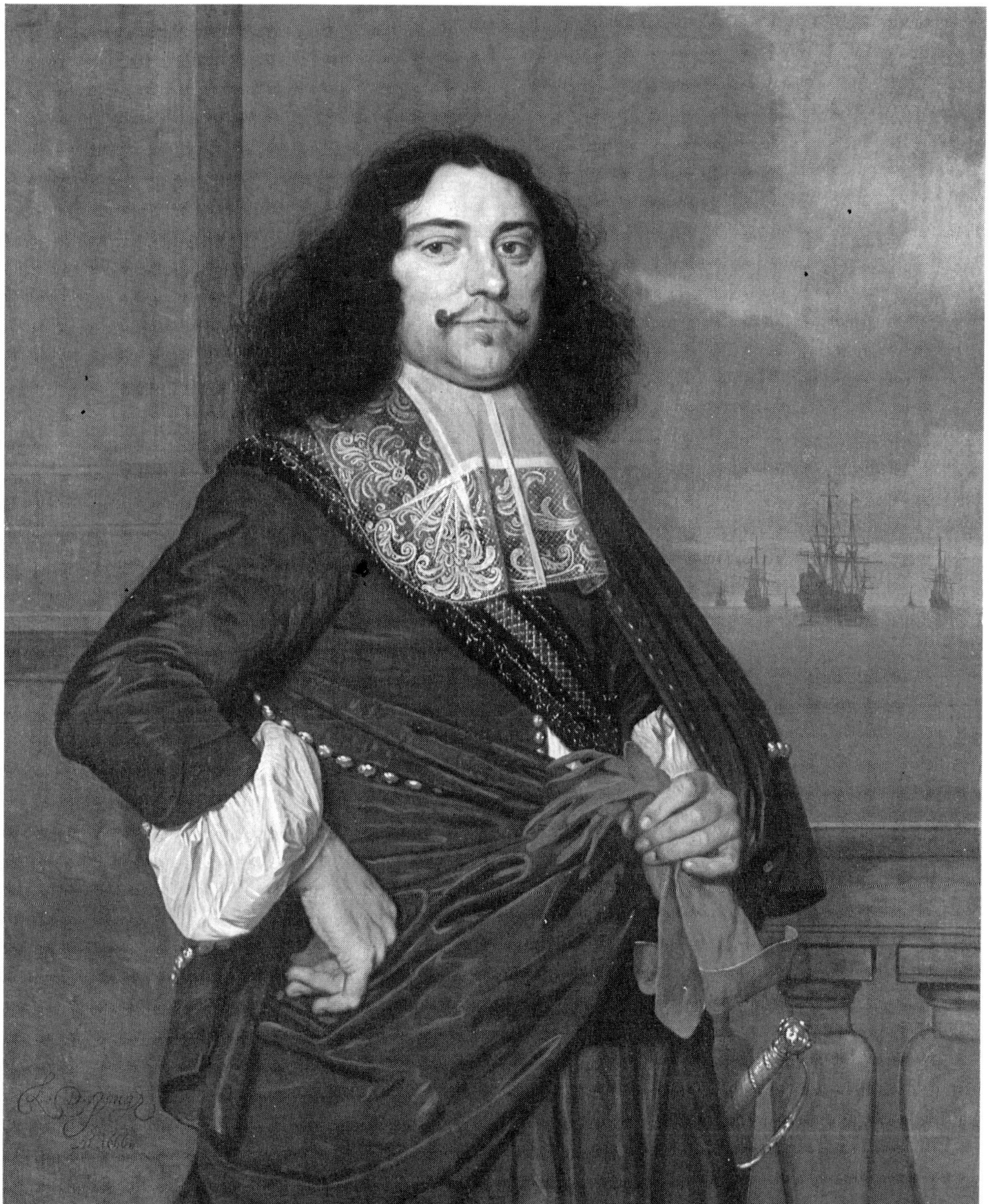

19. *Vice Admiral Jan van Nes*, signed and dated 1666. Canvas, 111 · 5 x 88 · 5 cm. Amsterdam, Rijksmuseum

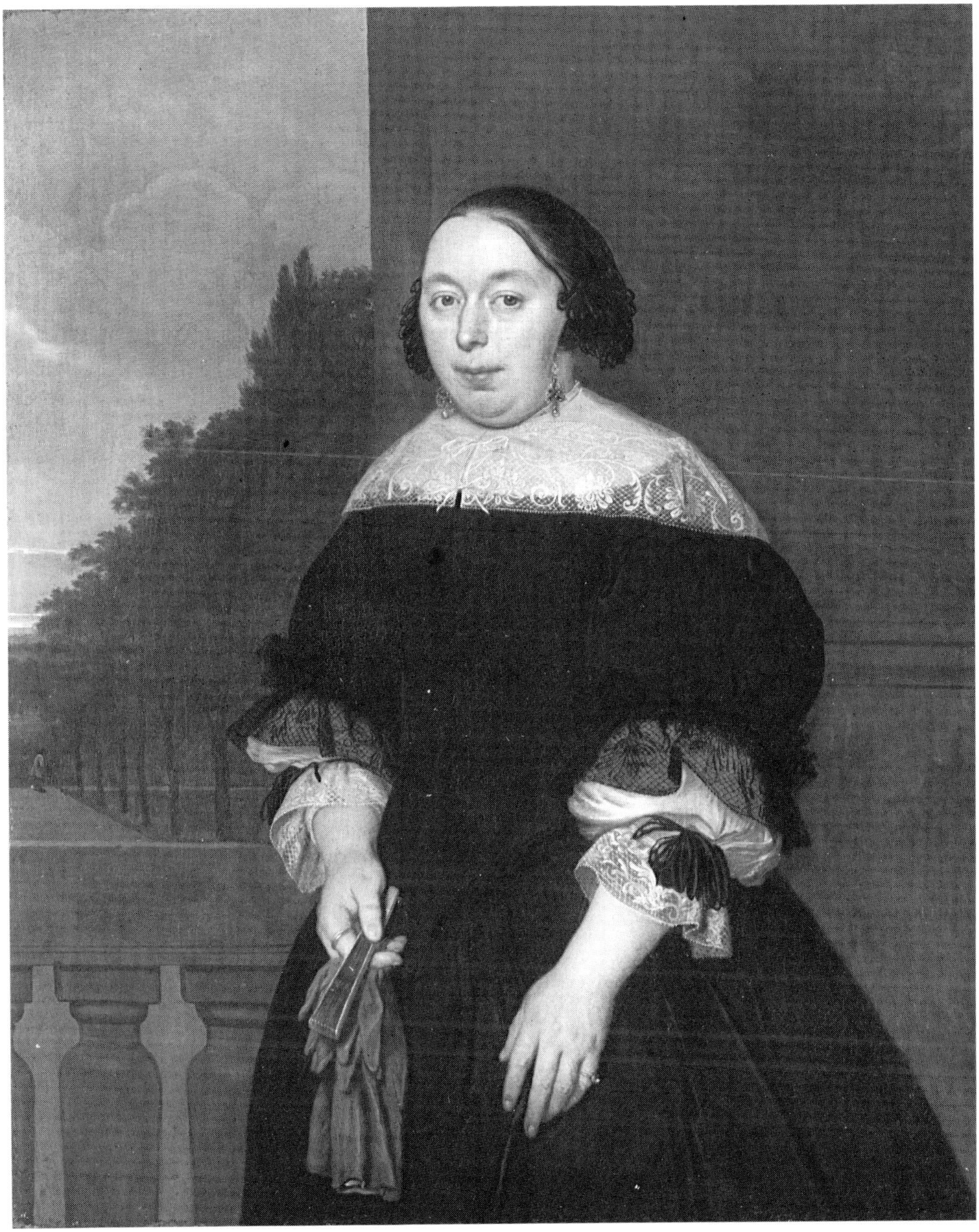

20. *Aletta van Ravensberg, Wife of Jan van Nes,* signed and dated 1668. Canvas, 111·5 x 88·5 cm. Amsterdam, Rijksmuseum

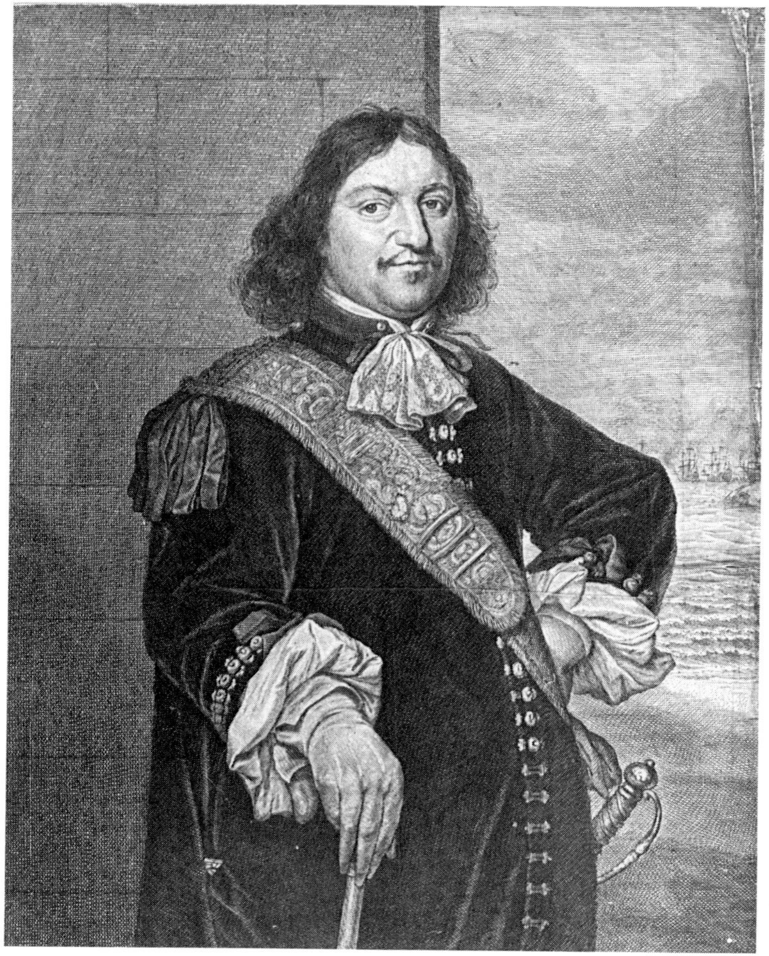

21. A. Blotelingh. *Lieutenant Admiral Aert van Nes*, dated 1667. Engraving after a painting by Ludolf de Jongh

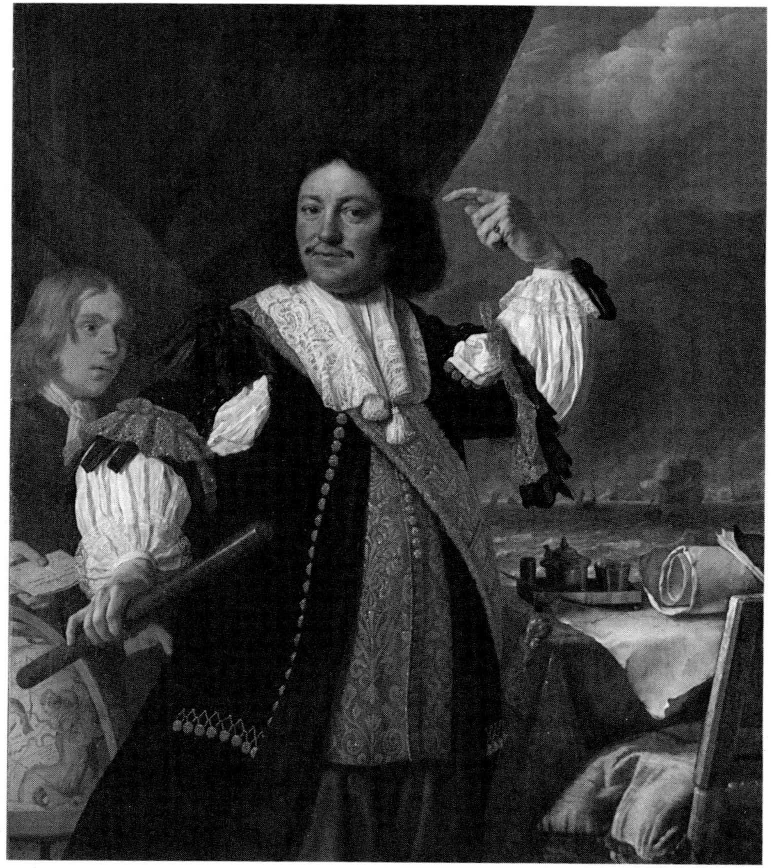

22. Bartholomeus van der Helst, *Lieutenanı Admiral Aert van Nes*, signed and dated 1668. Canvas, 139 x 125 cm. Amsterdam, Rijksmuseum

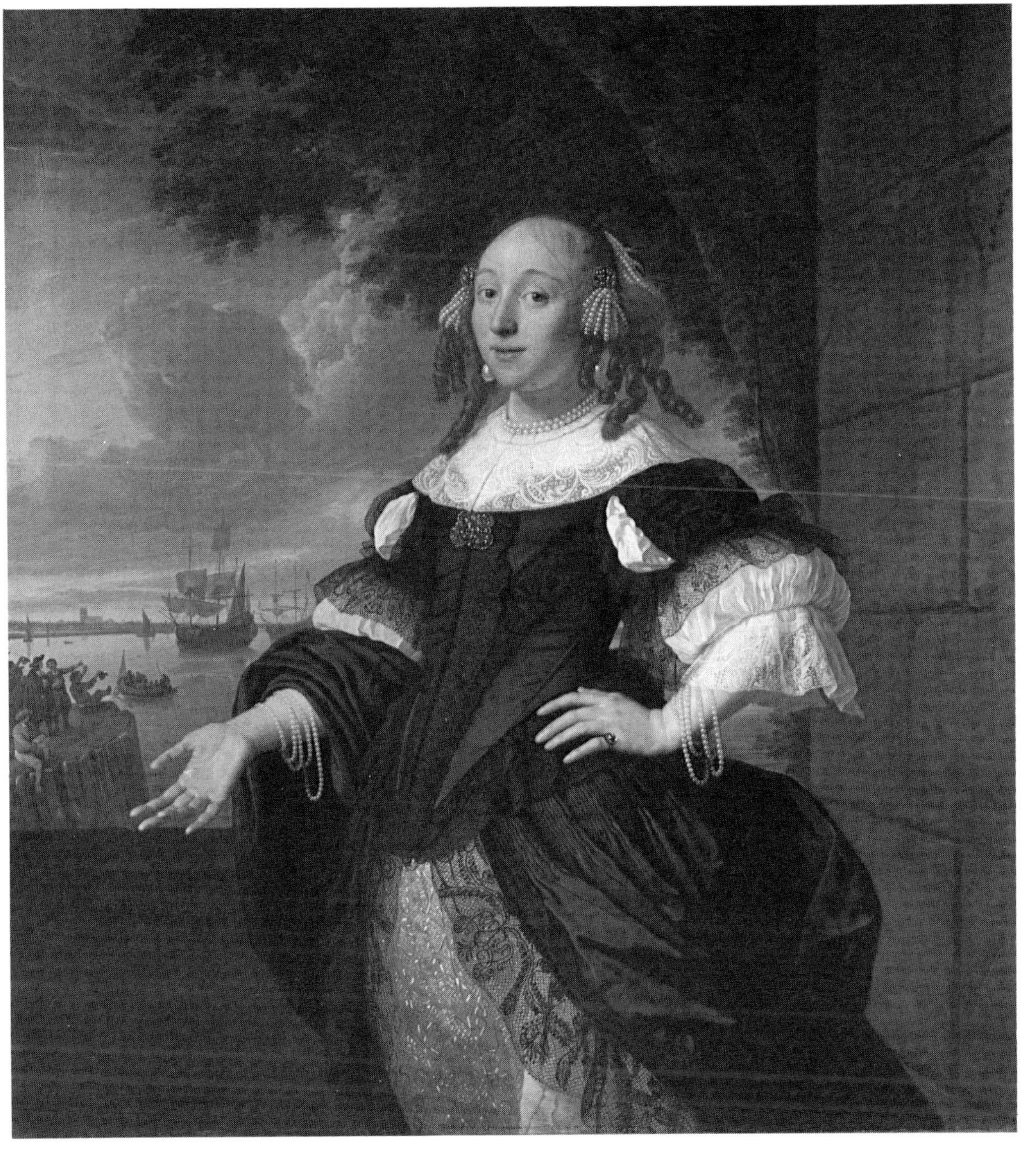

23. Bartholomeus van der Helst, *Geertruida den Dubbelde, Wife of Aert van Nes,* signed and dated 1668. Canvas, 139 x 125 cm. Amsterdam, Rijksmuseum

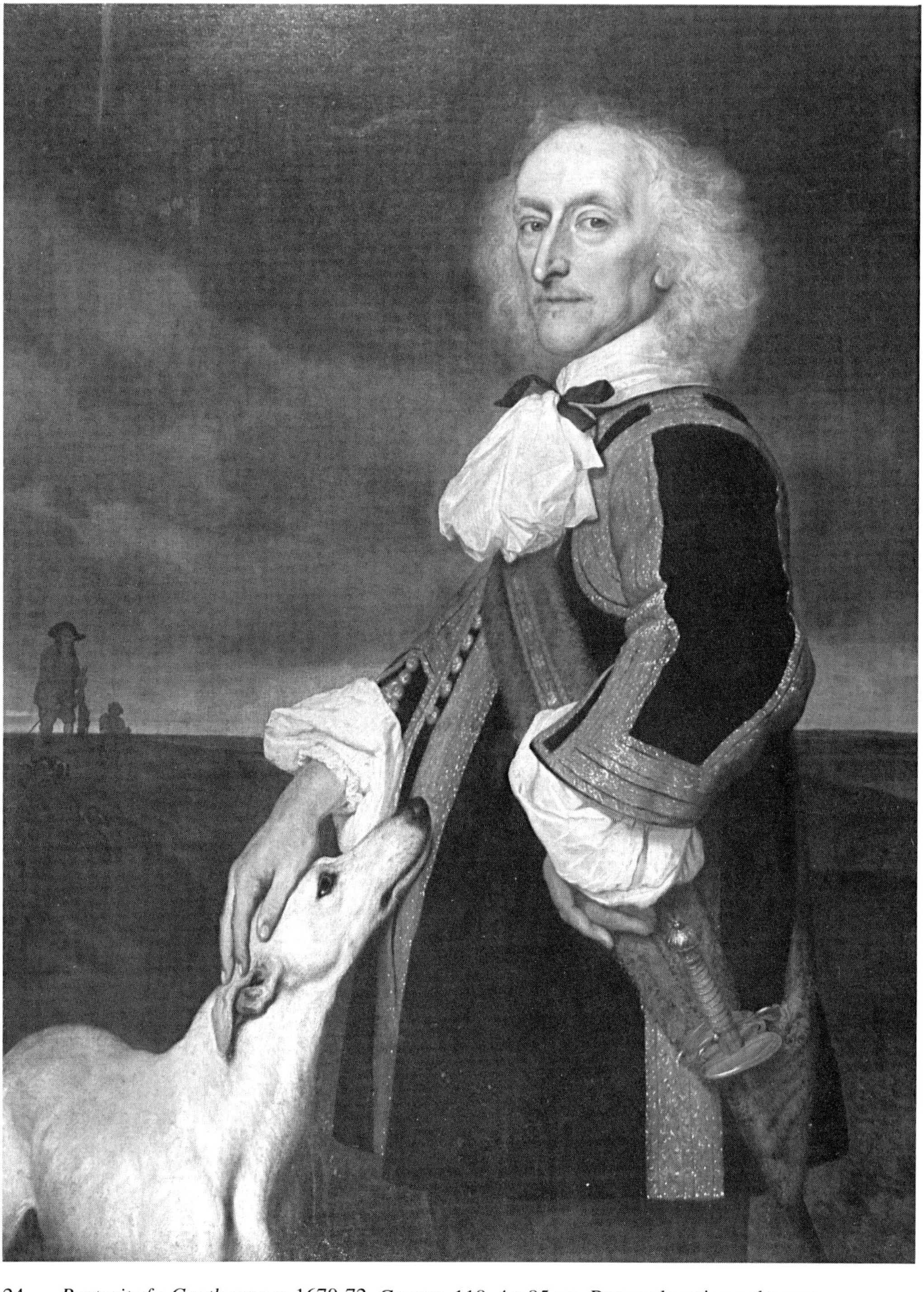

24. *Portrait of a Gentleman*, c. 1670-72. Canvas, 119·4 x 85 cm. Present location unknown

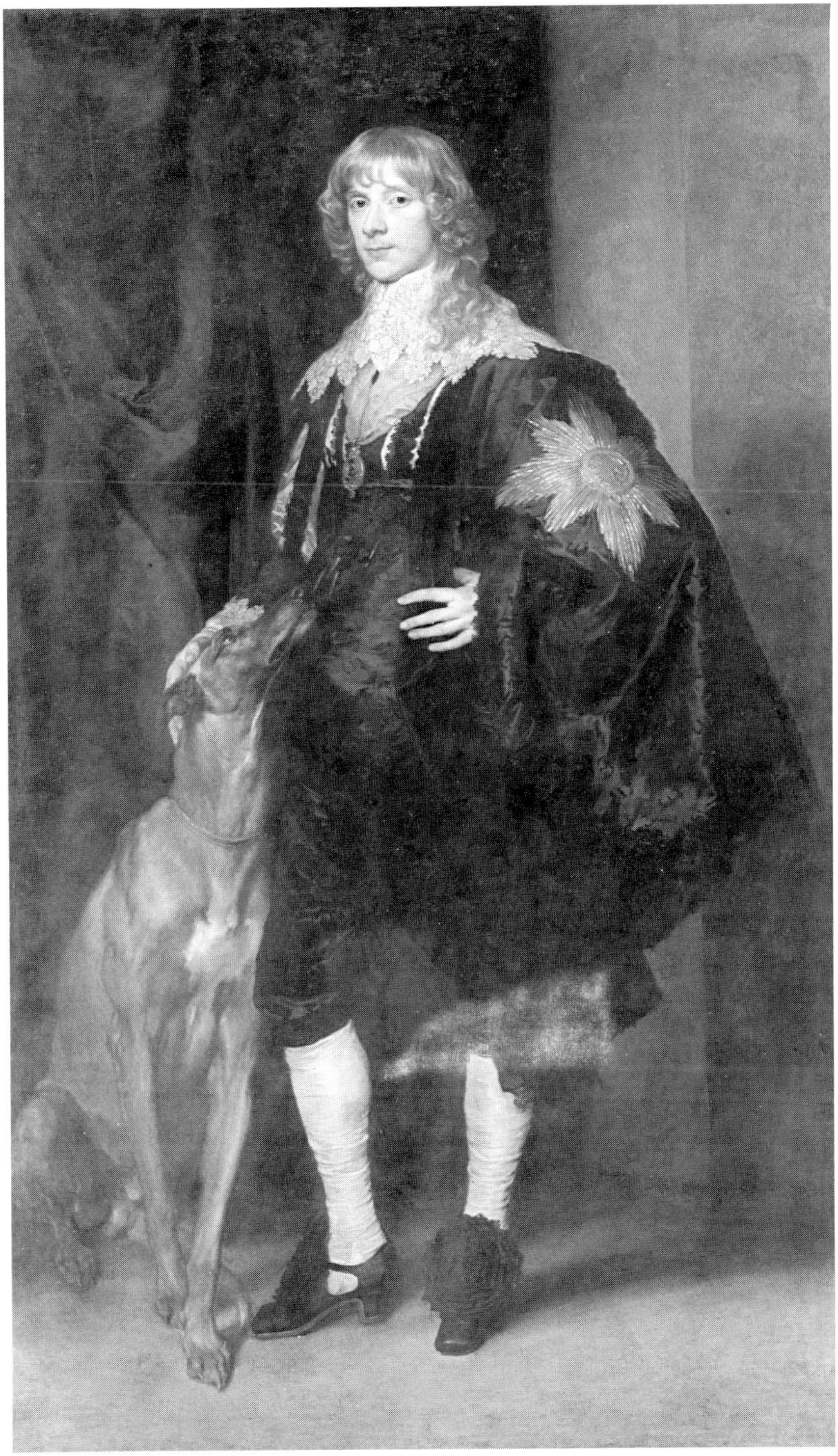

25. Anthony van Dyck, *James Stuart, Duke of Richmond and Lenox*. Canvas, 215·9 x 127·6 cm. New York, Metropolitan Museum of Art, Marquand Collection

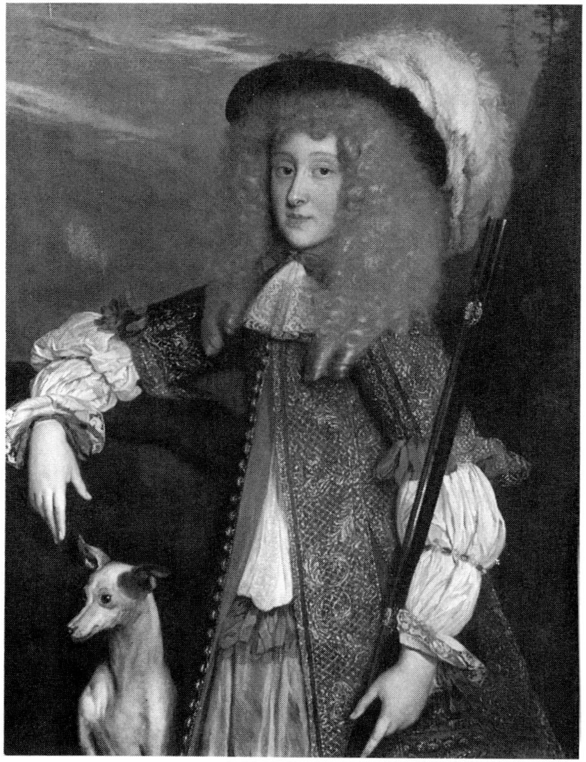

26. *Portrait of a Young Man with Dog and Musket*, c. 1675. Canvas, 112 x 83 cm. Present location unkown. Photograph courtesy of the Rijksbureau voor Kunsthistorische Documentatie, The Hague

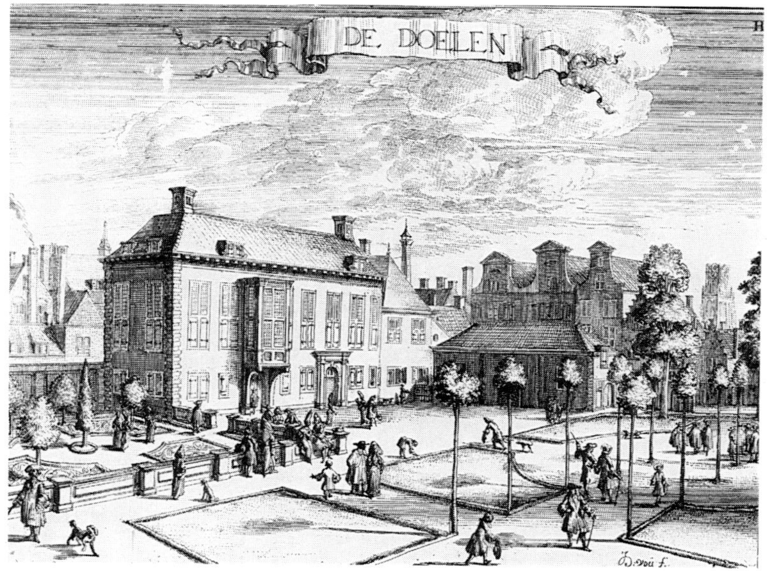

27. R. de Hooghe, *St. Joris Doelen*, Rotterdam, engraving, 1694. Rotterdam, Gemeentelijke Archiefdienst

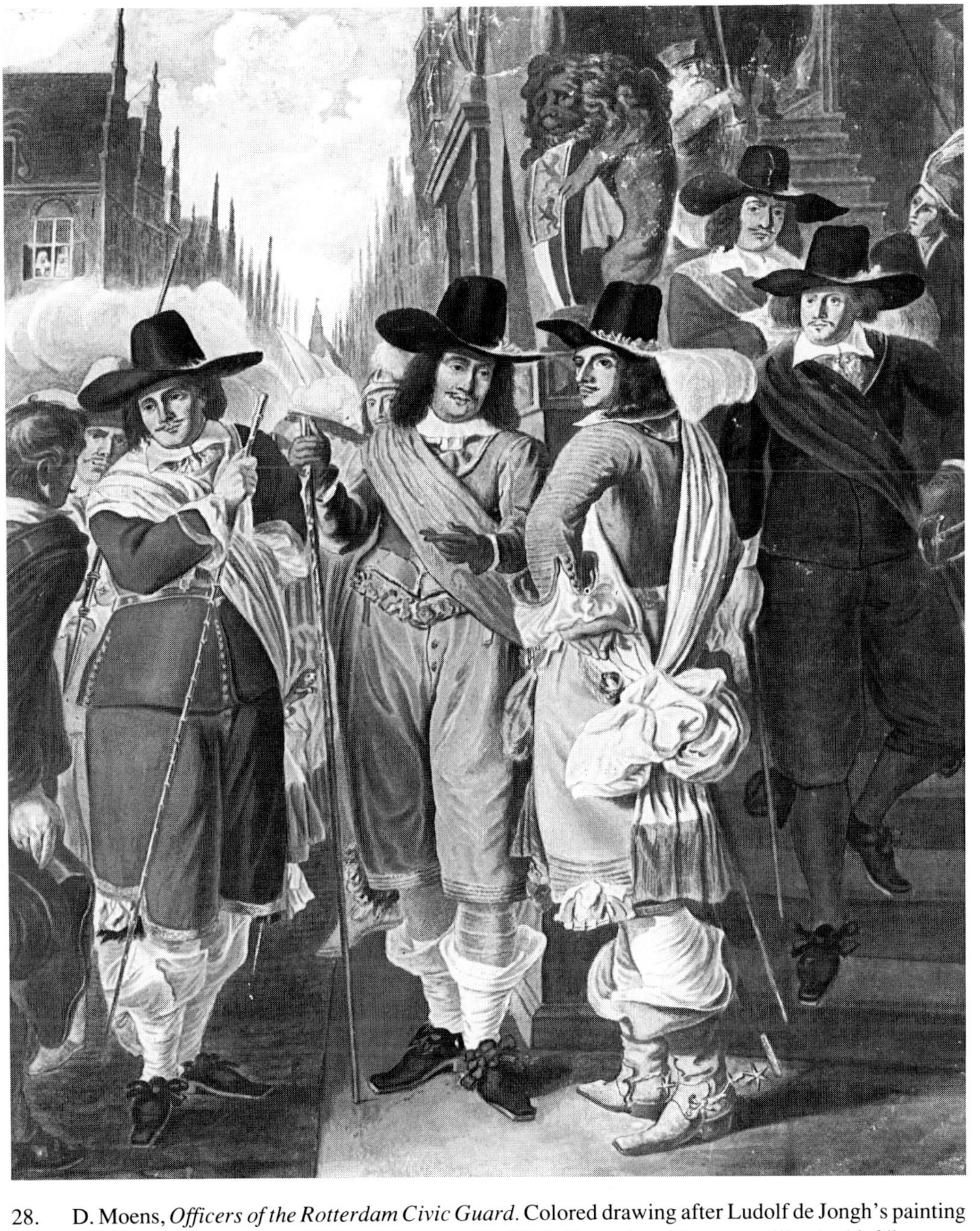

28. D. Moens, *Officers of the Rotterdam Civic Guard.* Colored drawing after Ludolf de Jongh's painting of c. 1655 (canvas, 265 x 200 cm) destroyed in 1864. Rotterdam, Gemeentelijke Archiefdienst

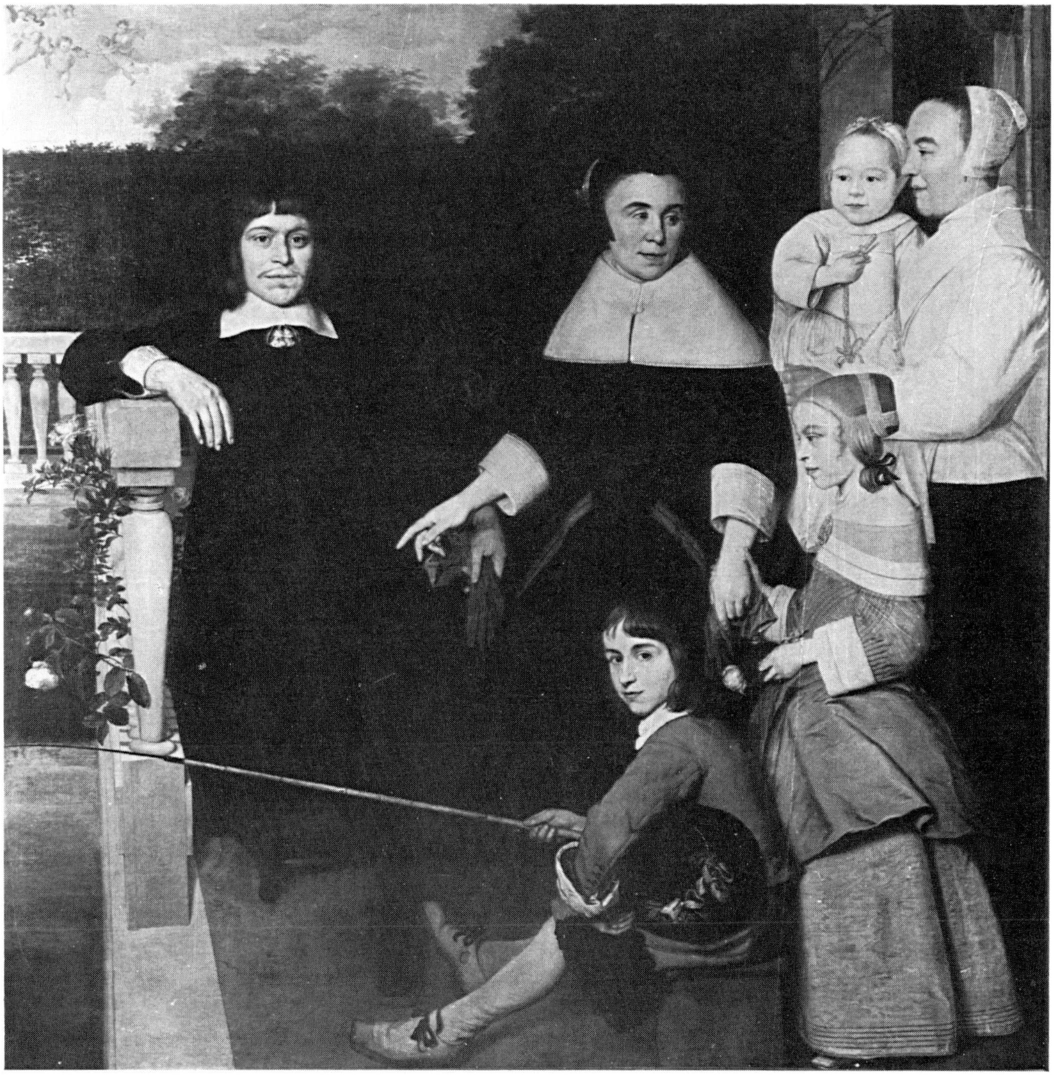

29. *A Family Group on a Terrace*, c. 1655. Canvas, 182 · 9 x 177 · 8 cm. Private Collection

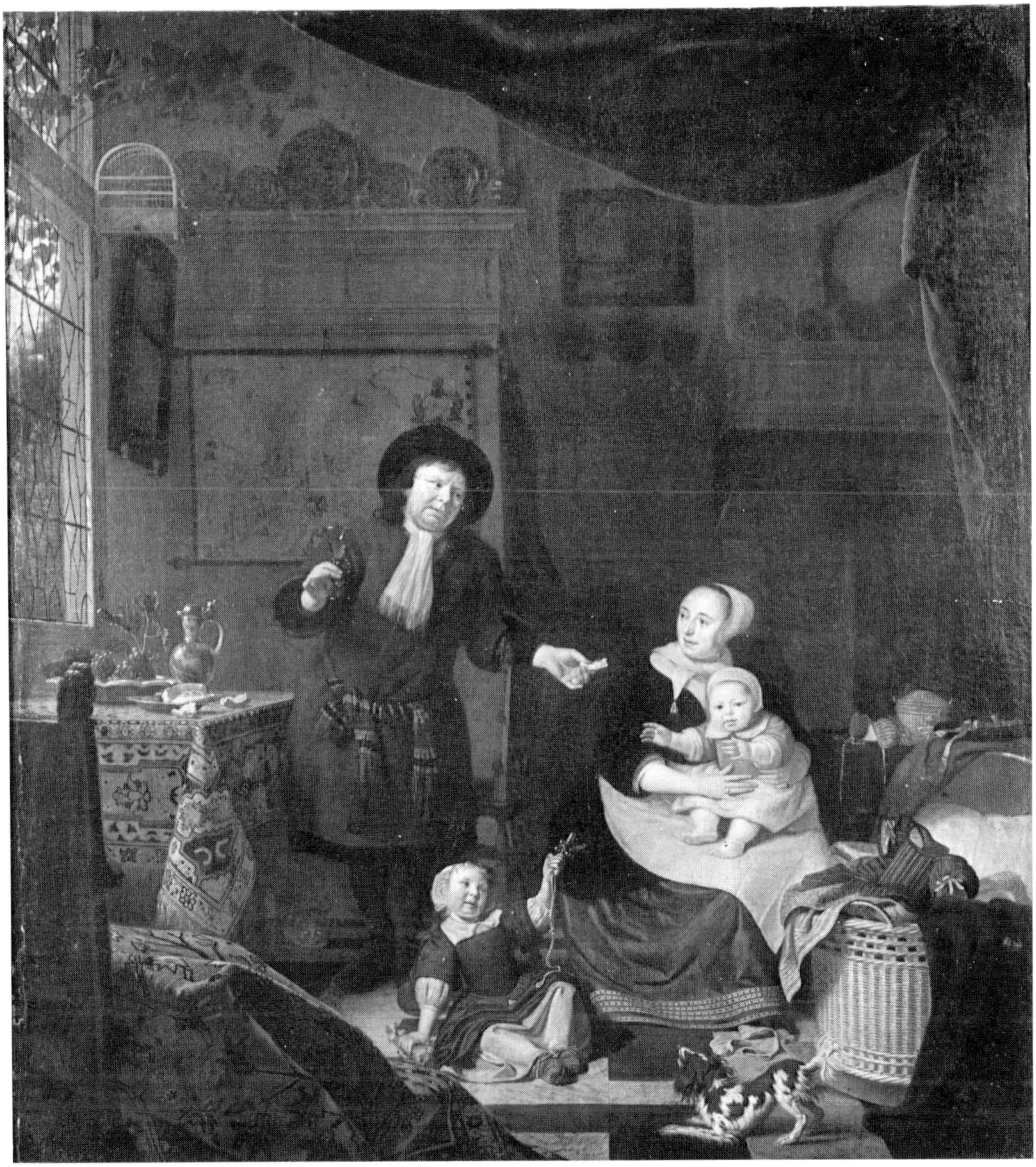

30. *Family Group in an Interior,* signed and dated 1673. Canvas, 72 · 5 x 63 · 5 cm. Amsterdam, Historisch Museum

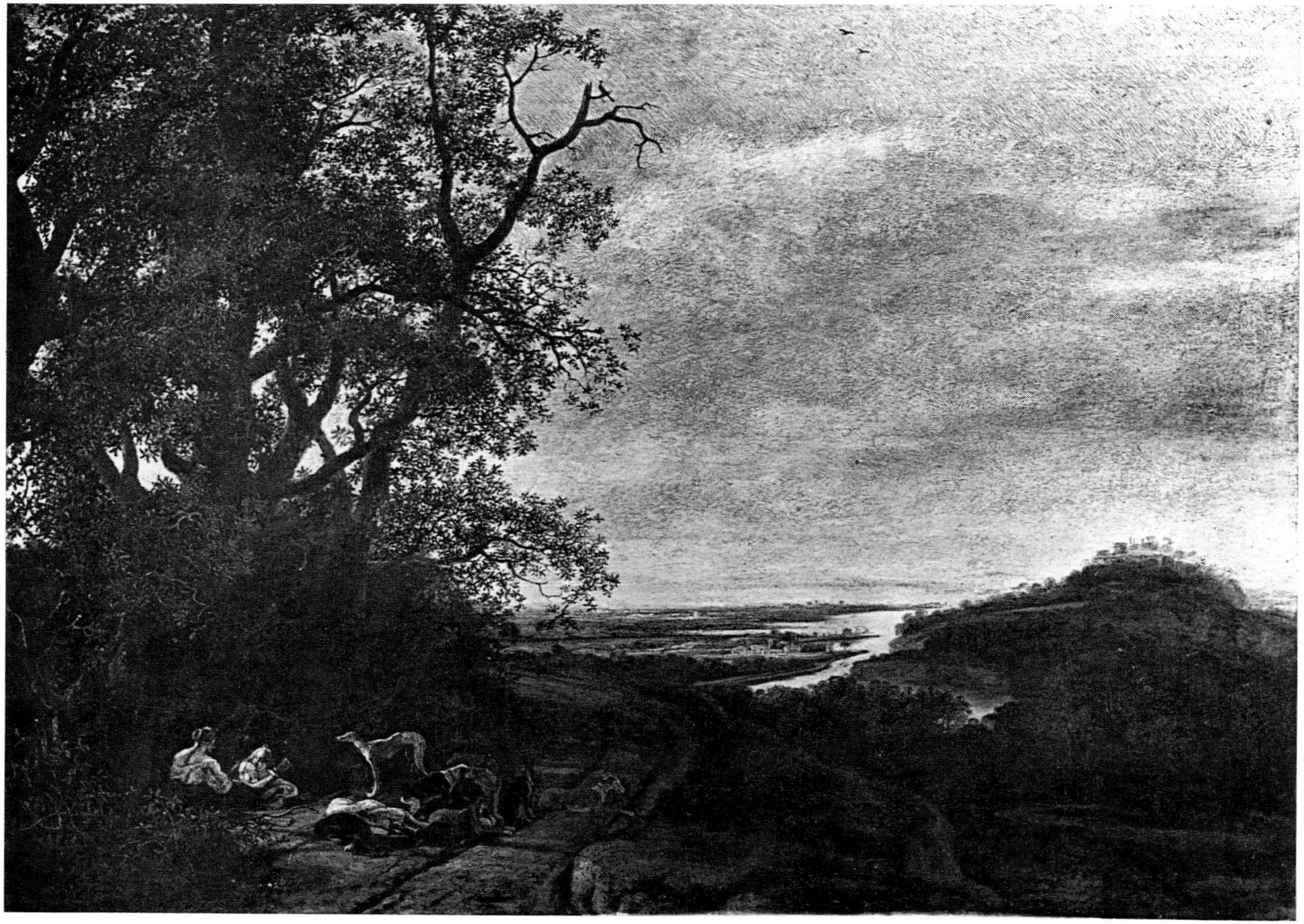

31. *Landscape with Diana and Her Nymphs*, signed (trace remains) and dated 1644. Panel, 75 x 107 cm. Present location unknown

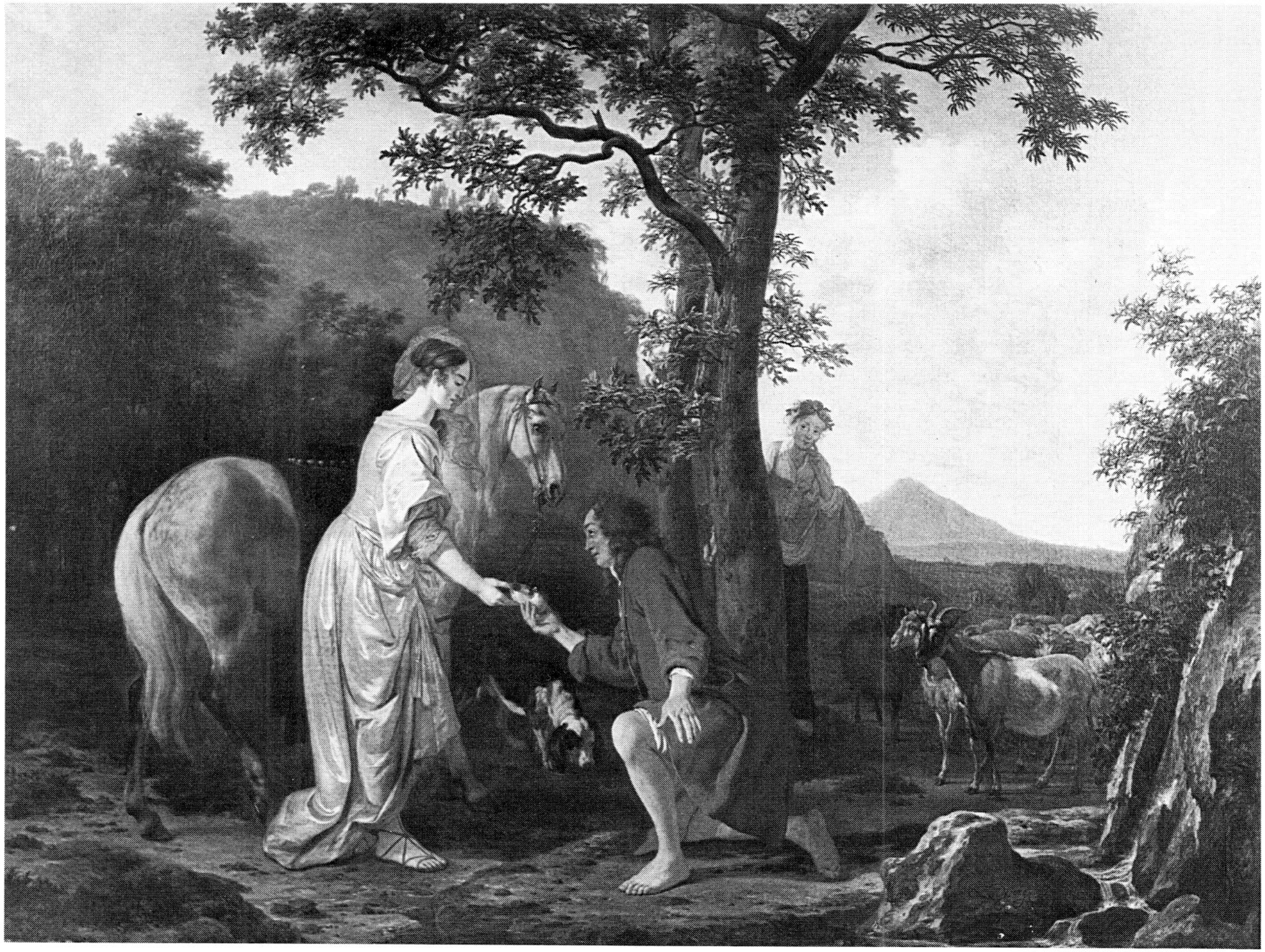

32. *Granida and Daifilo,* signed and dated 1654. Canvas, 107 x 145 cm. Osnabrück, Kulturgeschichtliches Museum

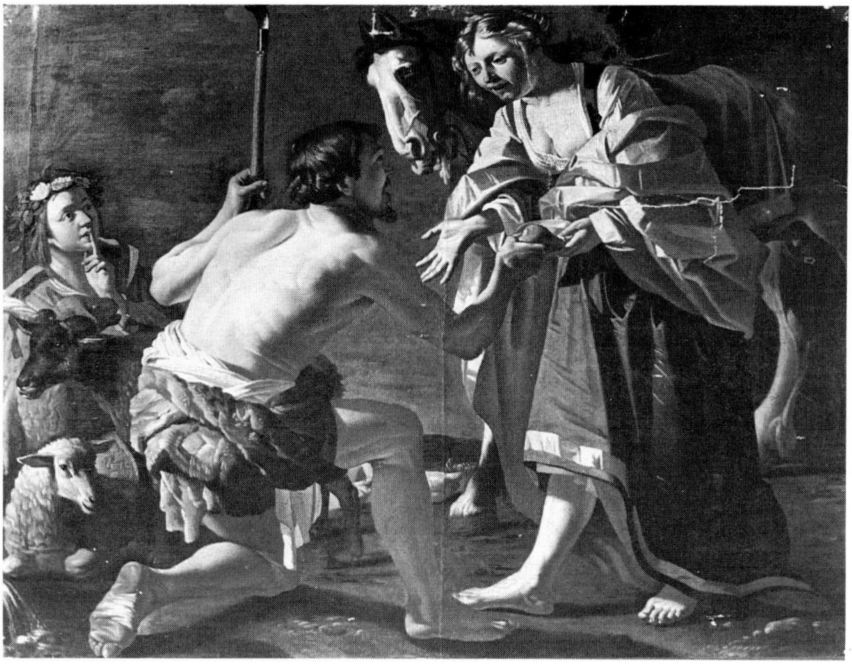

33. Dirck van Baburen, *Granida and Daifilo*, c. 1623. Canvas, 167 x 209 · 5 cm. Brussels, Koninklijke Musea voor Schone Kunsten van Belgie

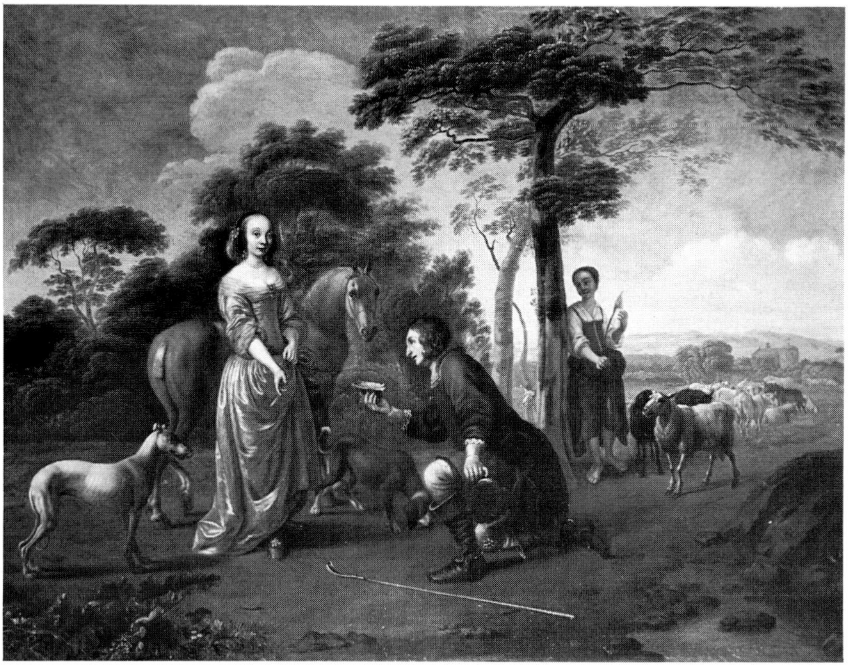

34. Jacob Ochtervelt, *Granida and Daifilo*, signed. c. 1655. 80 x 99 cm. Present location unknown. Photograph courtesy of the Rijksbureau voor Kunsthistorische Documentatie, The Hague

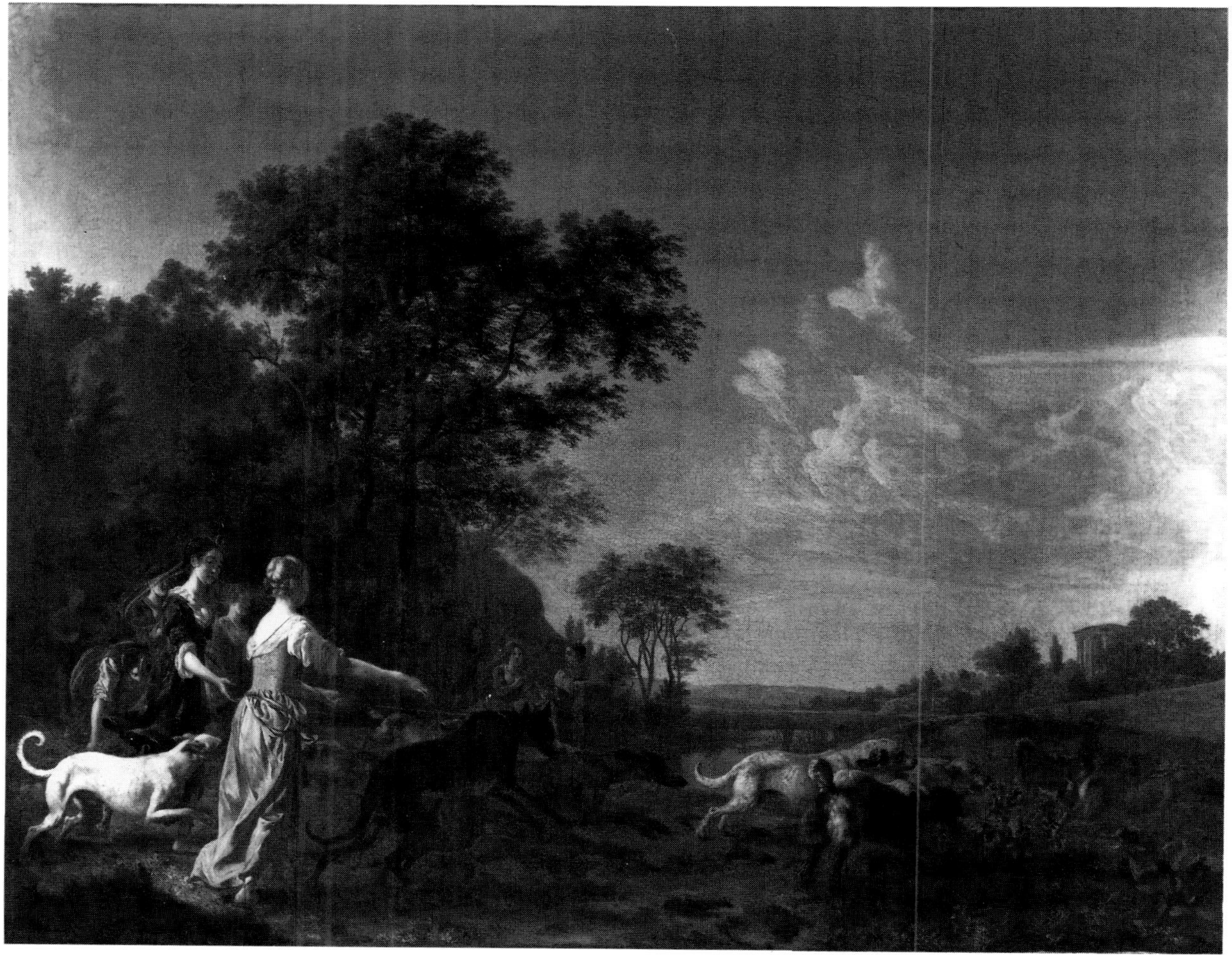

35. *Diana Hunting*. c. 1650-55. Canvas, 84·5 x 111·8 cm. Private collection

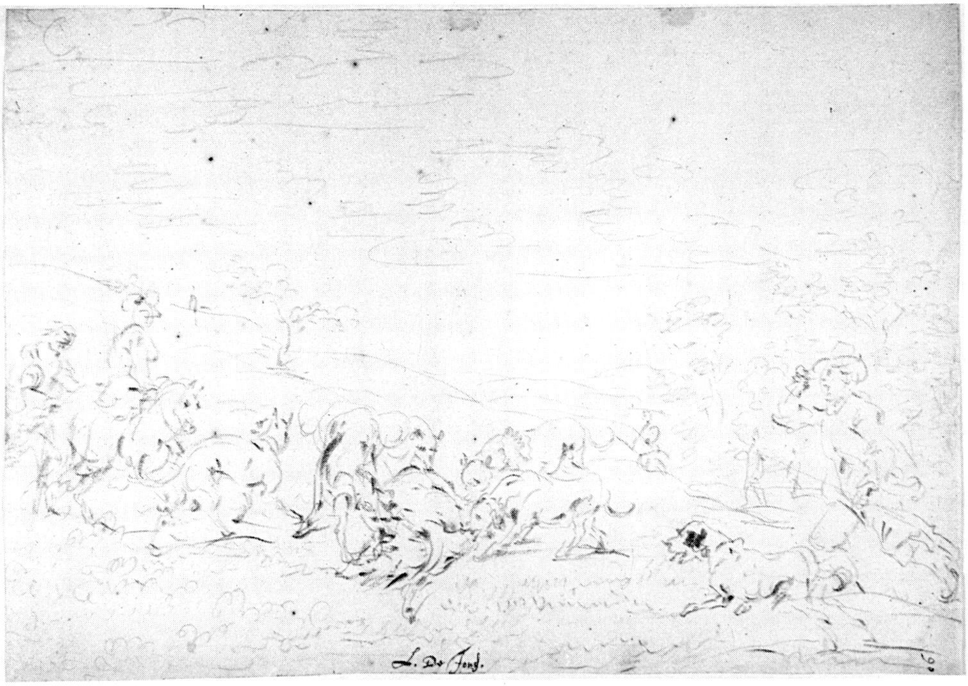

36. Leonard Bramer, *Landscape with the Death of a Fox*. Drawing after Ludolf de Jongh's painting of c. 1648-50 (Fig. 37). Amsterdam, Rijksprentenkabinet

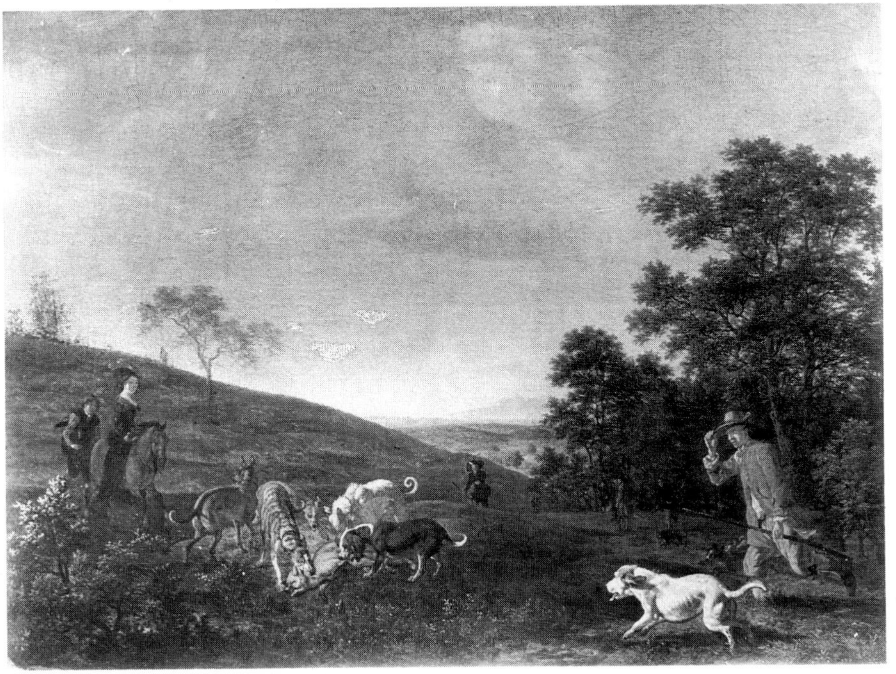

37. *Landscape with the Death of a Fox*. c. 1648-50. Canvas, 55 · 9 x 72 · 4 cm. Present location unknown. Photograph, Frick Art Reference Library, New York

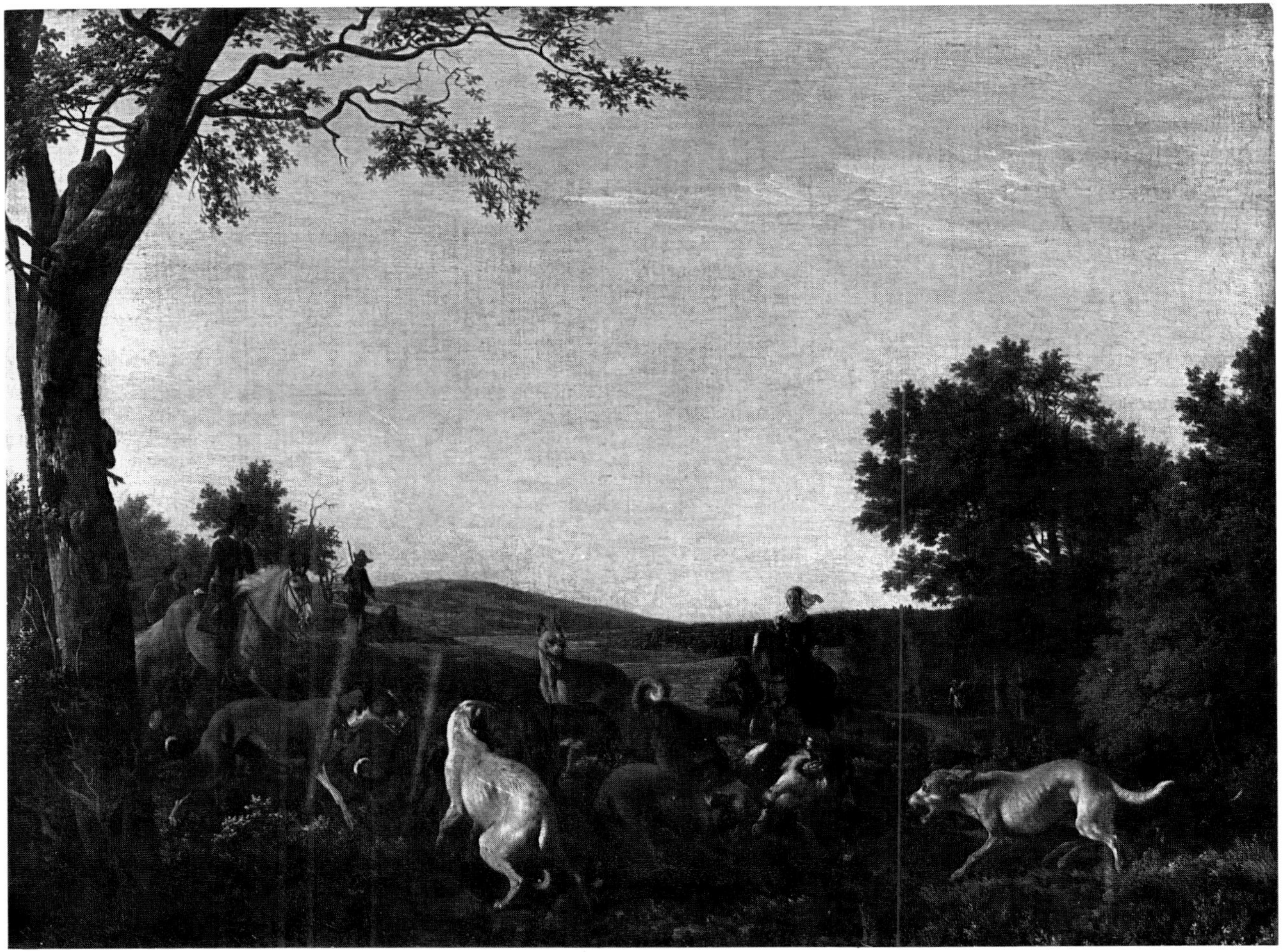

38. *Fox Hunt*, signed. c. 1648-50. Canvas, 51 x 71 cm. Amsterdam, Rijksmuseum

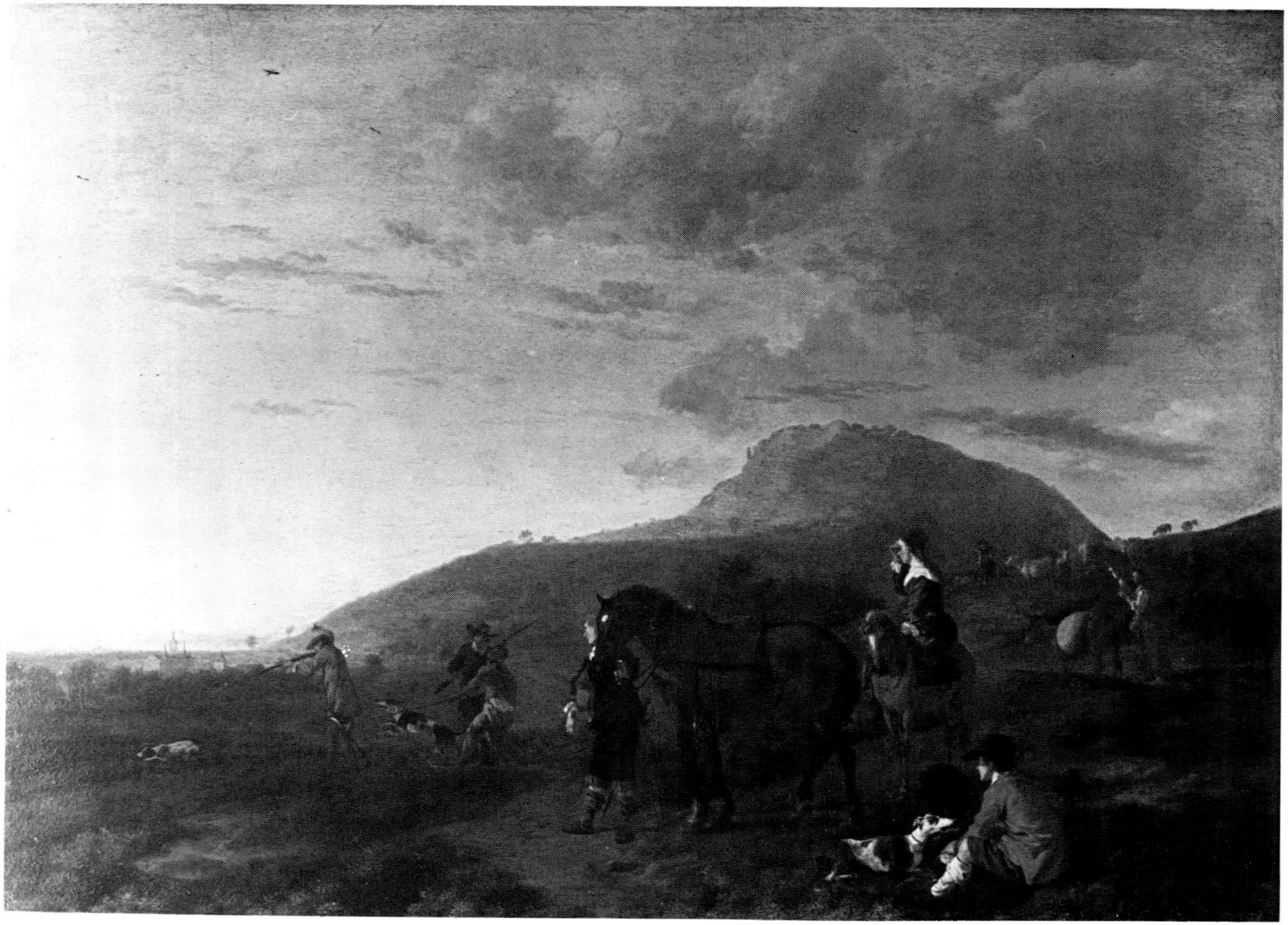

39. *A Shooting Party*. c. 1648-50. Panel, 56 x 83 cm. Dublin, National Gallery of Ireland

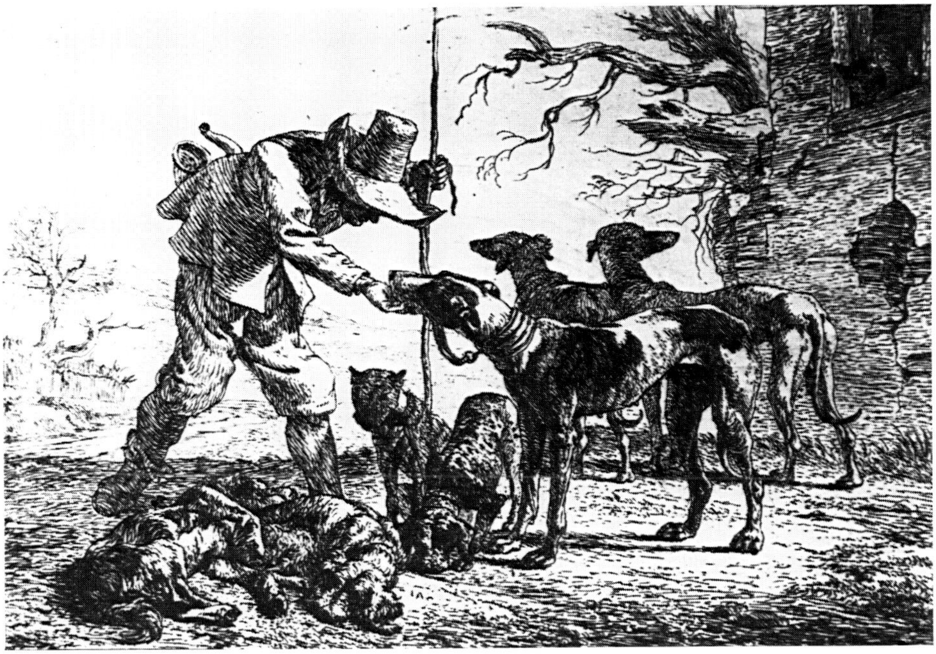

40. Pieter van Laer, *Sportsman with Dogs*. Print of 1636

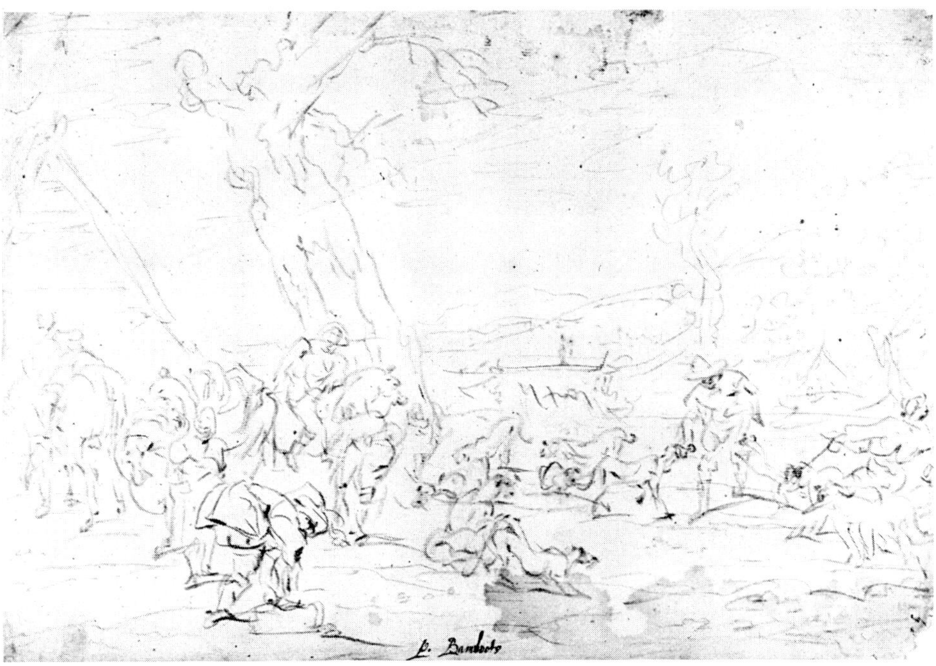

41. Leonard Bramer, *Rest on the Hunt*. Drawing after the original painting by Pieter van Laer. Amsterdam, Rijksprentenkabinet

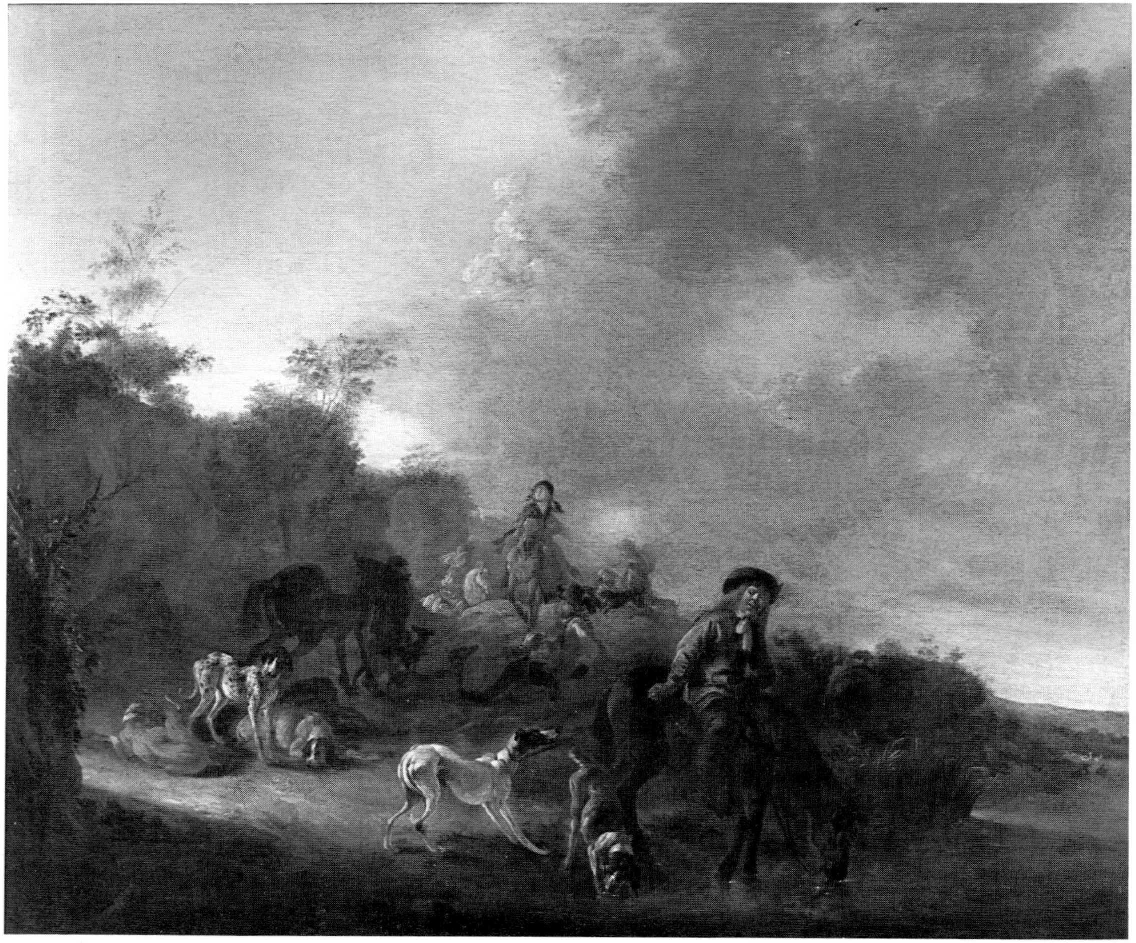

42. Dirck Stoop, *Landscape with Riders and Dogs*, signed and dated 1649. Panel, 52 · 5 x 63 · 5 cm. Utrecht, Centraal Museum

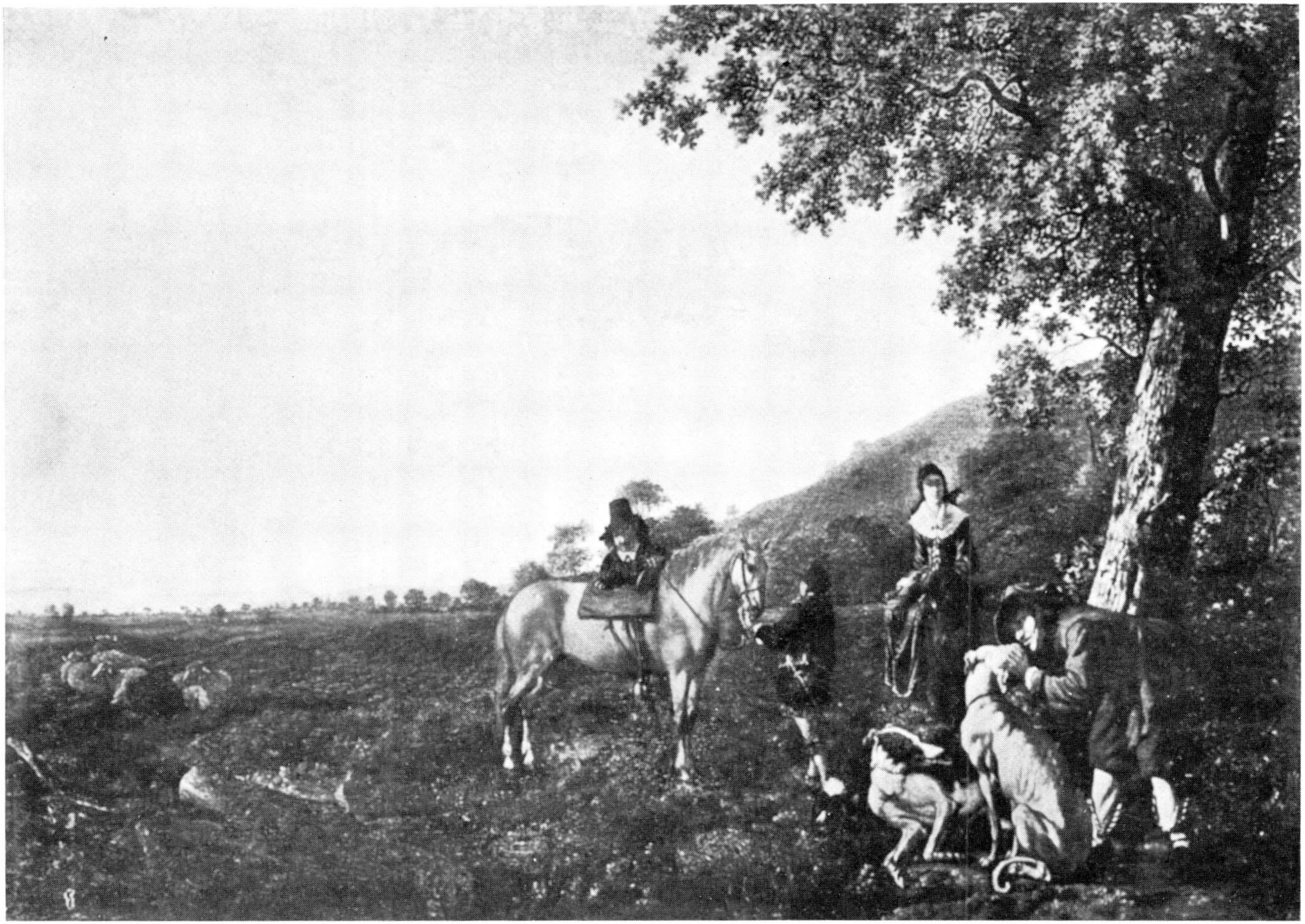

43. *Rest on the Hunt.* c. 1650. Panel, 58 · 5 x 82 · 5 cm. Present location unknown. Photograph courtesy of the Rijksbureau voor Kunsthistorische Documentatie, The Hague

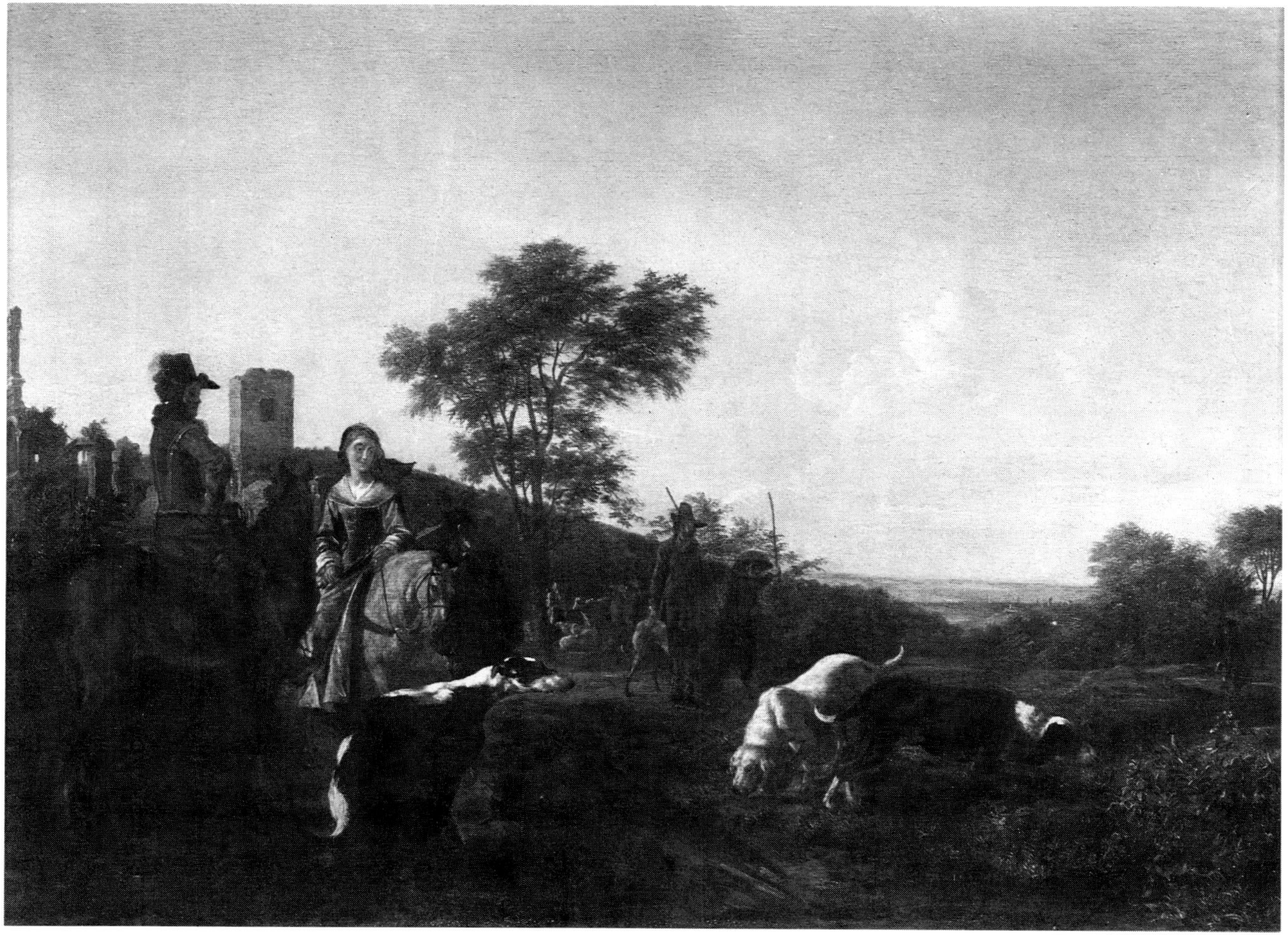

44. *Hunters in the Field,* signed. c. 1655. Panel, 59·5 x 82 cm. Schiedam, C. Roodenburg collection. Photograph courtesy of the Rijksbureau voor Kunsthistorische Documentatie, The Hague

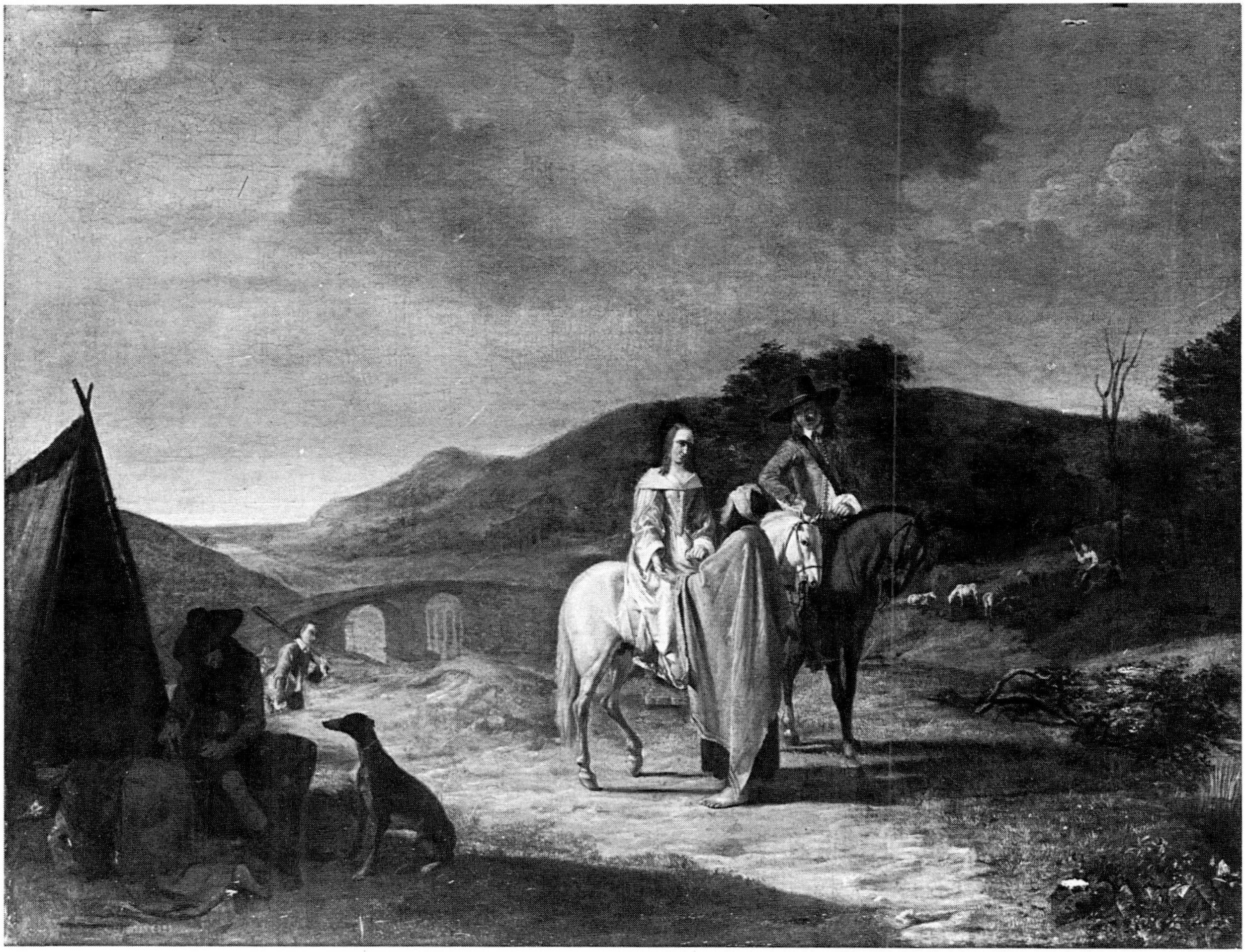

45. *The Cavaliers*. Formerly signed (?). c. 1650. Canvas, 97·5 x 130·5. The Hague, Dienst Verspreide Rijkskollekties, The Hague

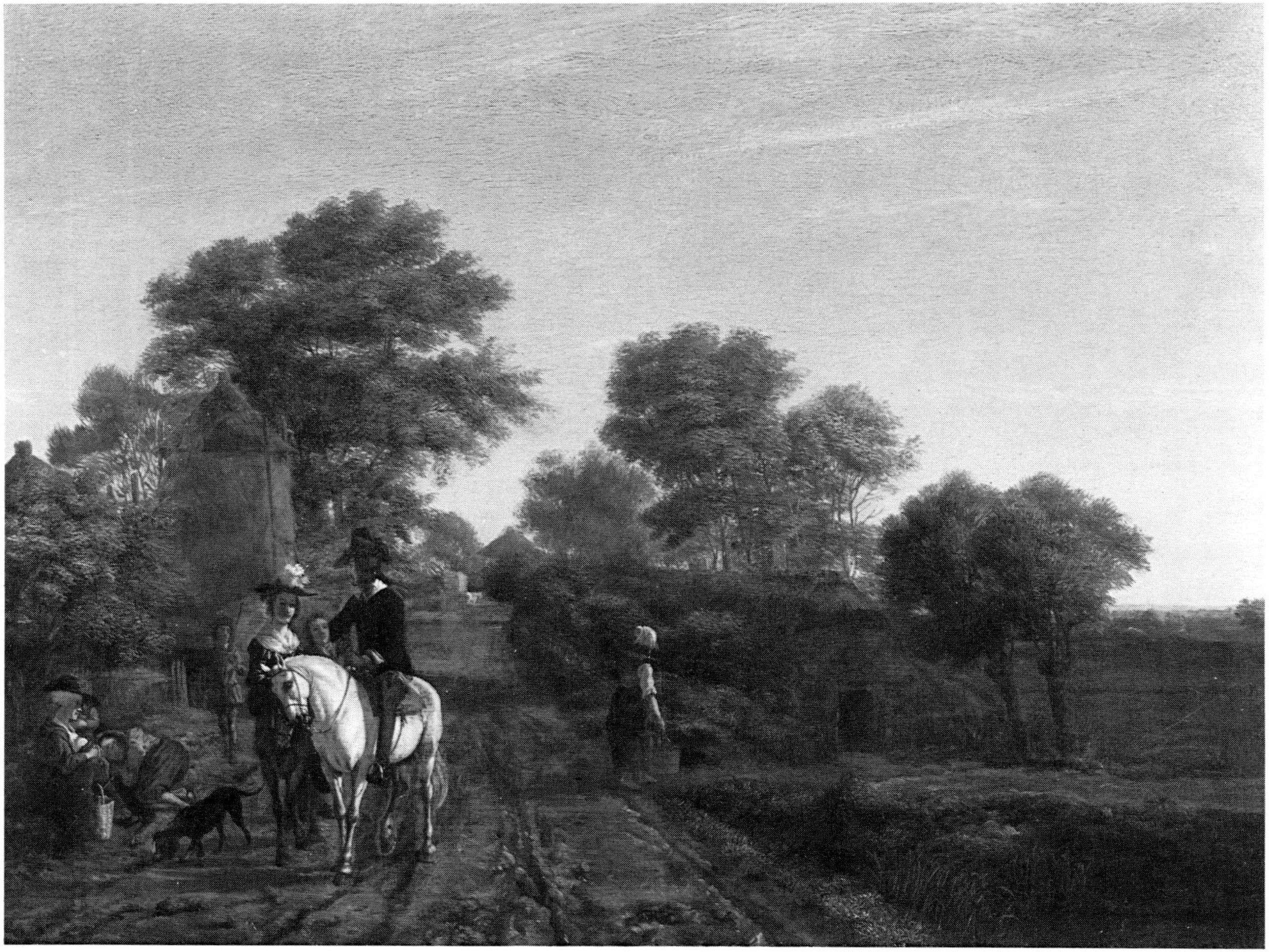

46. *Landscape with Riders*. c. 1650. Panel, 52 x 72 cm. Present location unknown.
Photograph courtesy of the Rijksbureau voor Kunsthistorische Documentatie, The Hague

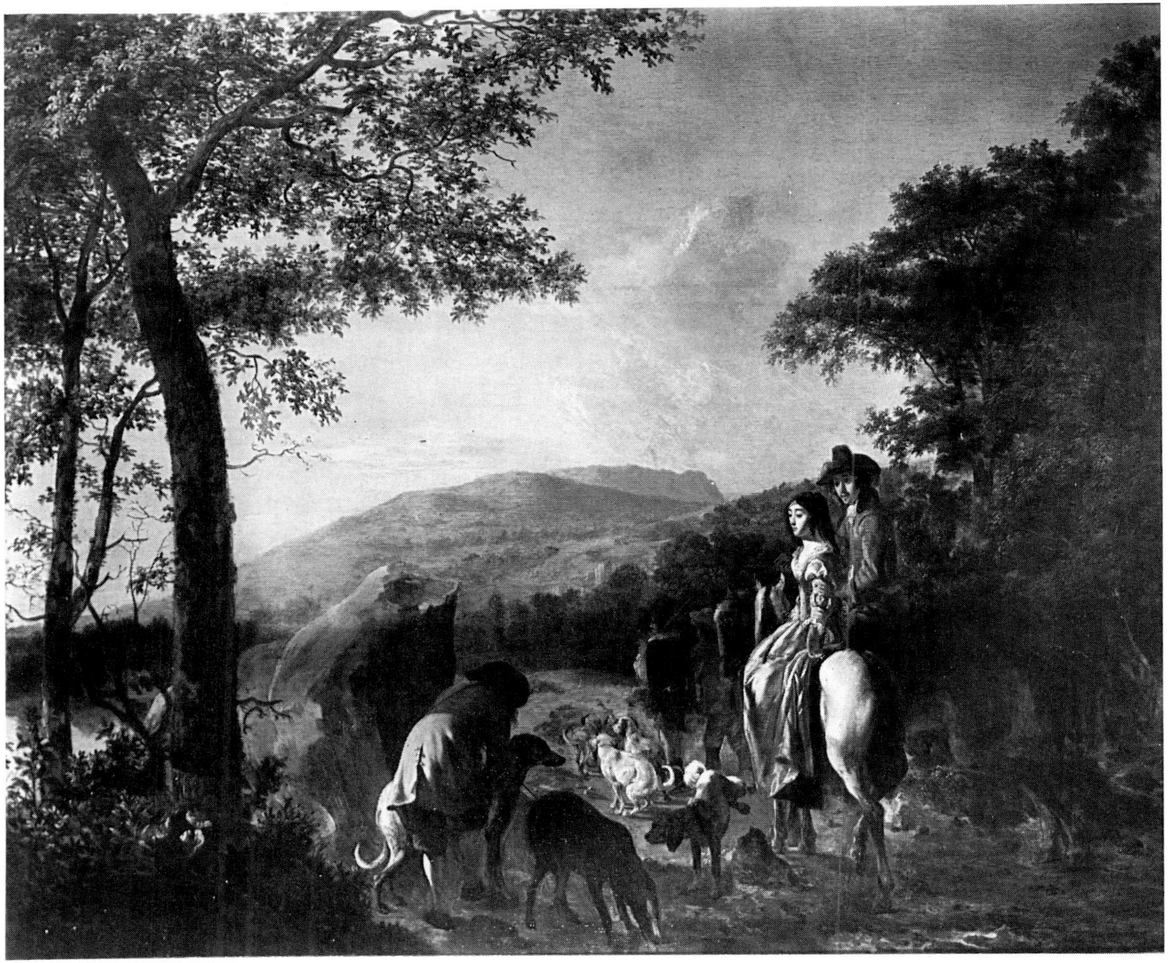

47. *Hunters in a Hilly Landscape.* c. 1655. Panel, 59 x 74 cm. Present location unknown. Photograph courtesy of the Rijksbureau voor Kunsthistorische Documentatie, The Hague

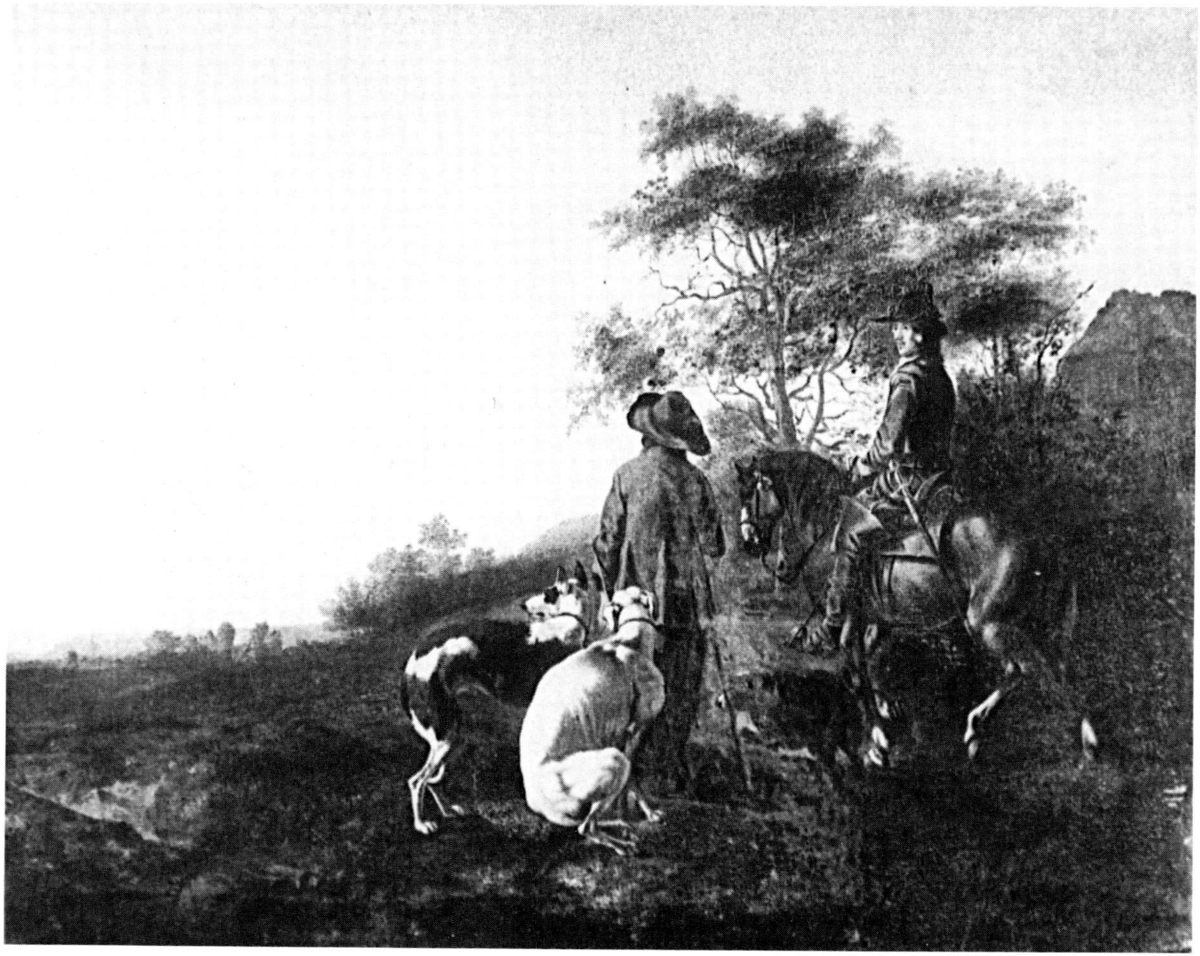

48. *Small Hunting Group*. c. 1655. Panel, 51 x 61 cm. Present location unknown. Photograph courtesy of the Rijksbureau voor Kunsthistorische Documentatie, The Hague

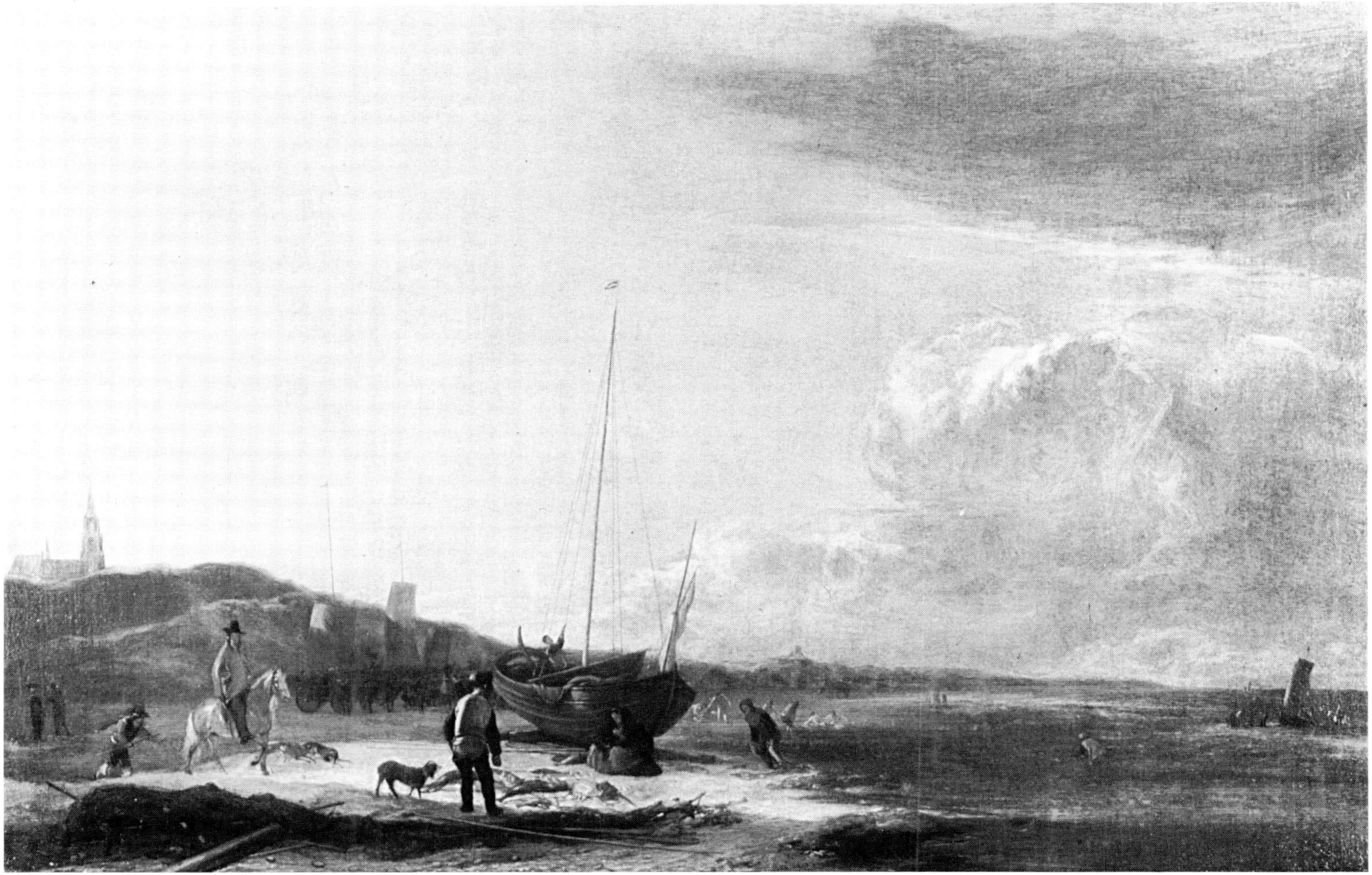

49. *Beach at Scheveningen*. c. 1646-48. Canvas, 67.3 x 109.2 cm. Stephen Reiss collection, Norwich

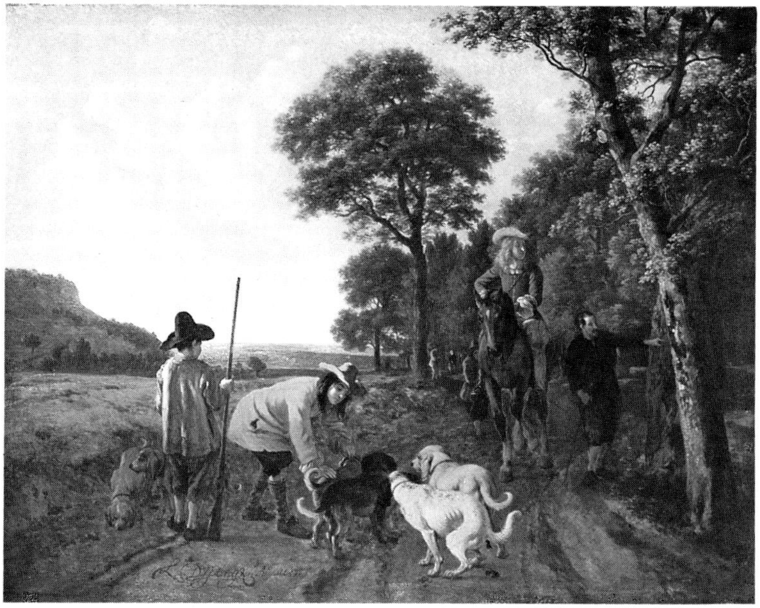

50. *Hunters with Dogs,* signed and dated 1665. Panel, 39 · 5 x 49 · 5 cm. Leningrad, Hermitage Museum

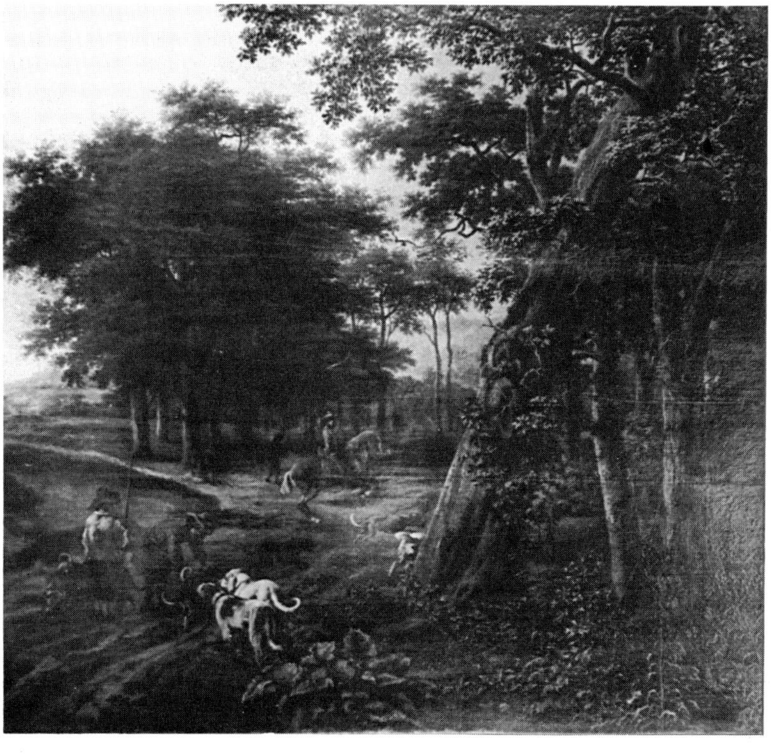

51. Joris van der Haagen and Ludolf de Jongh, *Hunt Scene.* c. 1665. Panel, 95 x 95 cm. Present location unknown. Photograph courtesy of the Rijksbureau voor Kunsthistorische Documentatie, The Hague

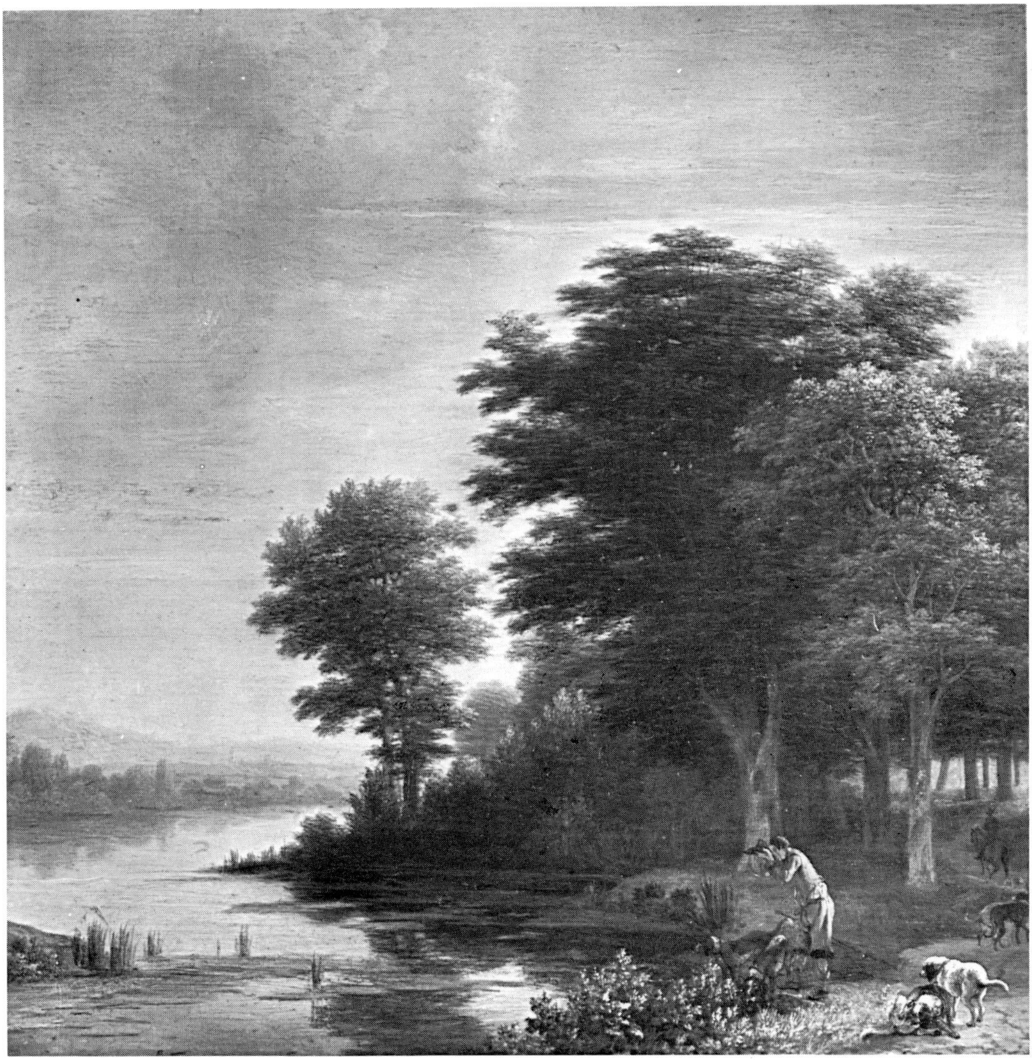

52. Joris van der Haagen and Ludolf de Jongh, *Landscape with a River*.
c. 1658-60. Panel, 25 x 25 cm. Present location unknown. Photograph courtesy of the Rijksbureau voor Kunsthistorische Documentatie, The Hague

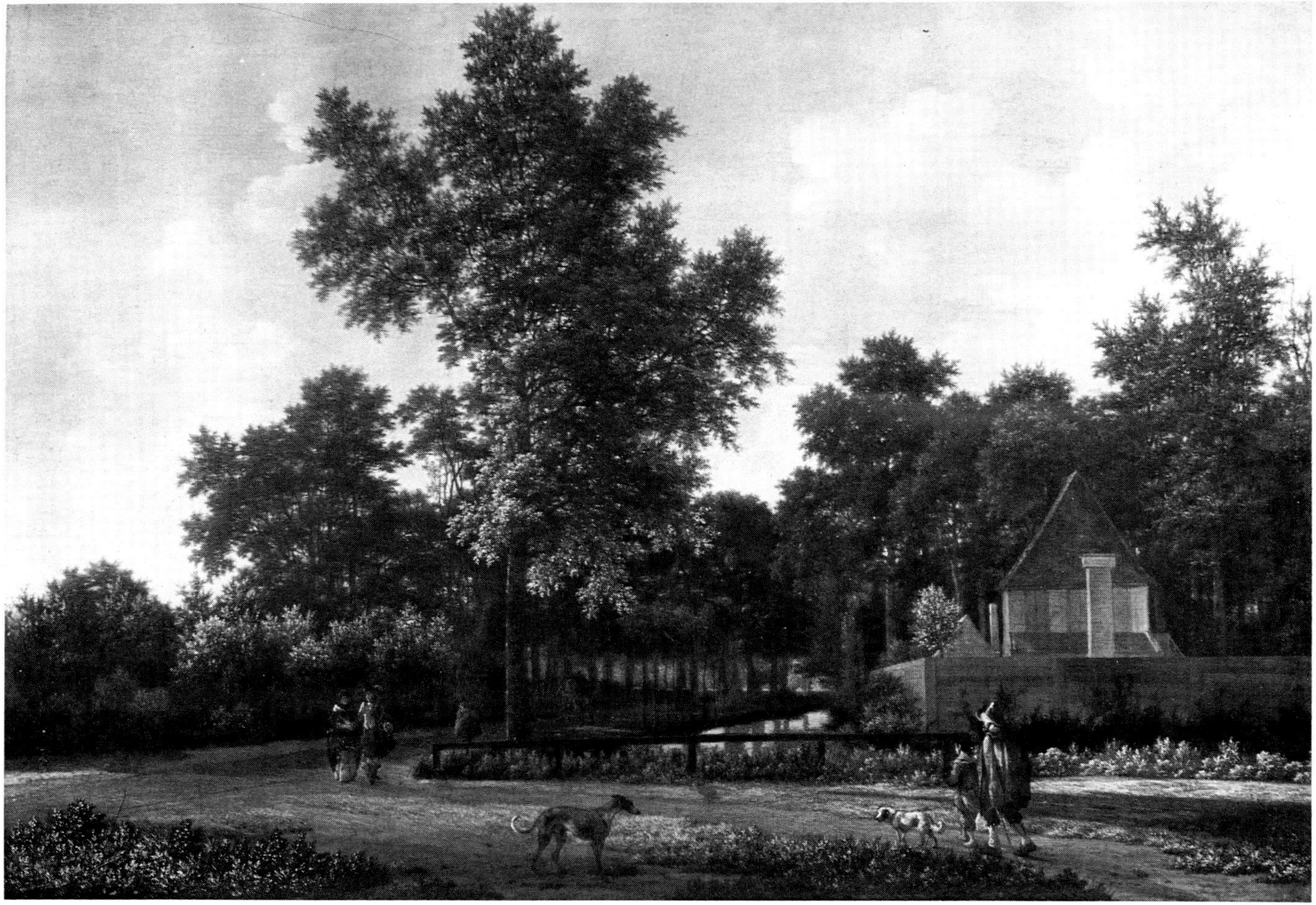

53. Joris van der Haagen and Ludolf de Jongh, *Forester's House in The Hague*. c. 1667. Panel, 40 x 58 cm. Present location unknown. Photograph courtesy of the Rijksbureau voor Kunsthistorische Documentatie, The Hague

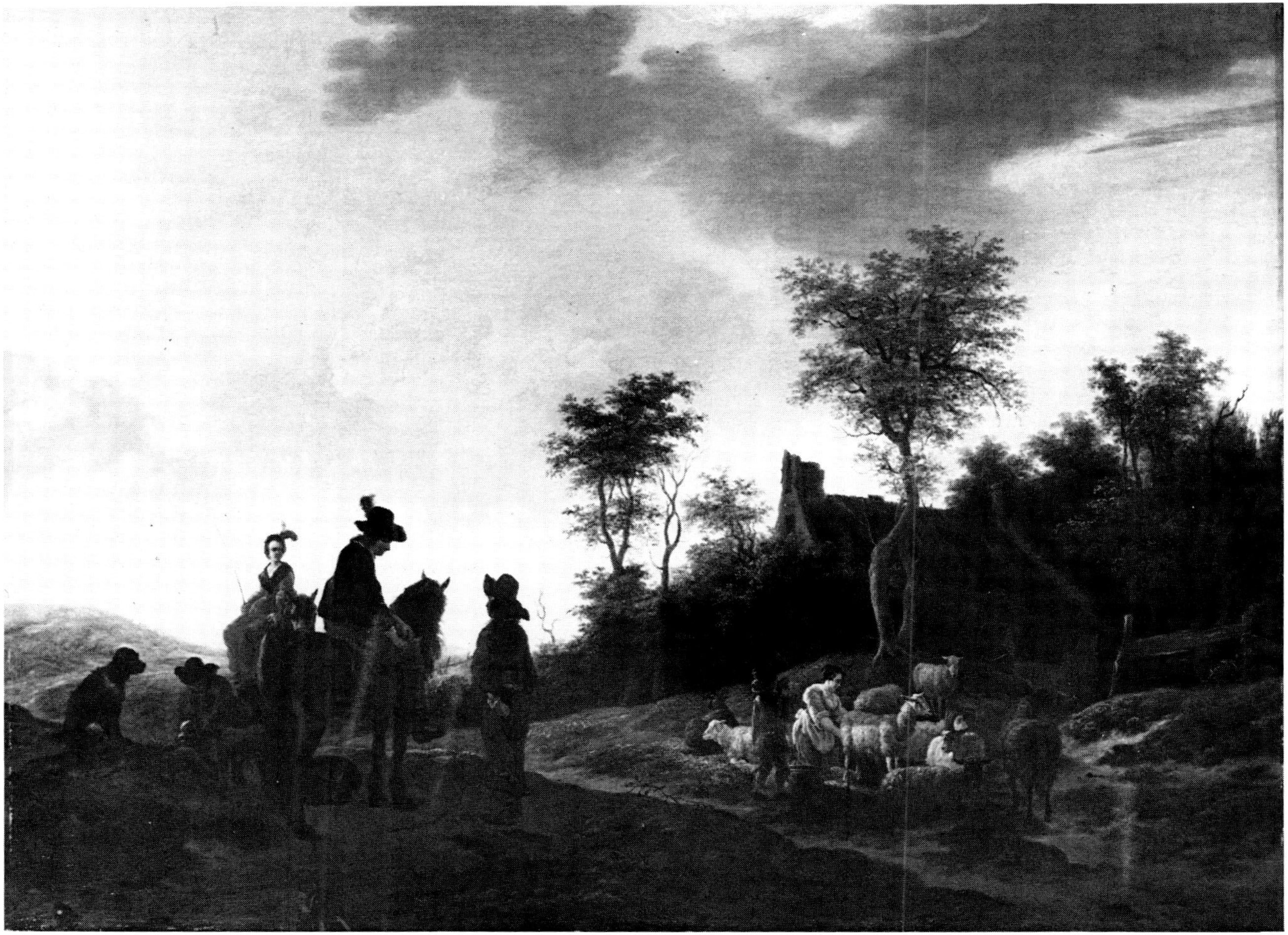

54. Joris van der Haagen and Ludolf de Jongh (?), *Landscape with Resting Herd and Two Riders*. c. 1662. Panel, 59 · 5 x 83 cm. Szépmüvészeti Müzeum, Budapest

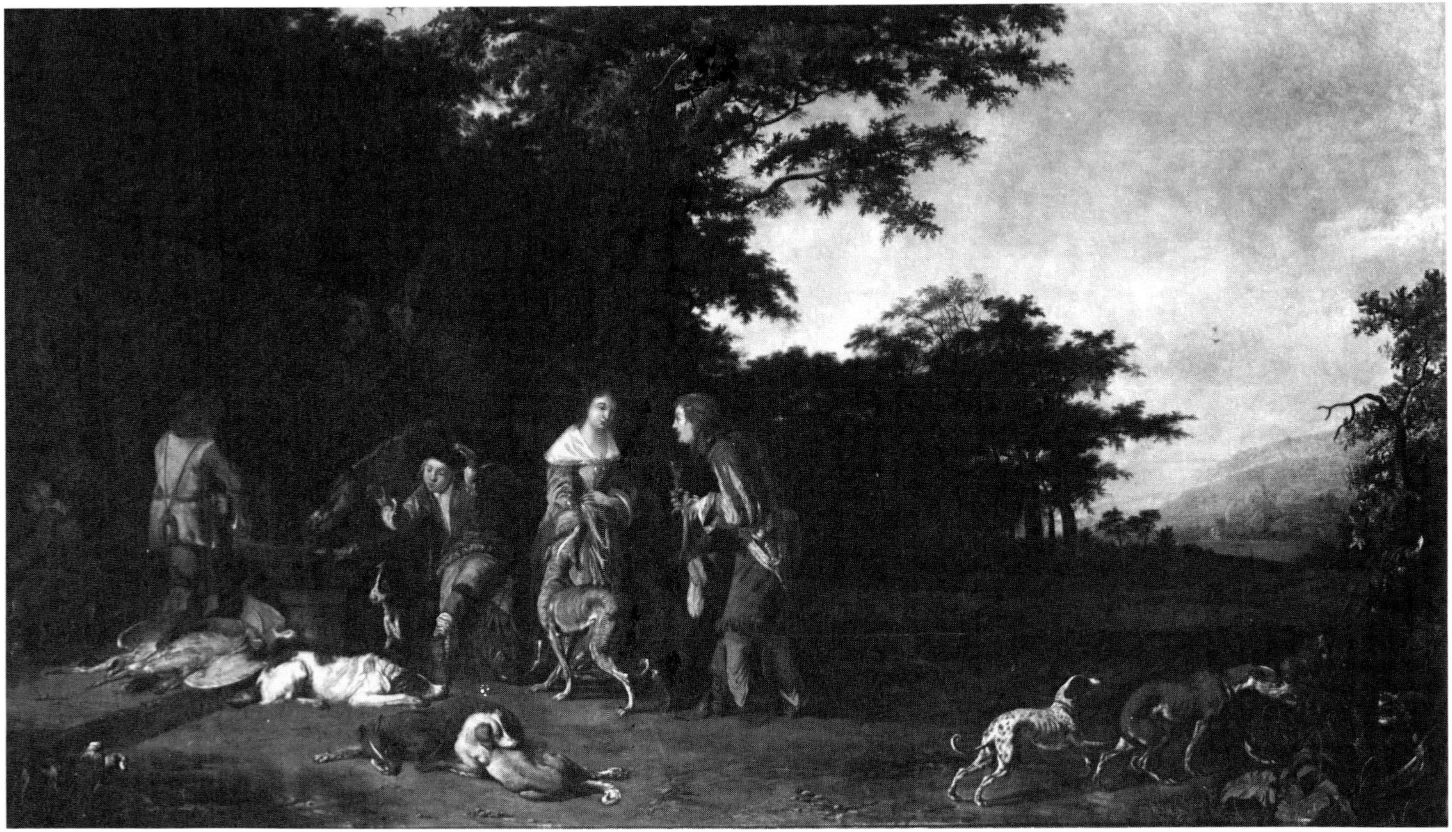

55. Abraham Hondius, *After the Hunt,* signed and dated1653. Panel, 92 x 163 · 2 cm. Present location unknown.
Photograph courtesy of the Rijksbureau voor Kunsthistorische Documentatie, The Hague

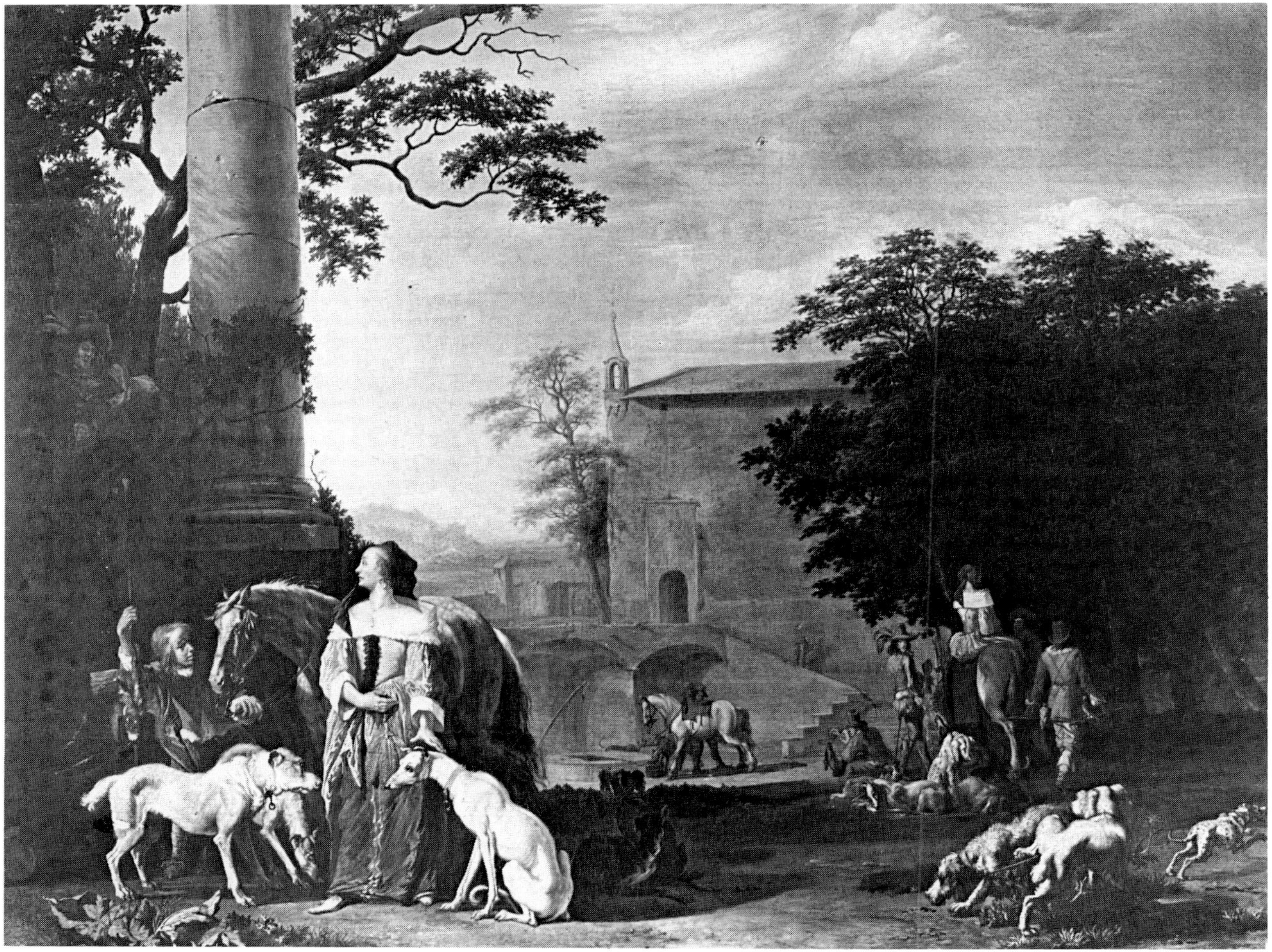

56. Abraham Hondius, *Hunters Resting,* signed and dated1654. Panel, 90 x 112 cm. Present location unknown. Photograph courtesy of the Rijksbureau voor Kunsthistorische Documentatie,The Hague

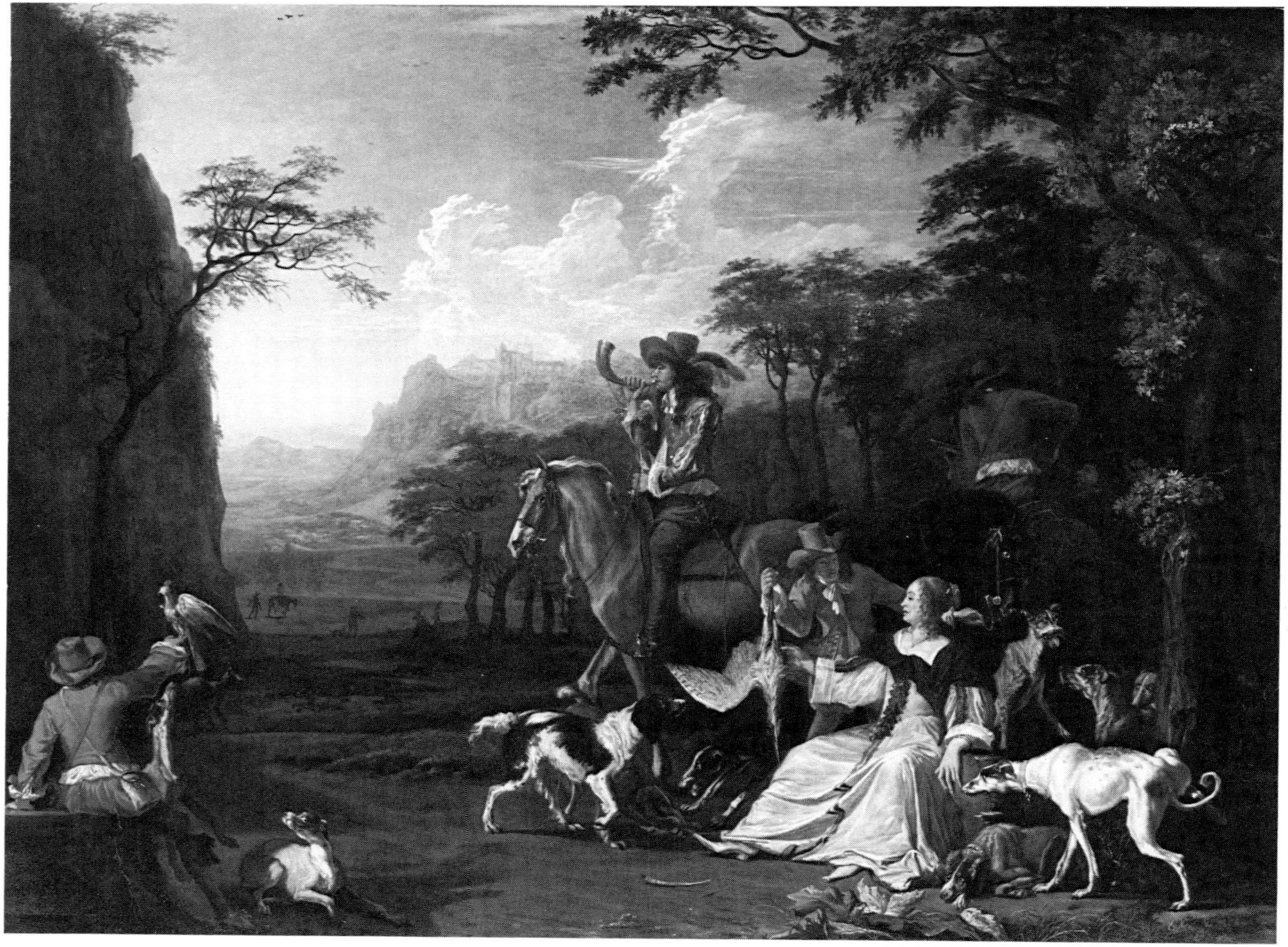

57. Abraham Hondius, *Rest on the Hunt*, signed. c. 1654. Panel, 92 · 5 x 125 cm. Present location unknown

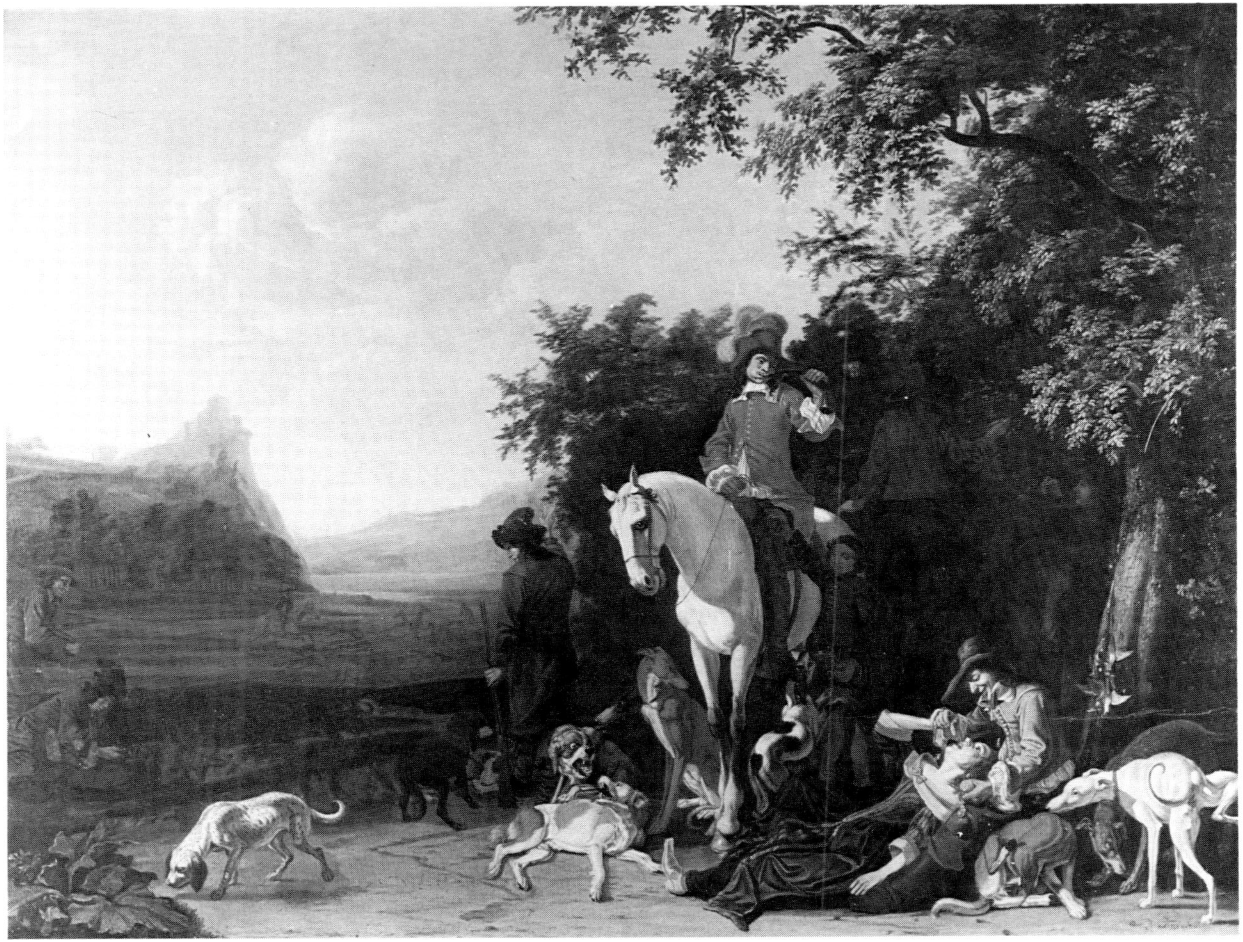

58. Abraham Hondius (?), *Halt on the Chase*. c. 1655.Panel, 92 x 124 cm. Present location unknown.
Photograph courtesy of the Rijksbureau voor Kunsthistorische Documentatie, The Hague

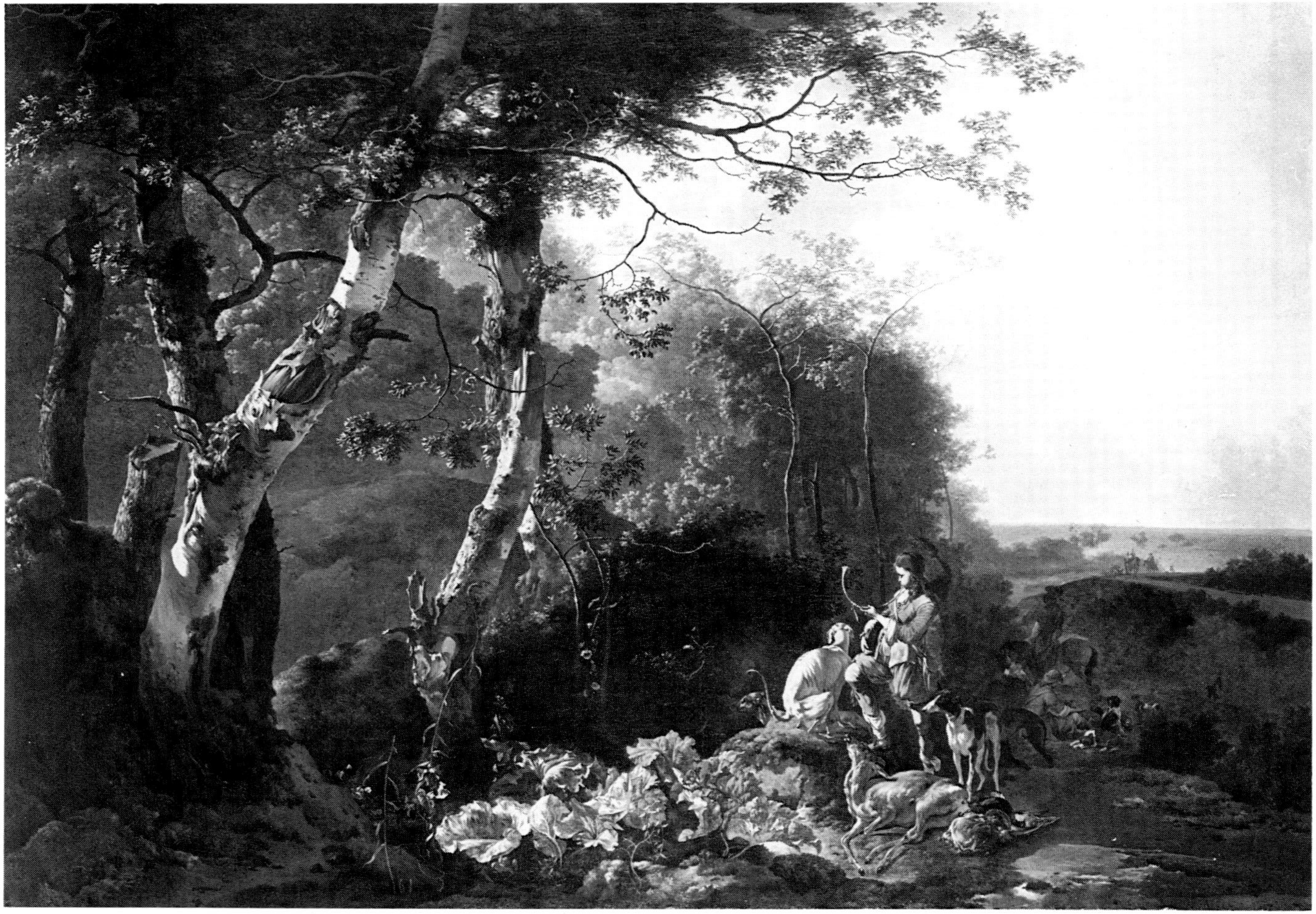

59. Adam Pynacker, *Landscape with Sportsmen and Game*. 1660s. Canvas, 137 · 8 x 198 · 8 cm.
By permission of the Governors of Dulwich Picture Gallery

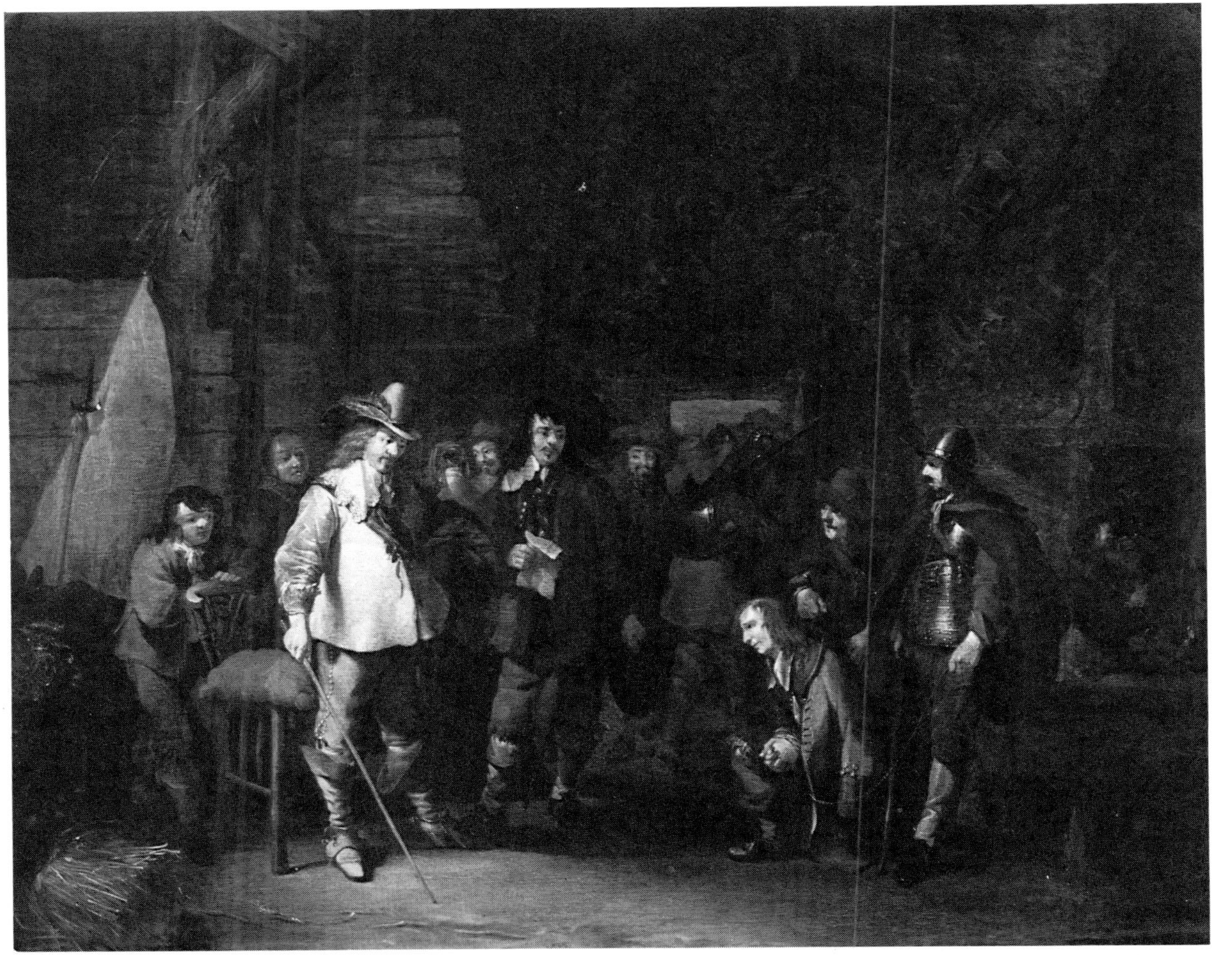

60. *Soldiers with a Kneeling Prisoner*, signed. c. 1642-45. Panel, 45 · 7 x 61 cm. Present location unknown

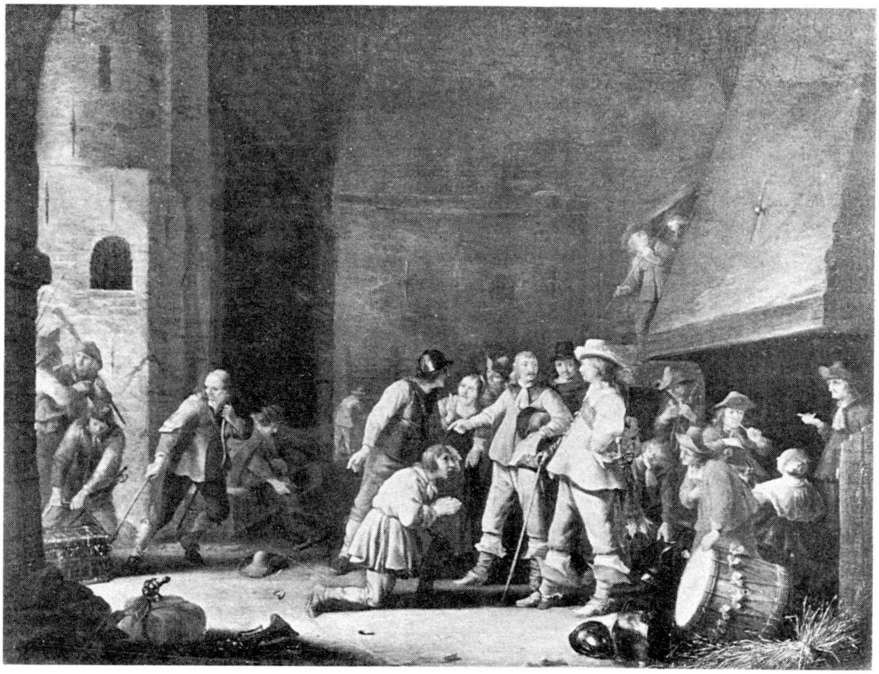

61. Anthonie Palamedesz., *Pillage of a Town.* c. 1642-45. Present location unknown. Photograph, Courtauld Institute of Art, London

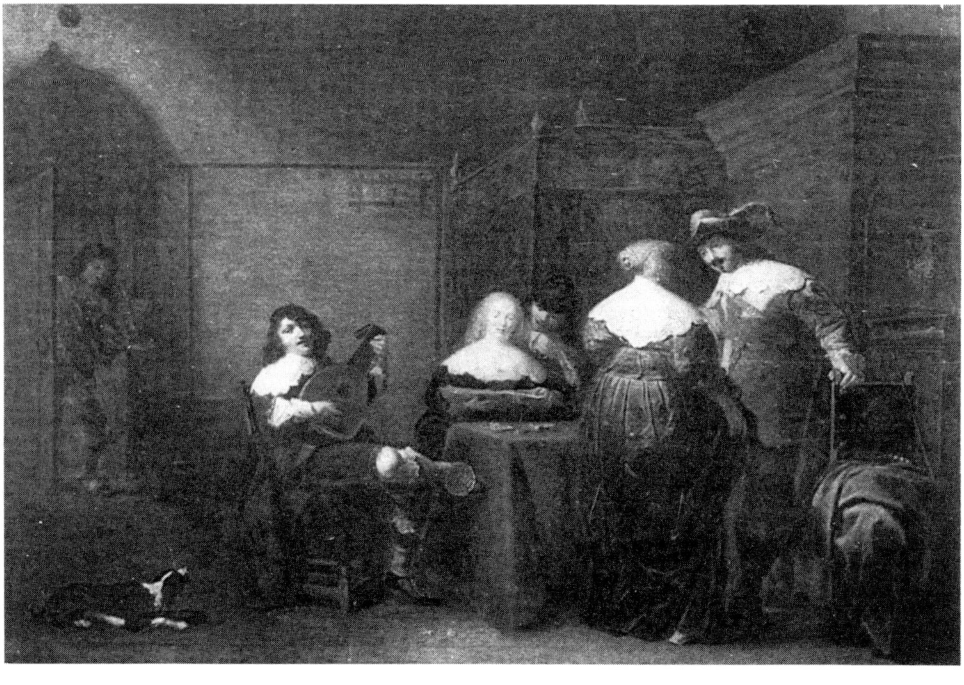

62. *House Concert,* signed. c. 1642. Panel, 51 x 69 cm. Present location unknown. Photograph, Courtauld Institute of Art, London

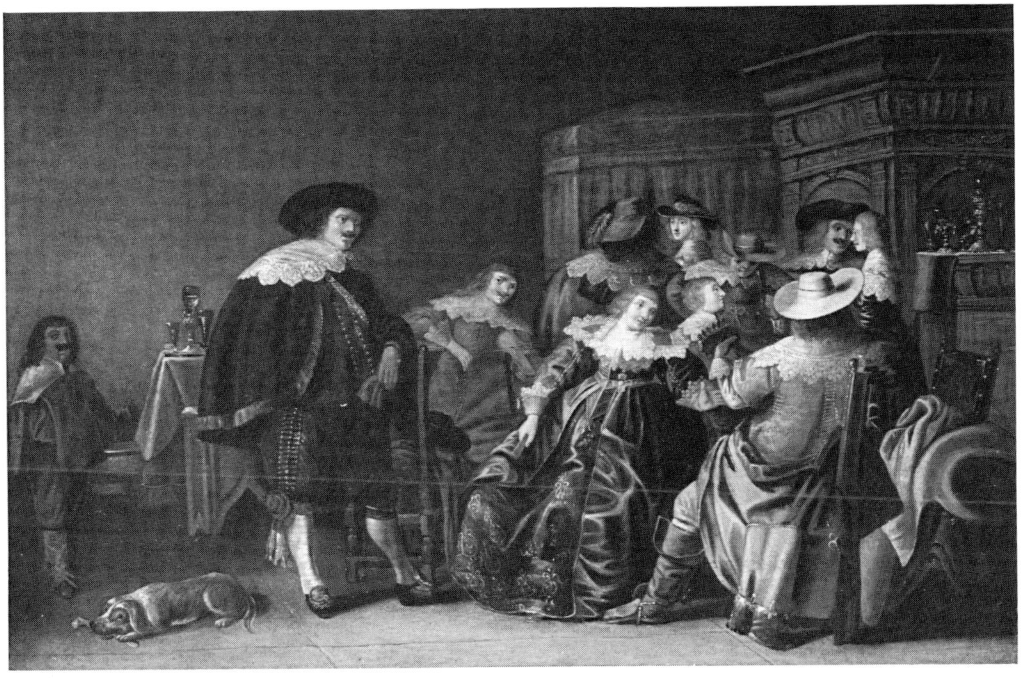

63. Anthonie Palamedesz., *Musical Gathering,* signed D. Hals. 1630s. Canvas, 50 x 65 cm. Present location unknown. Photograph courtesy of the Rijksbureau voor Kunsthistorische Documentatie, The Hague

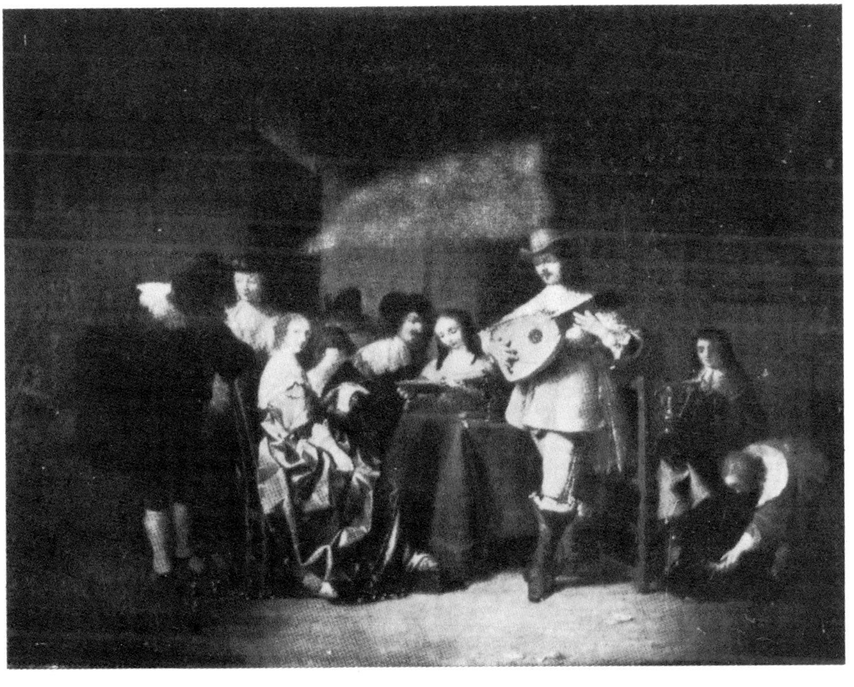

64. *Musical Company,* signed. c. 1642. Panel, 55 x 69 cm. Present location unknown. Photograph, Courtauld Institute of Art, London

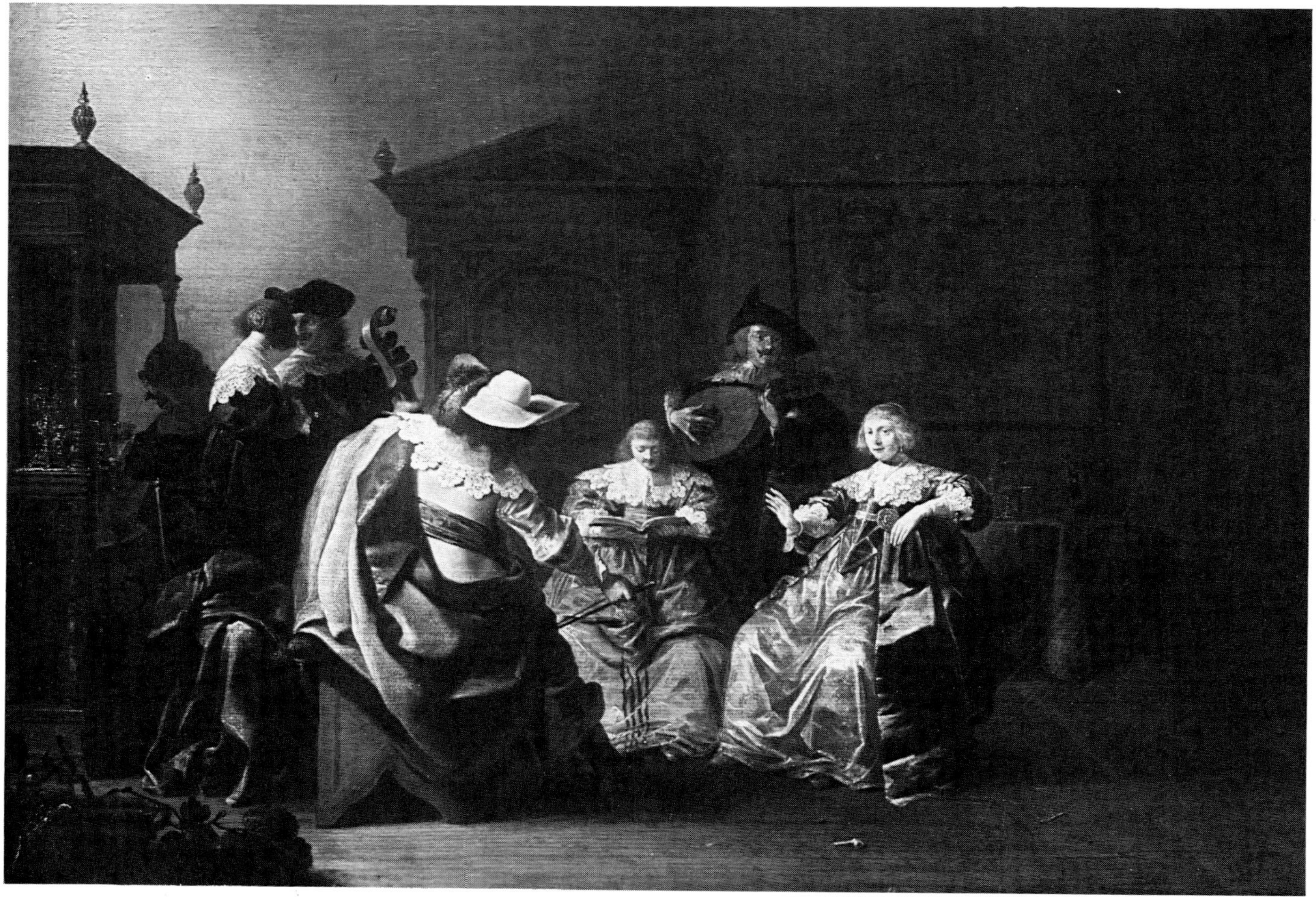

65. Anthonie Palamedesz., *Musical Group*. 1630s. Panel, 52 x 77 cm. Present location unknown. Photograph courtesy of the Rijksbureau voor Kunsthistorische Documentatie, The Hague

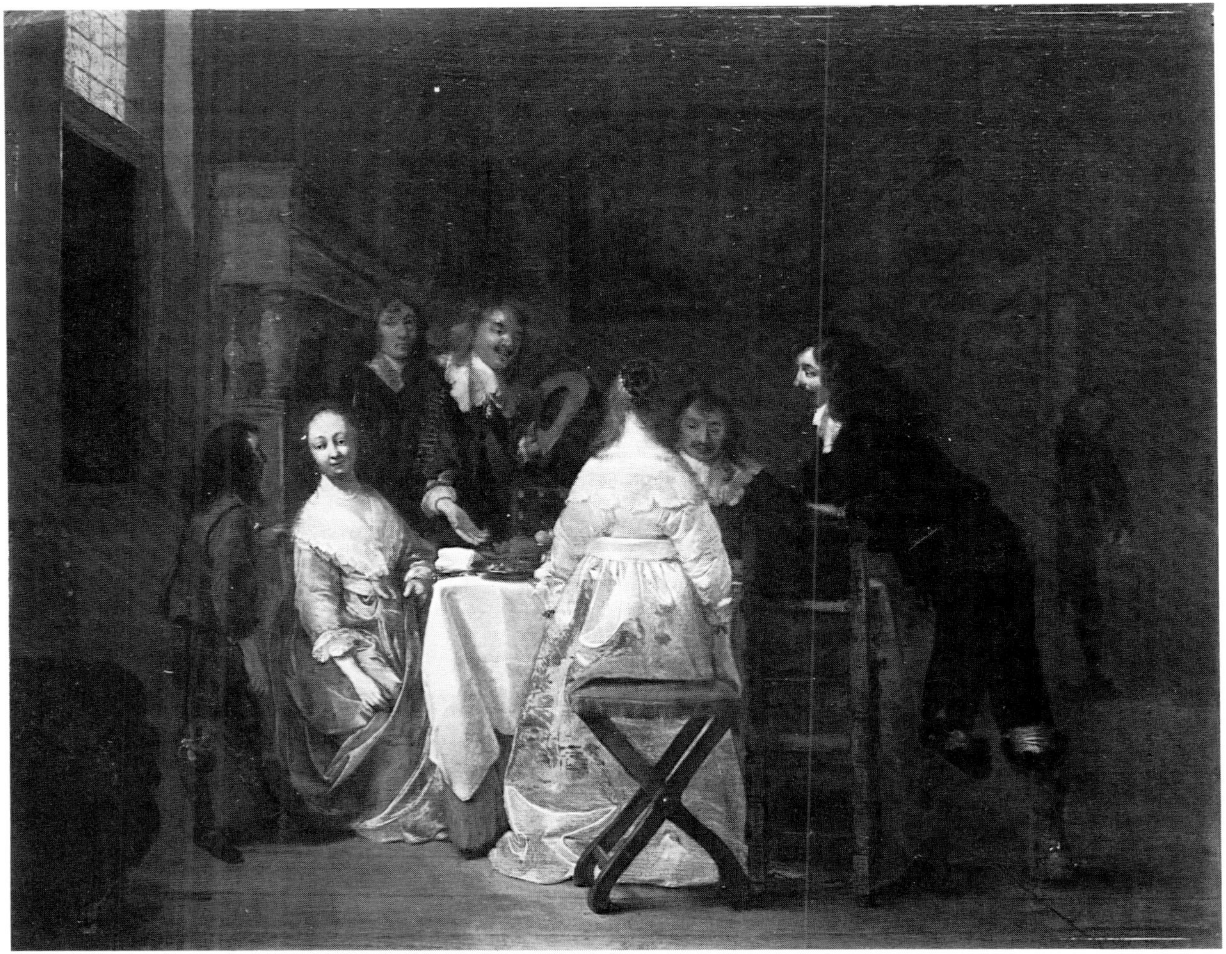

66. *Gathering at a Table,* signed. c. 1648. Canvas, 44 · 2 x 57 · 7 cm. Museum der bildenden Künste, Leipzig

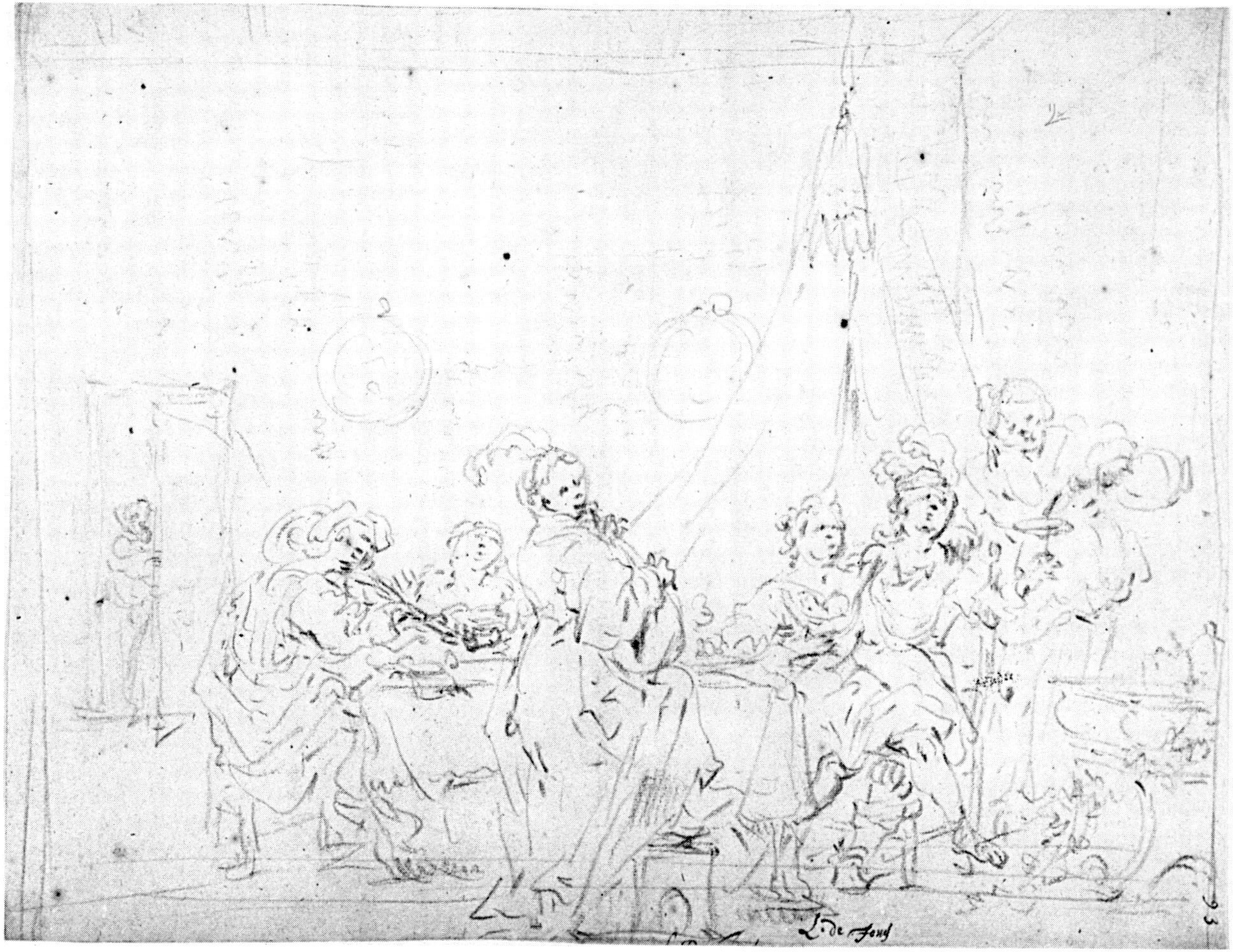

67. Leonard Bramer, *Prodigal Son*. Drawing after Ludolf de Jongh's painting of c. 1648-50. Amsterdam, Rijksprentenkabinet

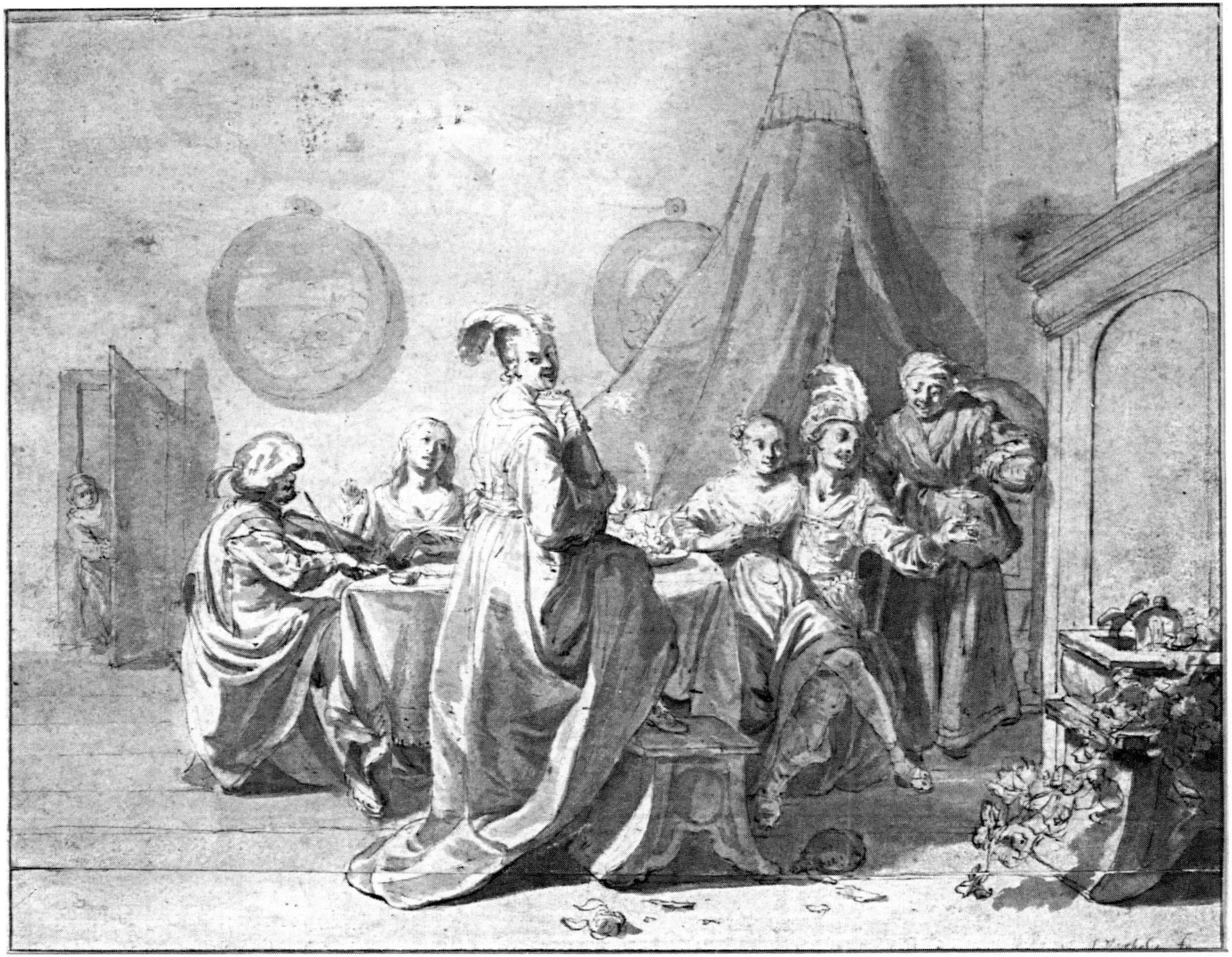

68. Jan Verkolje, *Prodigal Son.* Drawing after Ludolf de Jongh's painting of c. 1648-50. Amsterdam, Rijksprentenkabinet

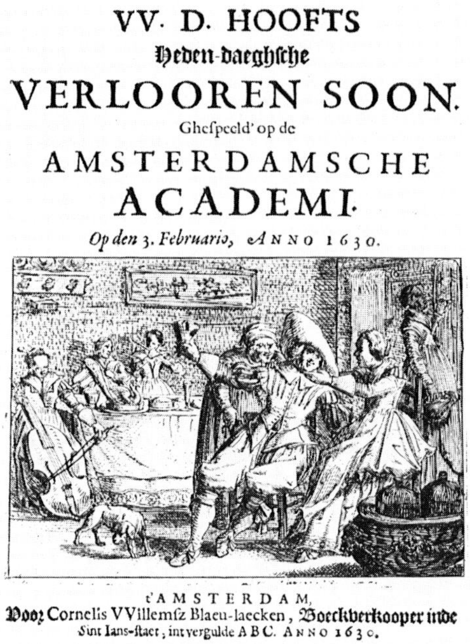

VV. D. HOOFTS
Heden-daeghsche
VERLOOREN SOON.
Ghespeeld' op de
AMSTERDAMSCHE
ACADEMI.
Op den 3. Februario, ANNO 1630.

t'AMSTERDAM,
Voor Cornelis VVillemsz Blaeu-laecken, Boeckverkooper inde
Sint Ians-straet, int vergulde ABC. ANNO 1630.

69. Engraving from the title page of W. D. Hooft, *Hedendaeghsche Verlooren Soon,* Amsterdam, 1630. Leiden, Rijksuniversiteit

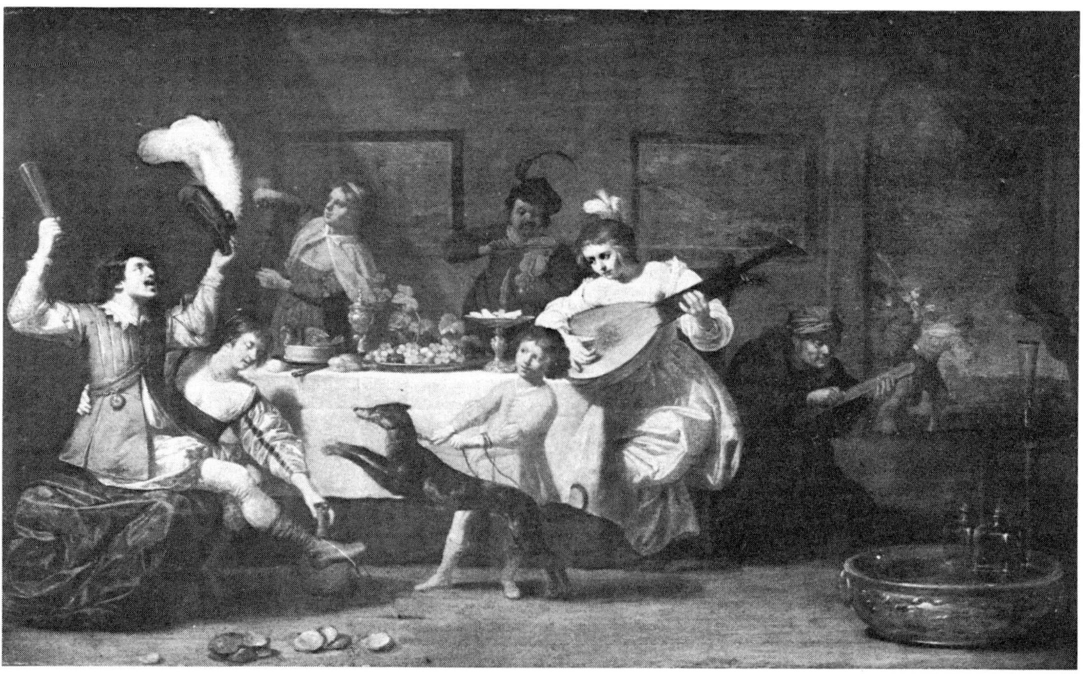

70. Jan van Bylert, *Prodigal Son,* signed. 1640s. Panel, 44 · 5 x 71 cm. Present location unknown. Photograph courtesy of the Rijksbureau voor Kunsthistorische Documentatie, The Hague

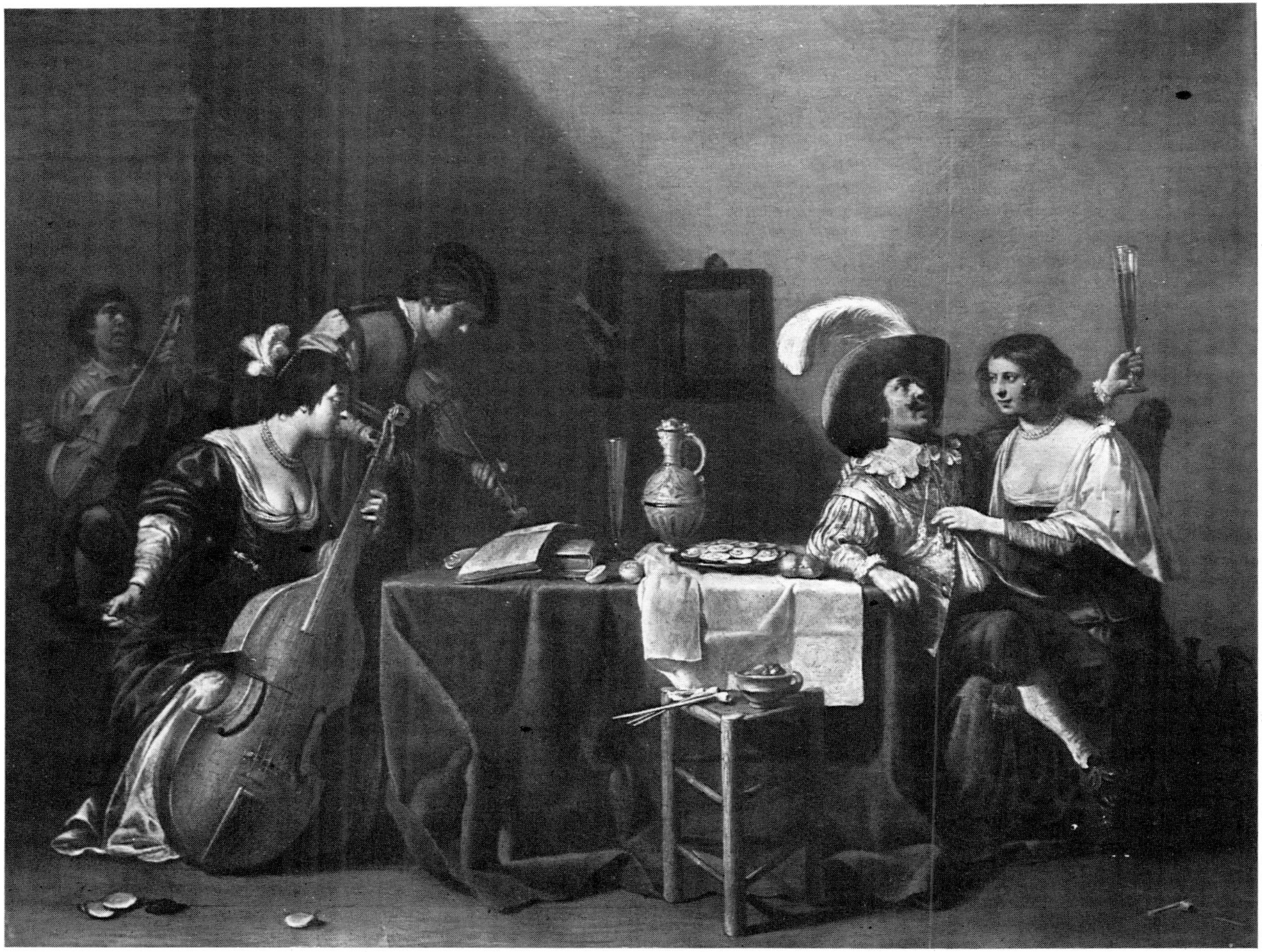

71. Jan van Bylert, *Prodigal Son,* signed. 1640s. Panel, 52x 70 cm. Present location unknown. Photograph courtesy of the Rijksbureau voor Kunsthistorische Documentatie, The Hague

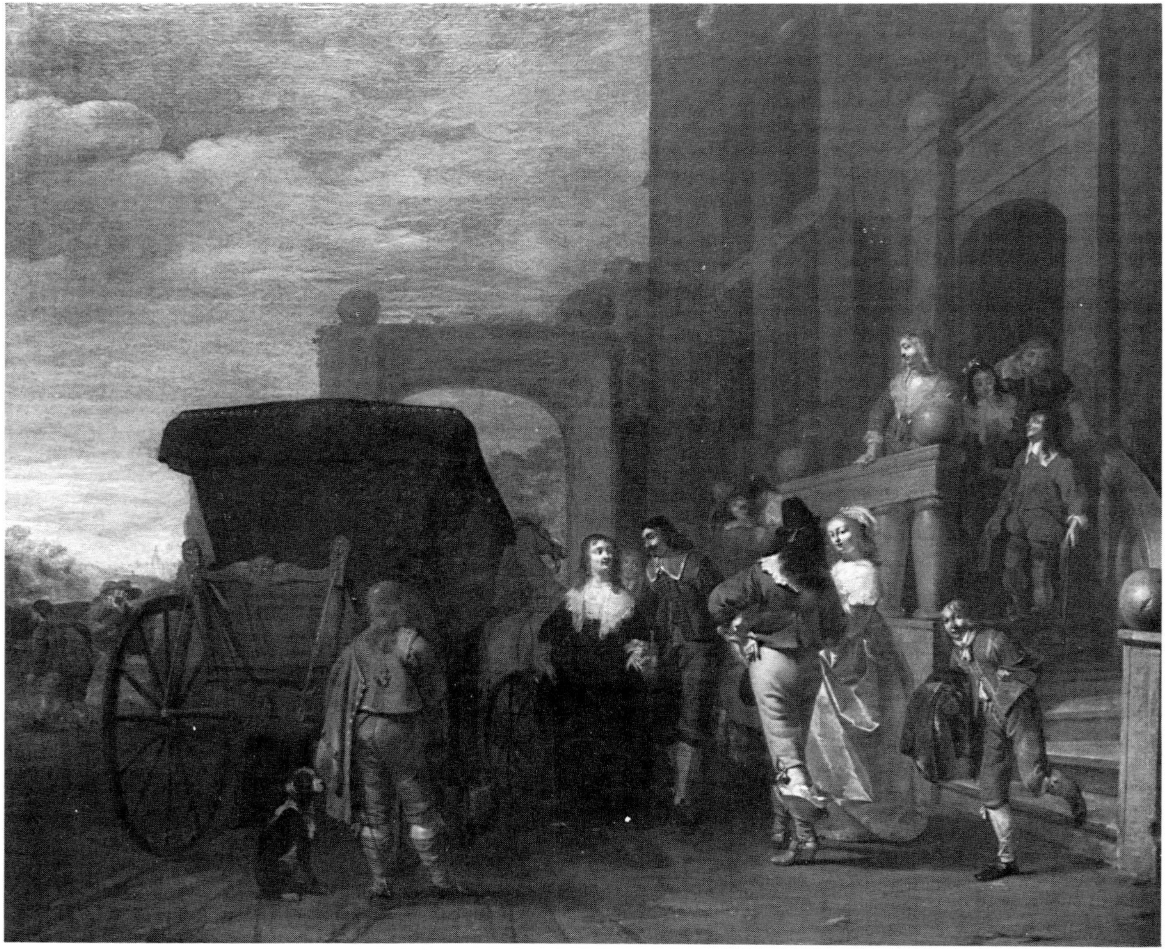

72. *Departure for the Country*, signature no longer visible. c. 1648. Panel, 80 x 102 cm. Milan, Castello Sforzesco

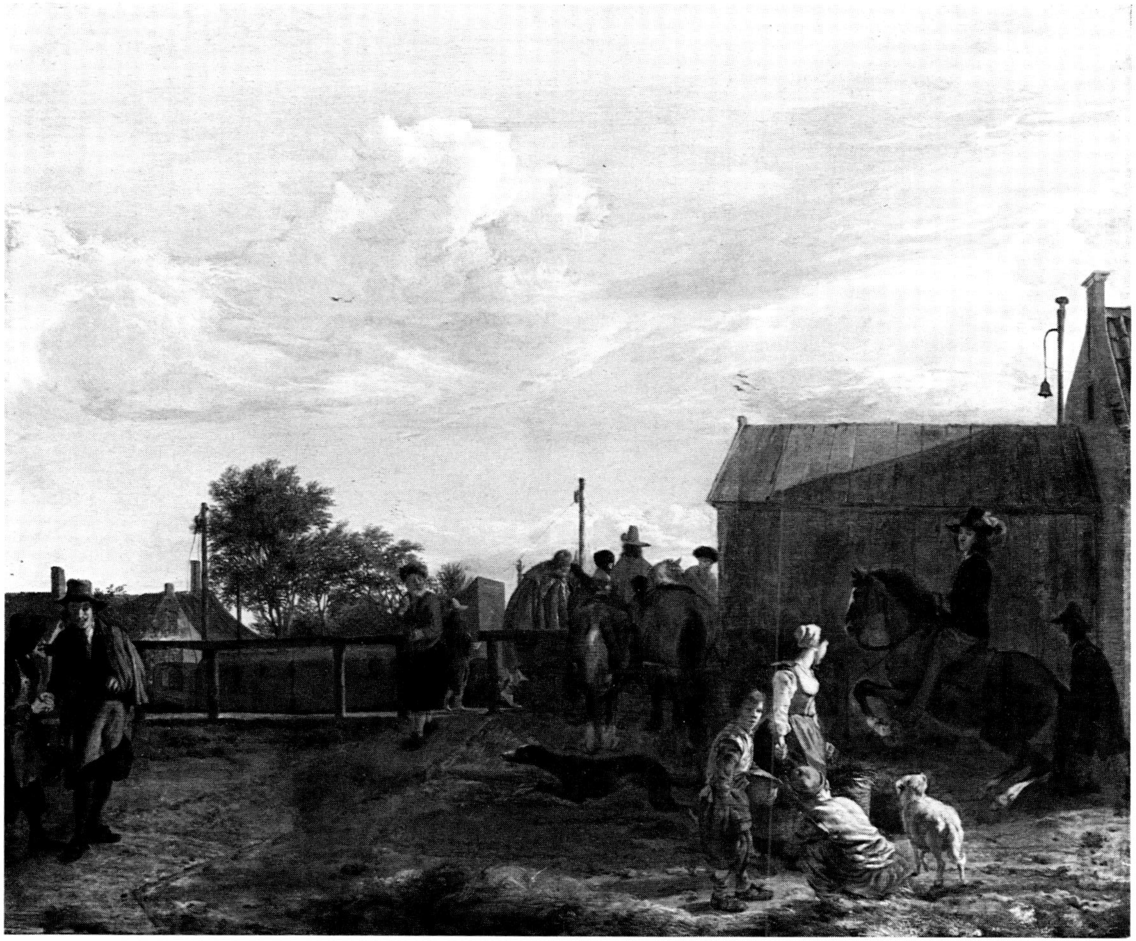

73. *Canal Boat Station*, signed. c. 1648-50. Panel, 52·6 x 65·4 cm. Dublin, National Gallery of Ireland

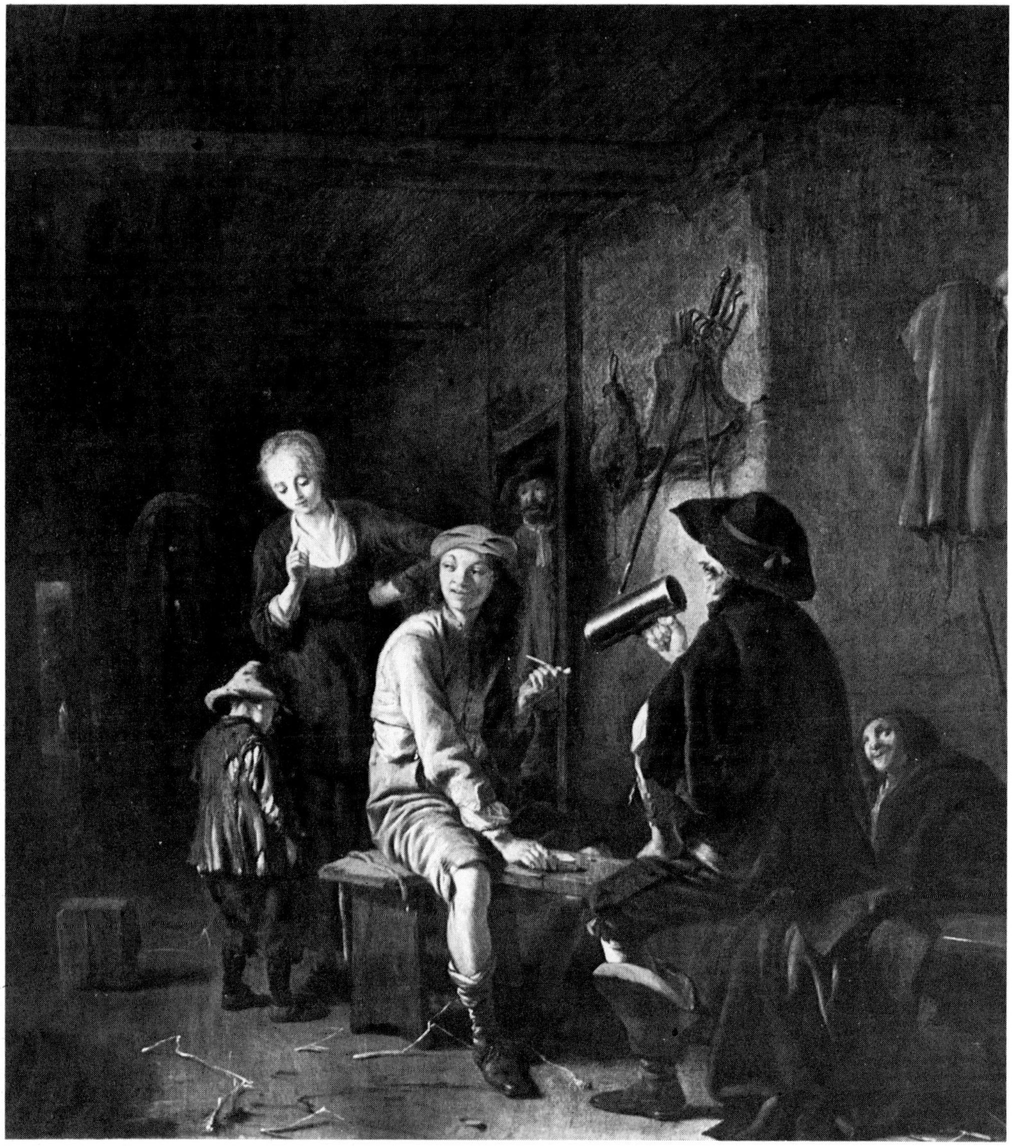

74. *The Reprimand,* signed. c. 1650. Panel, 50 · 5 x 43 · 5 cm. Present location unknown. Photograph courtesy of the Rijksbureau voor Kunsthistorische Documentatie, The Hague

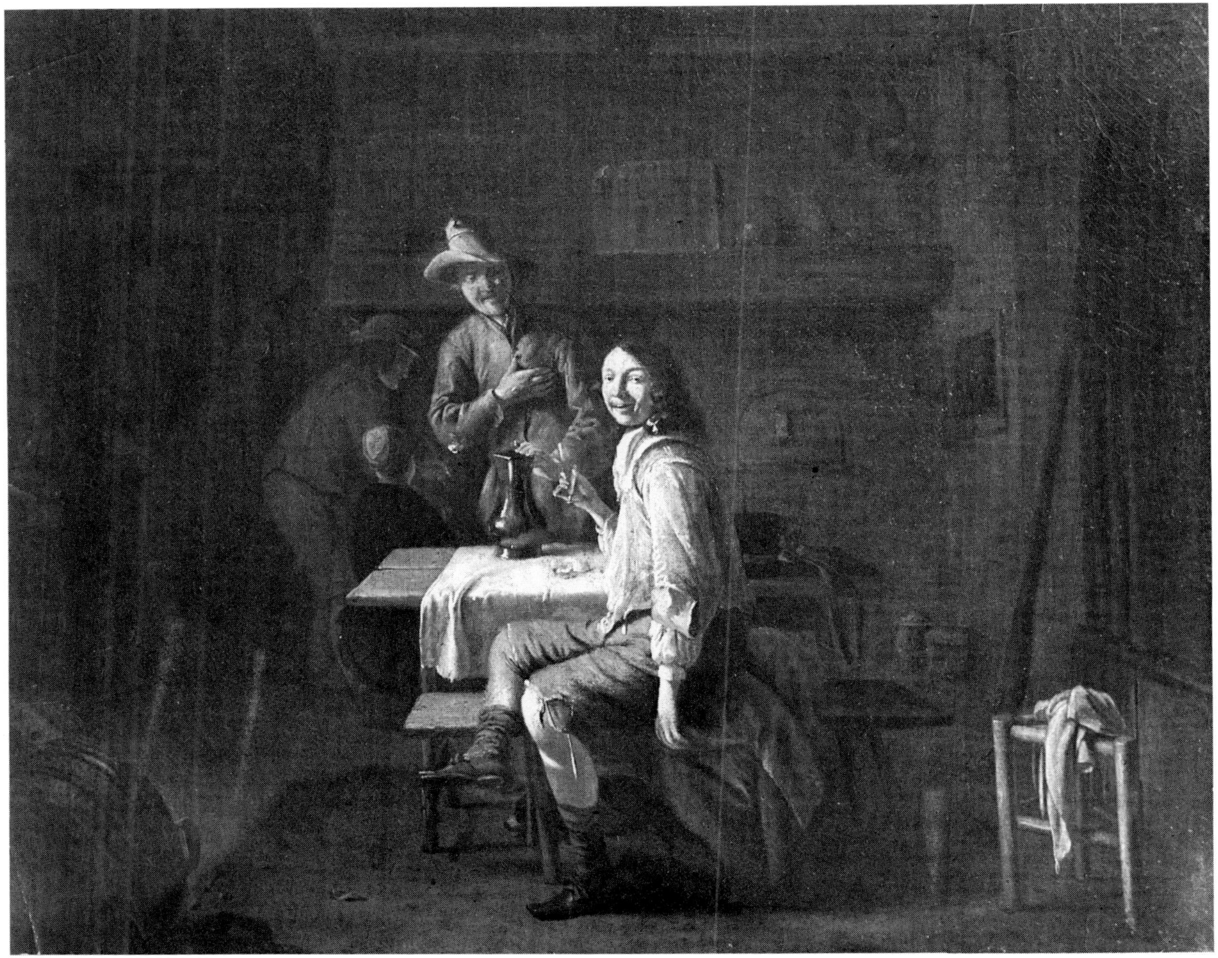

75. *A Public House*. c. 1650. Canvas, 45 · 7 x 53 · 3 cm. Present location unkown.
Photograph courtesy of the Rijksbureau voor Kunsthistorische Documentatie, The Hague

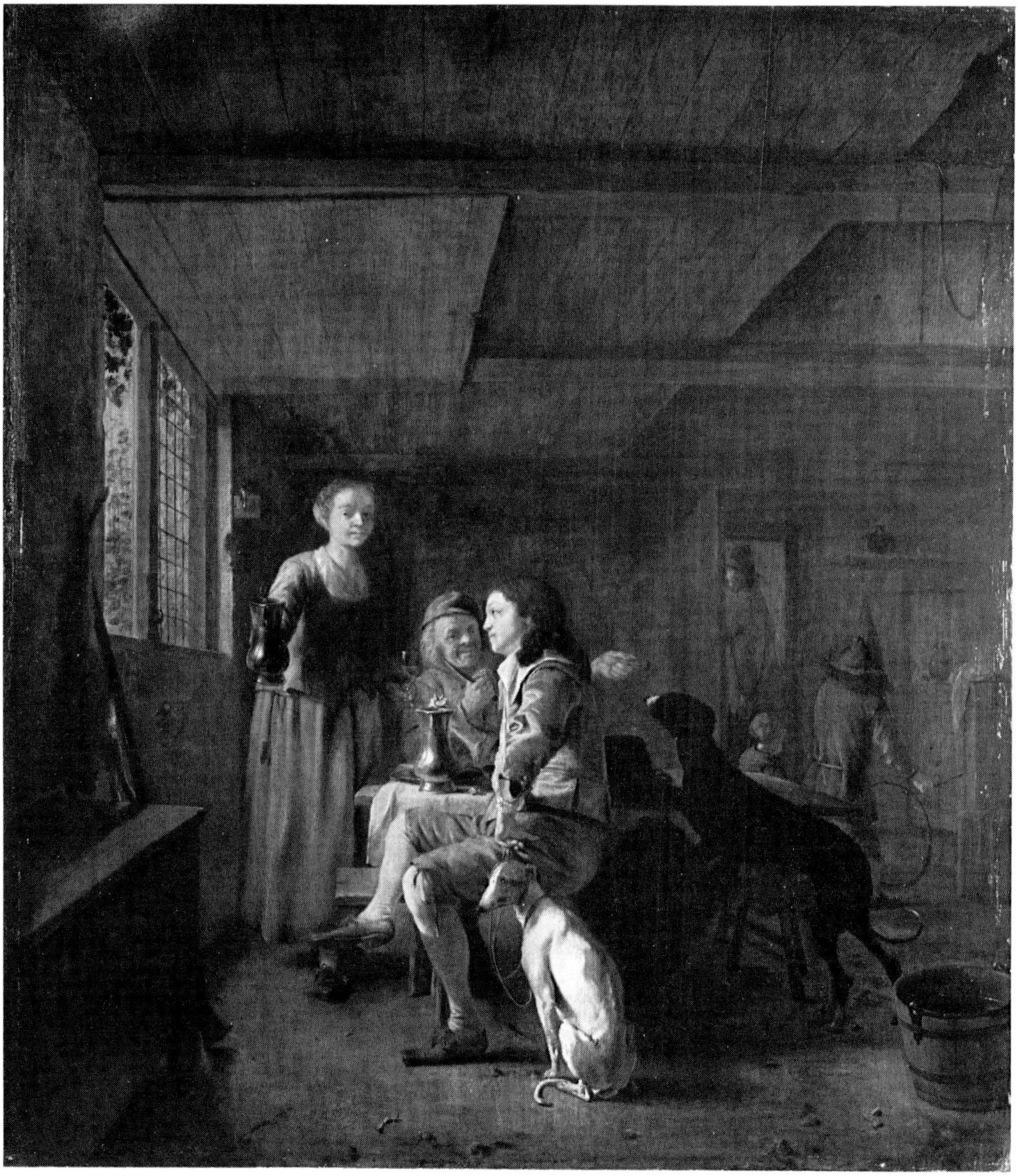

76. *Hunters in an Inn*. c. 1650. Panel, 72 x 62 · 5 cm. Basel, Öffentliche Kunstsammlung

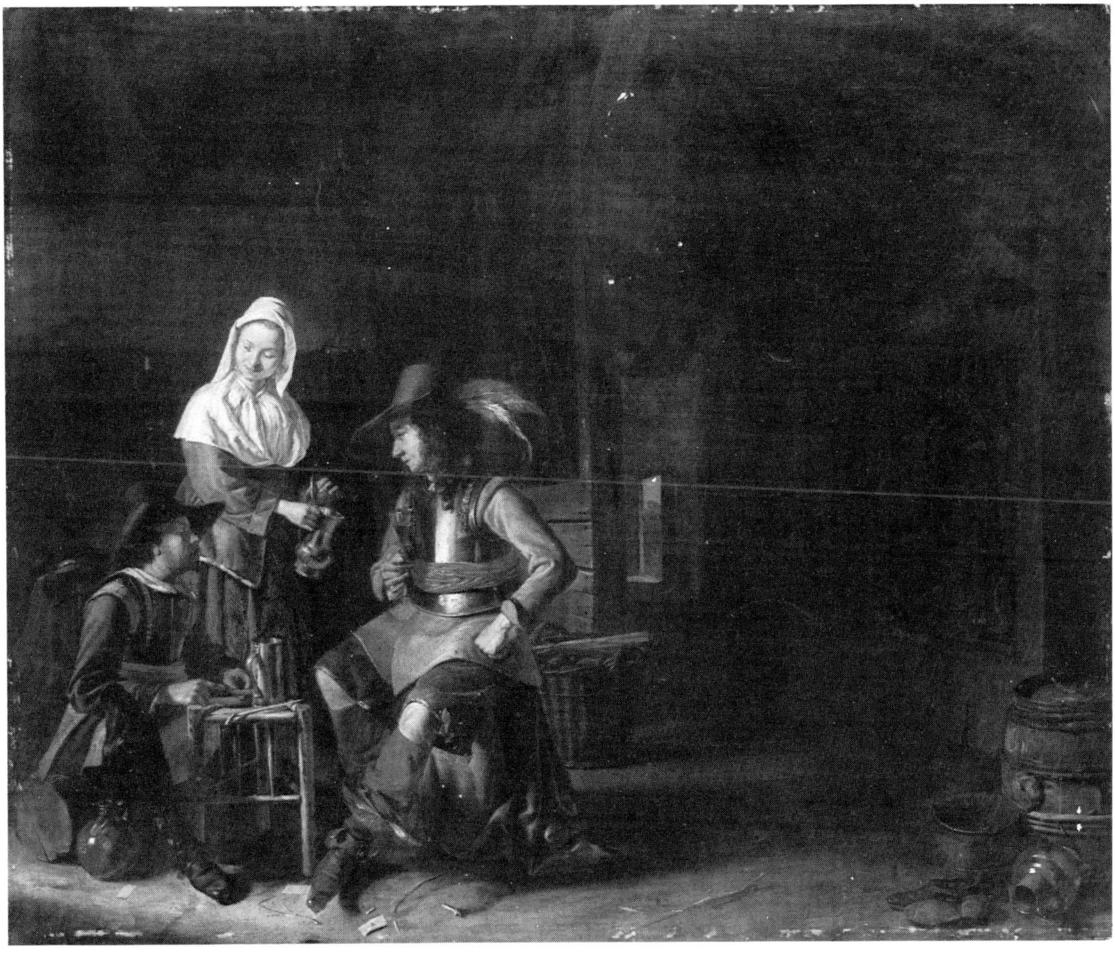

77. *Tavern Scene*. 1650-55. Panel, 59 x 70 cm. Prague, National Gallery

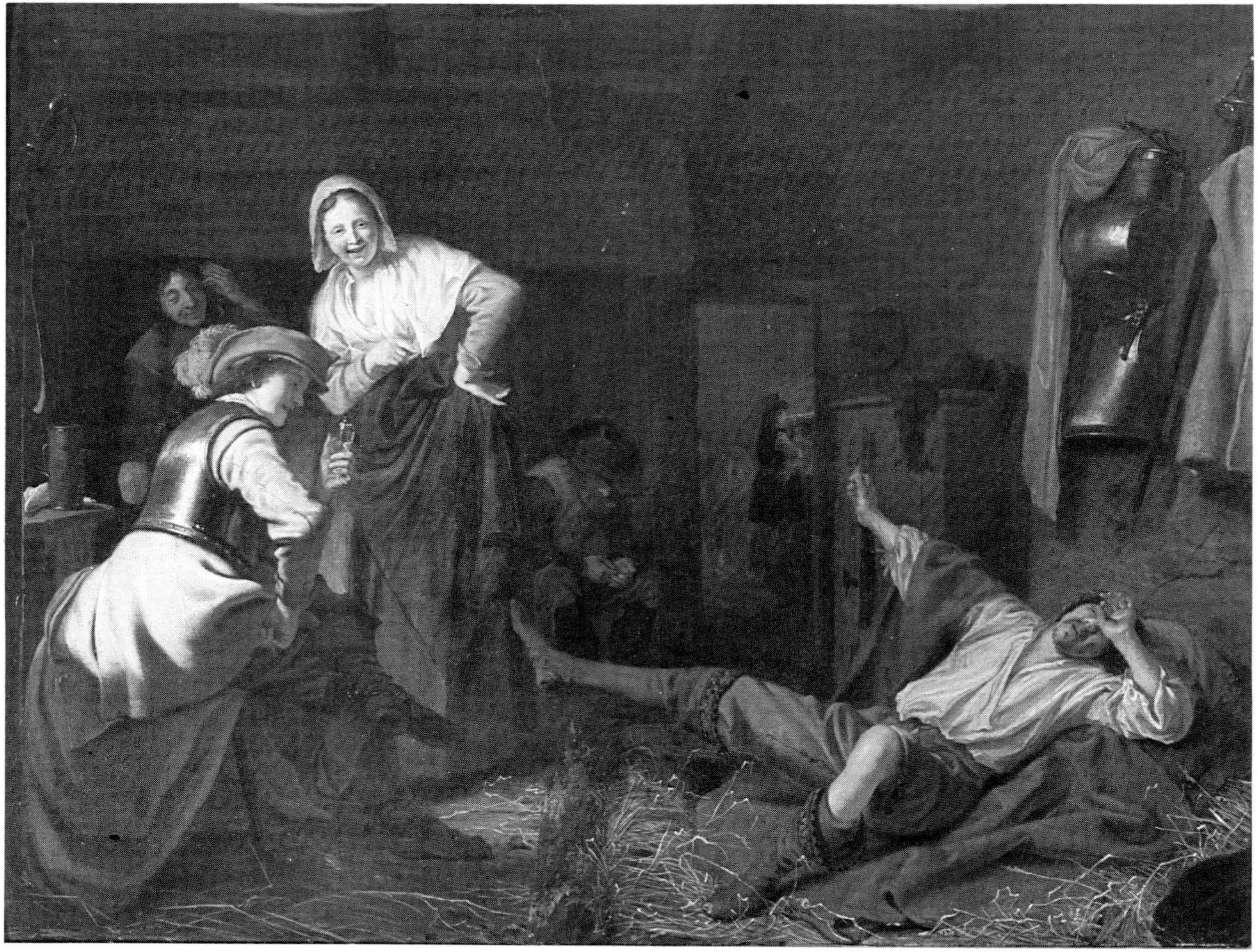

78. *Soldiers at Reveille*. 1650-55. Panel, 48 x 63 · 5 cm. Raleigh, North Carolina Museum of Art

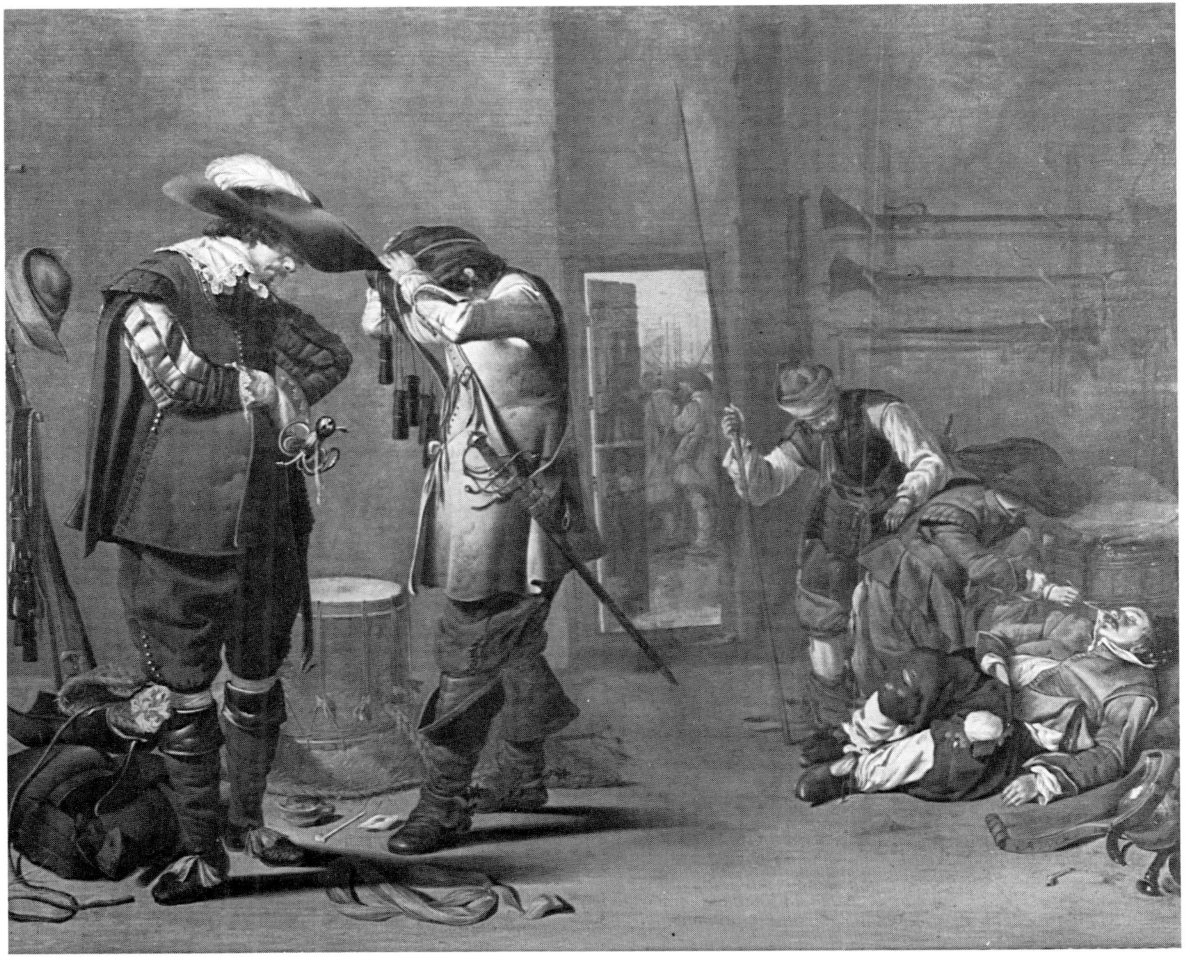

79. Jacob Duck, *Soldiers Arming Themselves*, signed. c. 1635. Panel, 43 x 57 cm. New York, H. Shickman Gallery

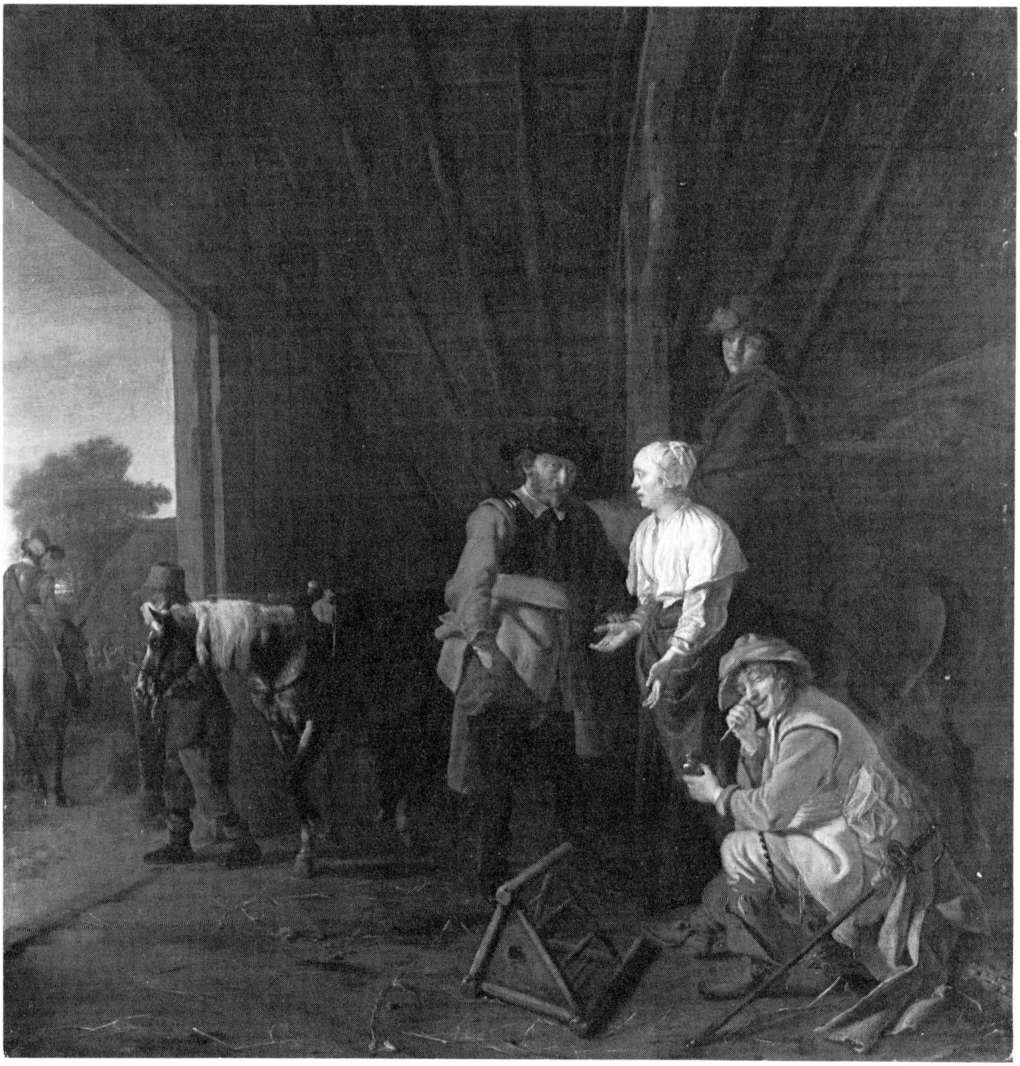

80. *Paying the Hostess,* signed Pr. d. Hooch. 1650-55. Panel, 66 x 63 cm. Private collection

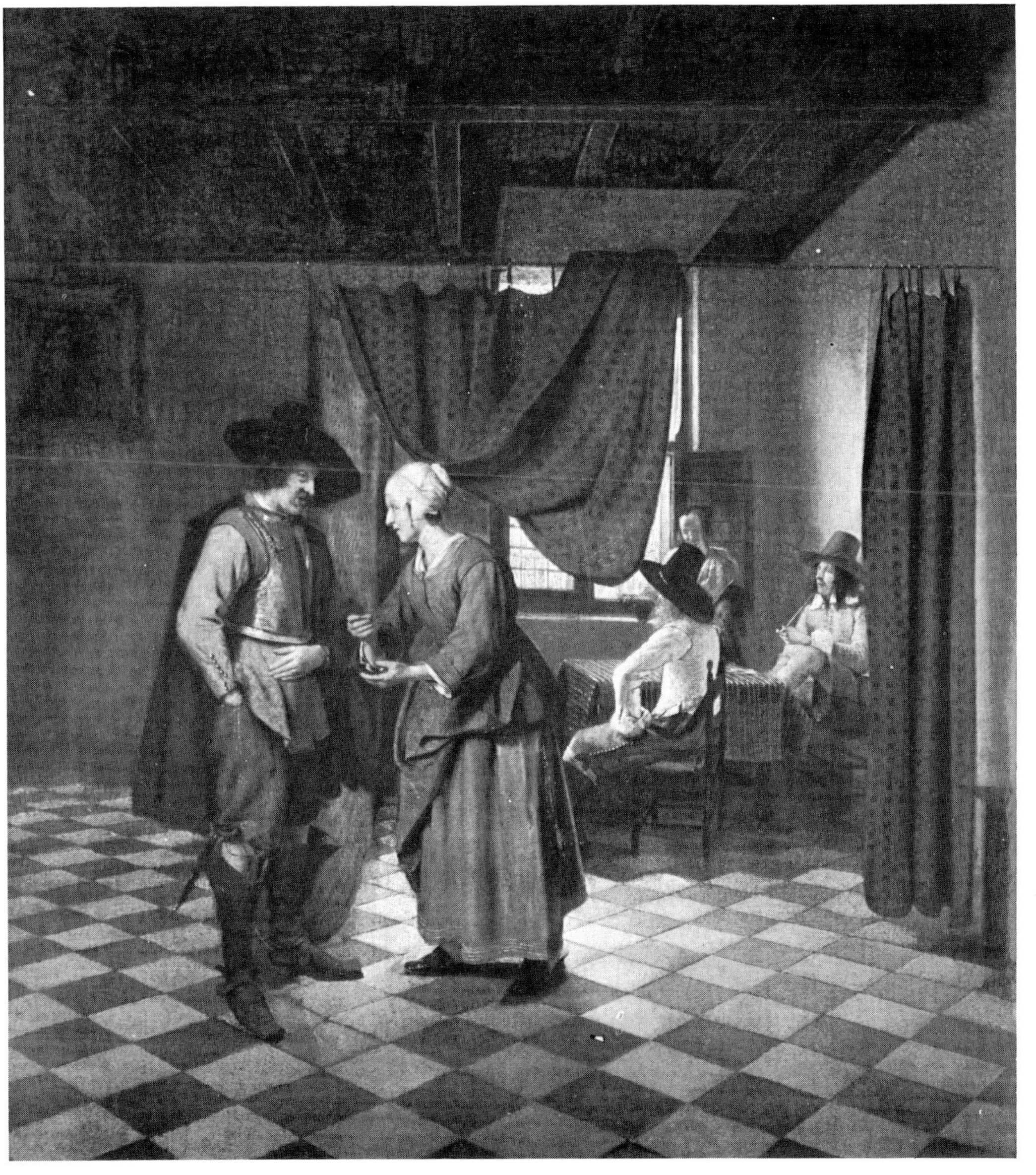

81. Pieter de Hooch, *Paying the Hostess,* signed and dated 1658. Canvas, 71 x 63 · 5 cm. London, Marquis of Bute collection

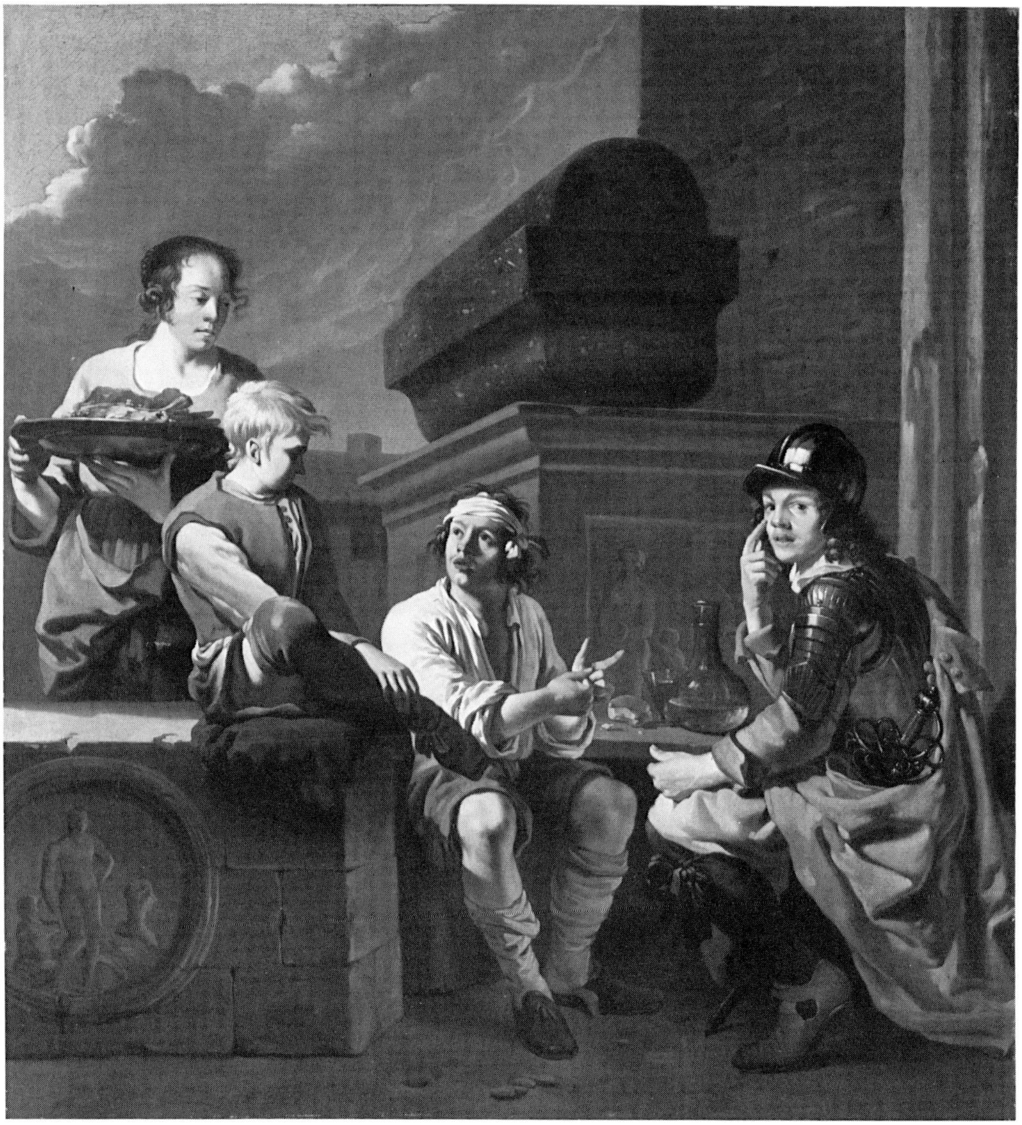

82. Karel Dujardin, *The Story of the Soldier*. 1650s. Canvas, 89 · 5 x 80 cm.
New Haven, Yale University Art Gallery, Leonard C. Hanna, Jr. Fund

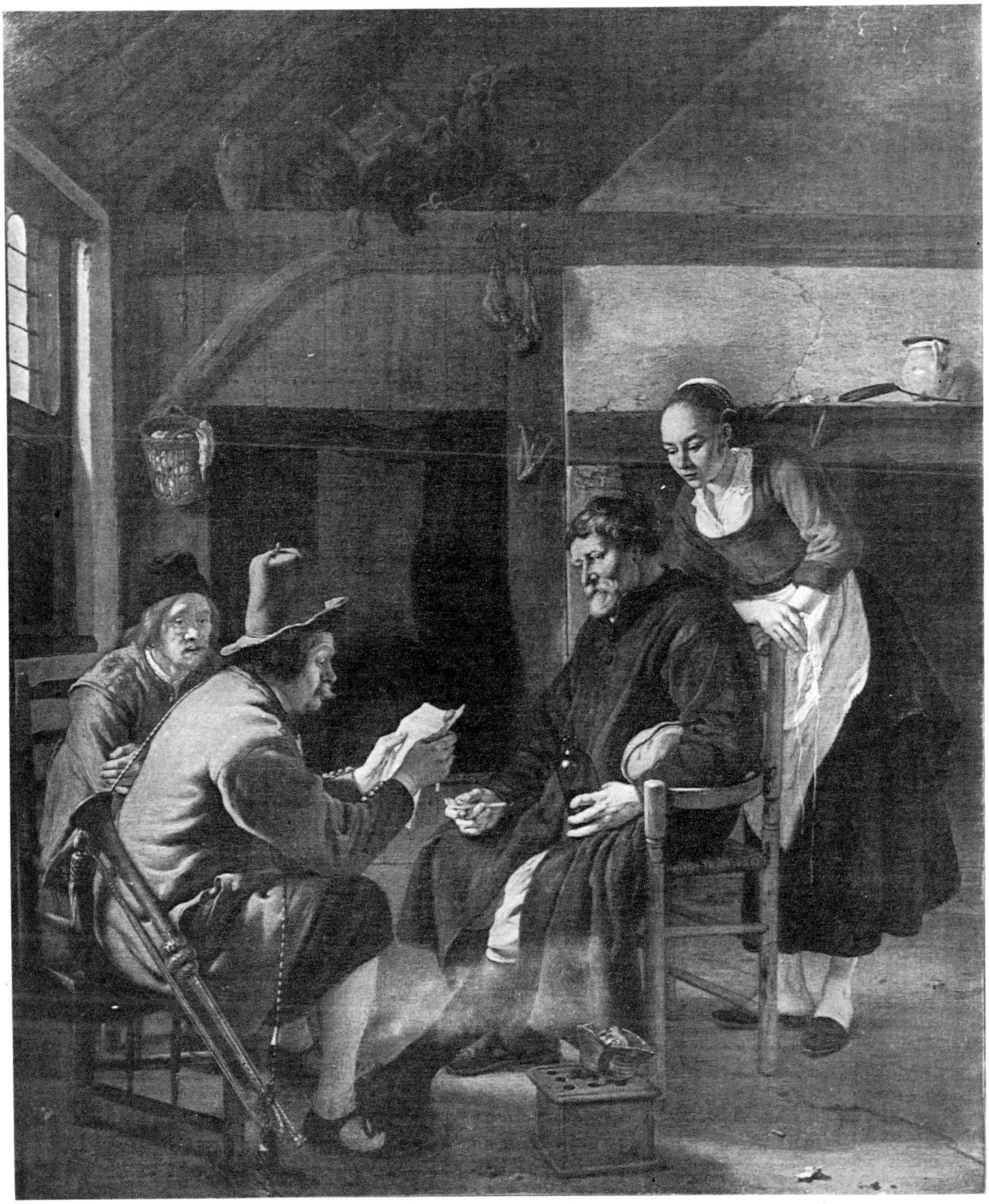

83. *The Message*, signed and dated 1657. Canvas, 66·5 x 54 cm. Mainz, Mittelrheinisches Landesmuseum

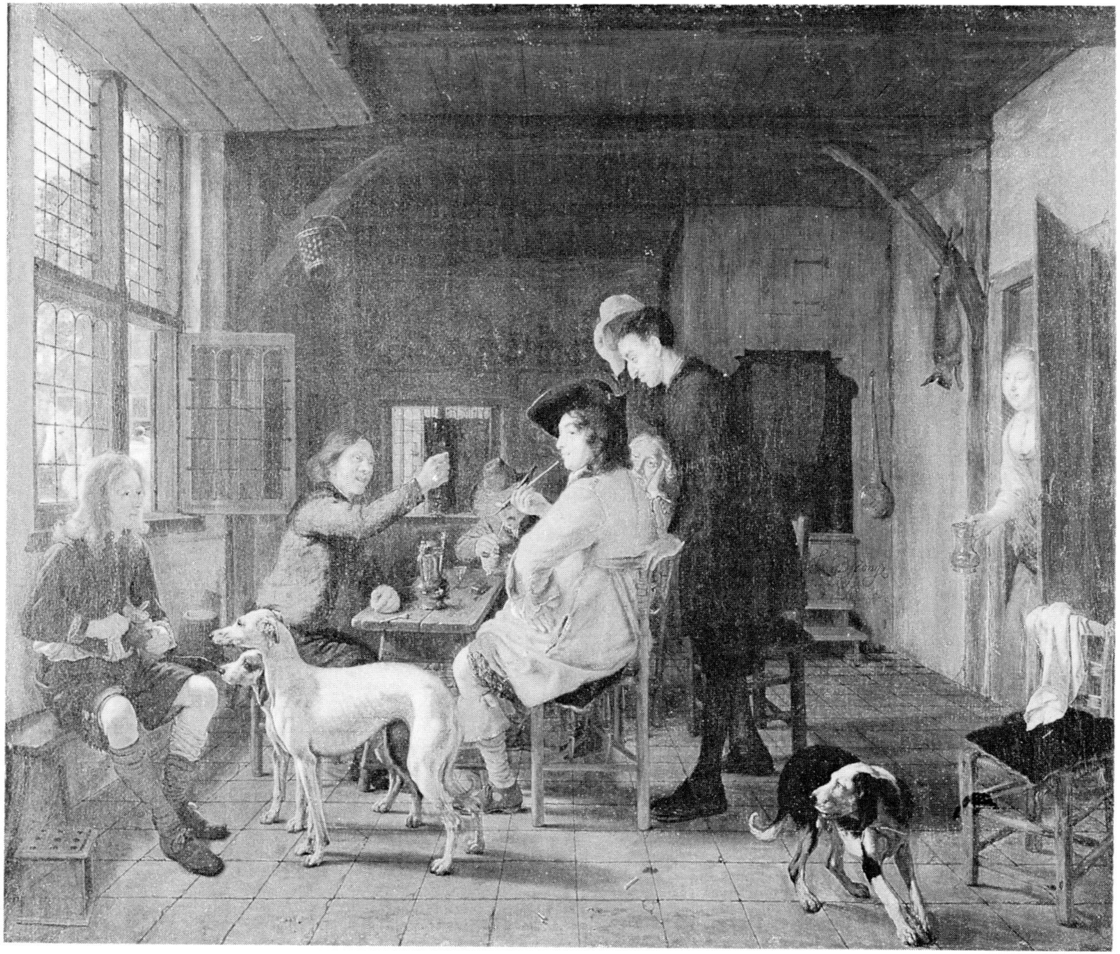

84. *Hunters in an Inn,* signed and dated 1658. Canvas, 67 x 81 cm. Groningen, Museum van Oudheden

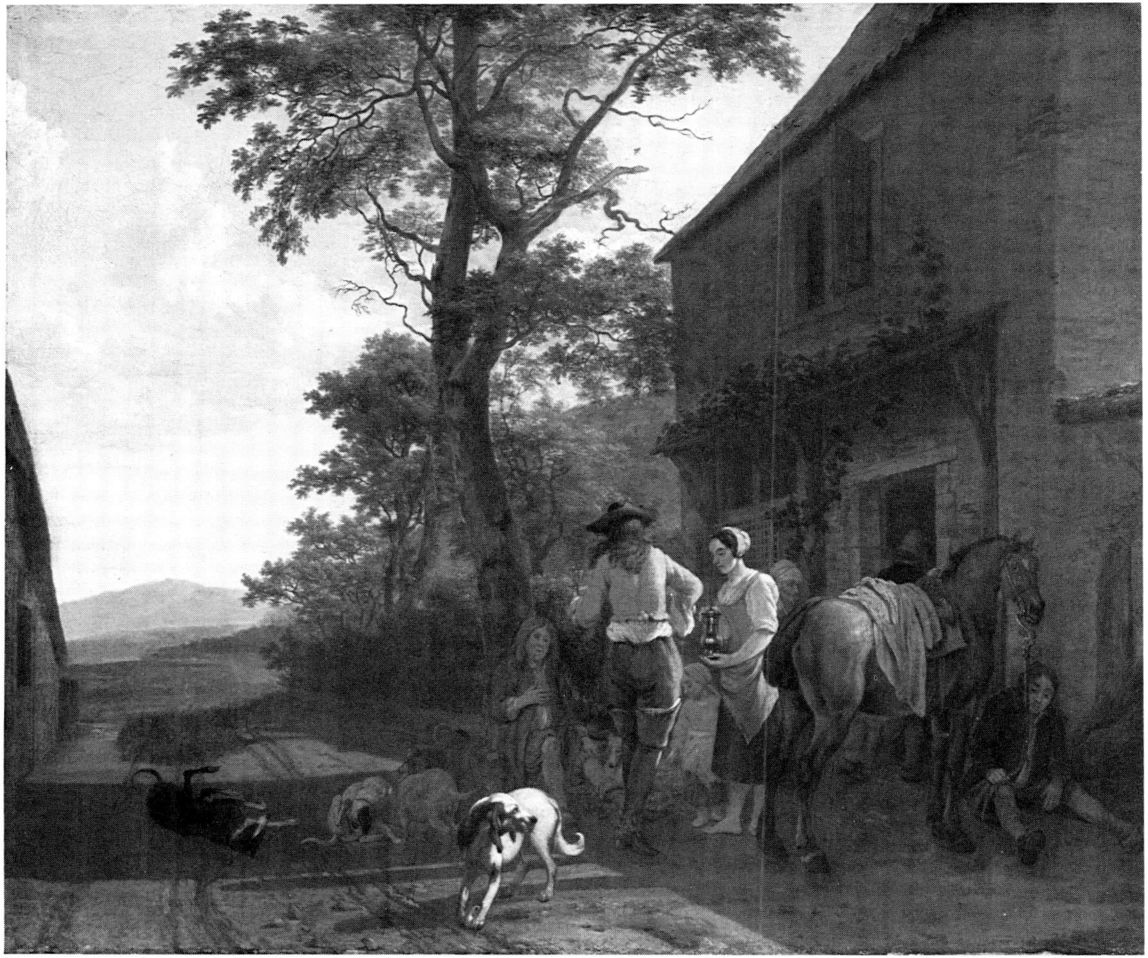

85. *Hunters Outside an Inn*. c. 1655. Canvas, 65 x 81 cm. Geneva, Musée d'Art et d'Histoire

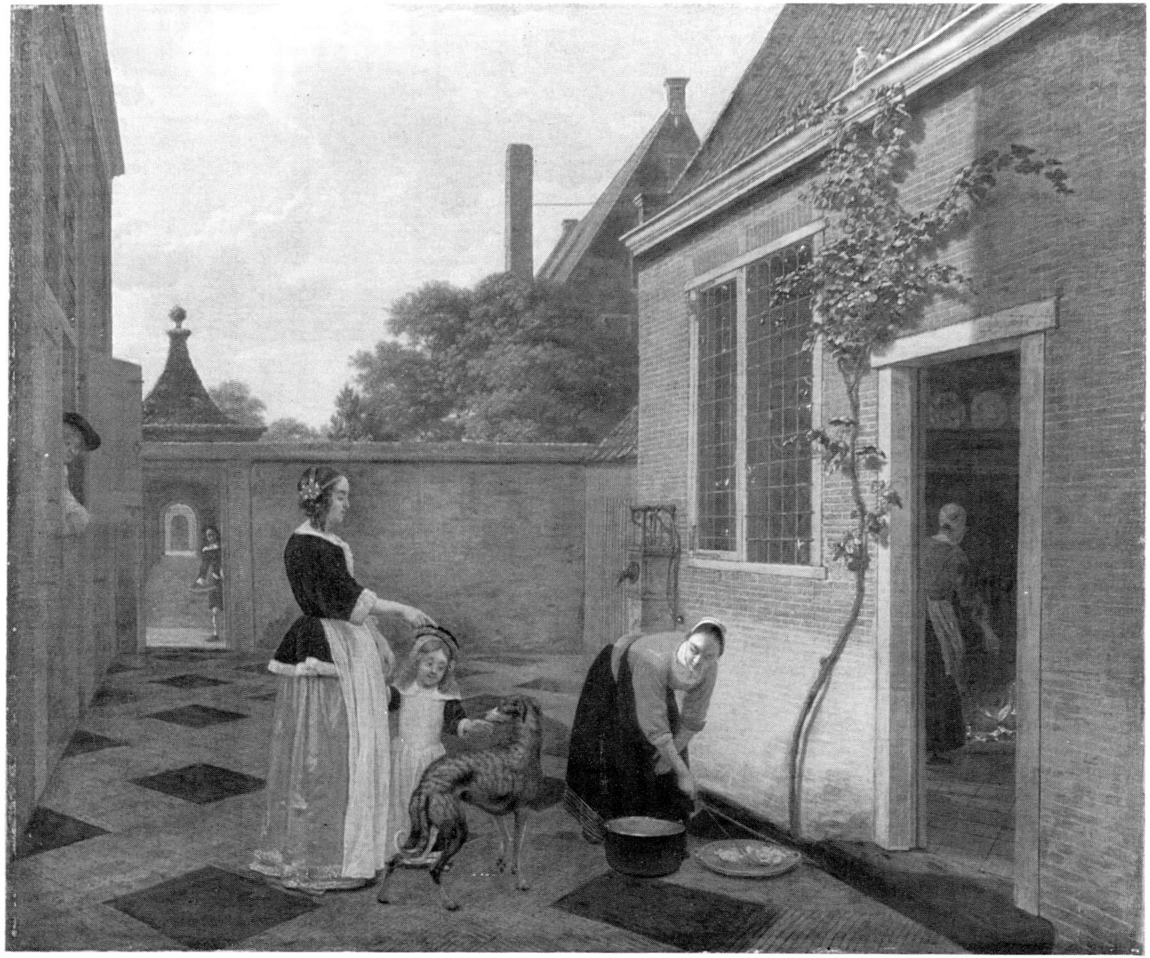

86. *Scene in a Courtyard*. c. 1660. Canvas, 67·3 x 82·2 cm.
New York, Metropolitan Museum of Art, Bequest of William K. Vanderbilt, 1920.

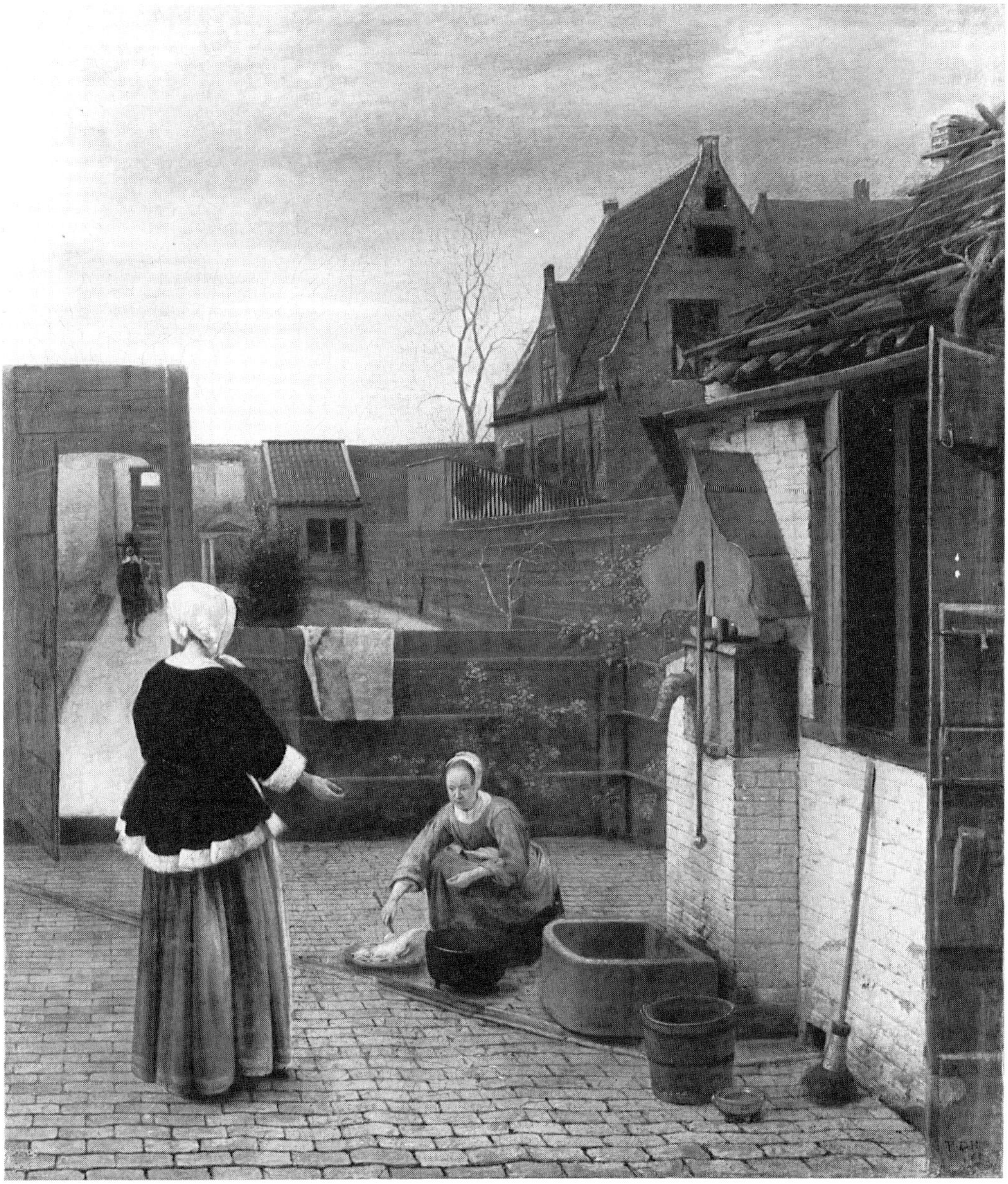

87. Pieter de Hooch, *A Woman and a Maid in a Courtyard,* signed and dated 166(?). 1660-63. Canvas, 73 · 7 x 62 · 6 cm. Reproduced by Courtesy of the Trustees, The National Gallery, London

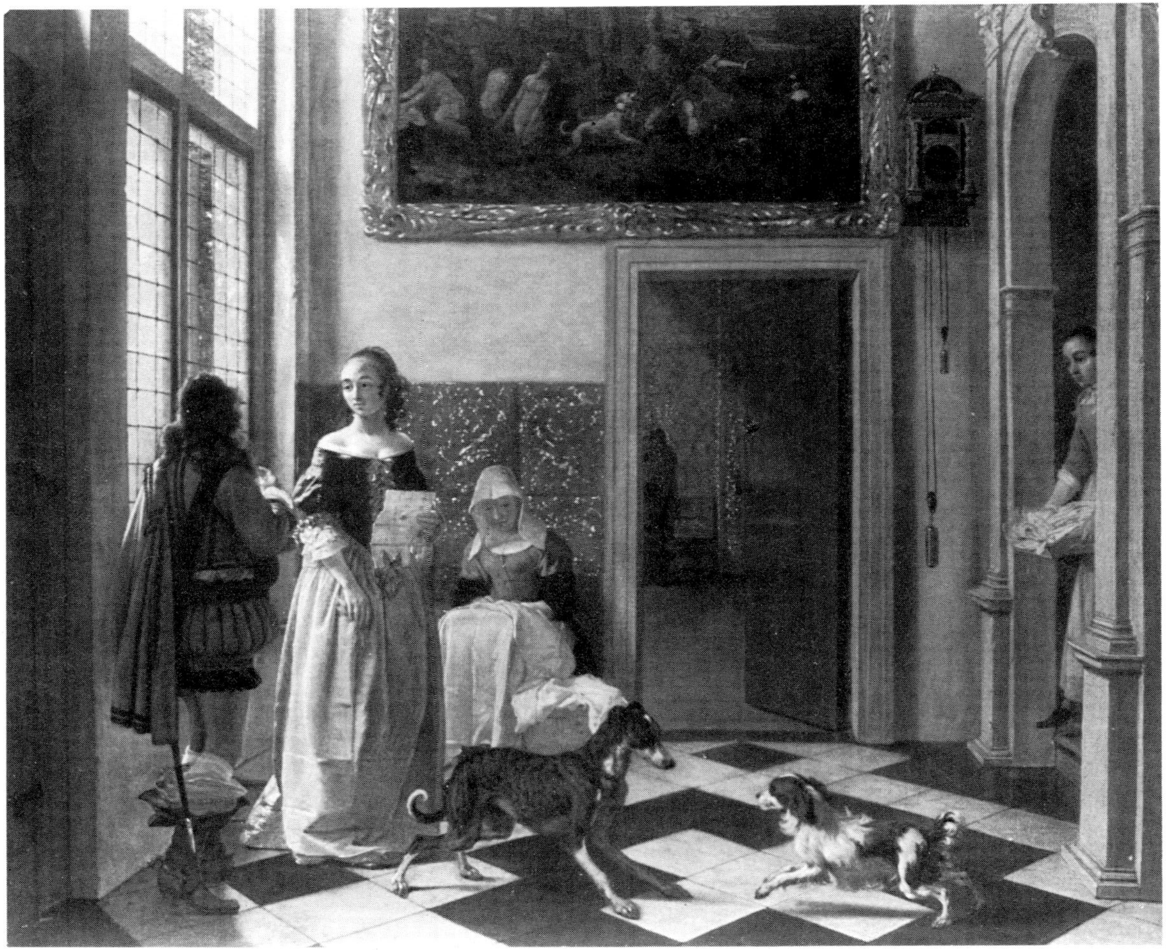

88. *Woman Receiving a Letter*, signed. 1663-65. Canvas, 59 · 6 x 72 · 3 cm.
Ascott House, Rothschild Collection, The National Trust

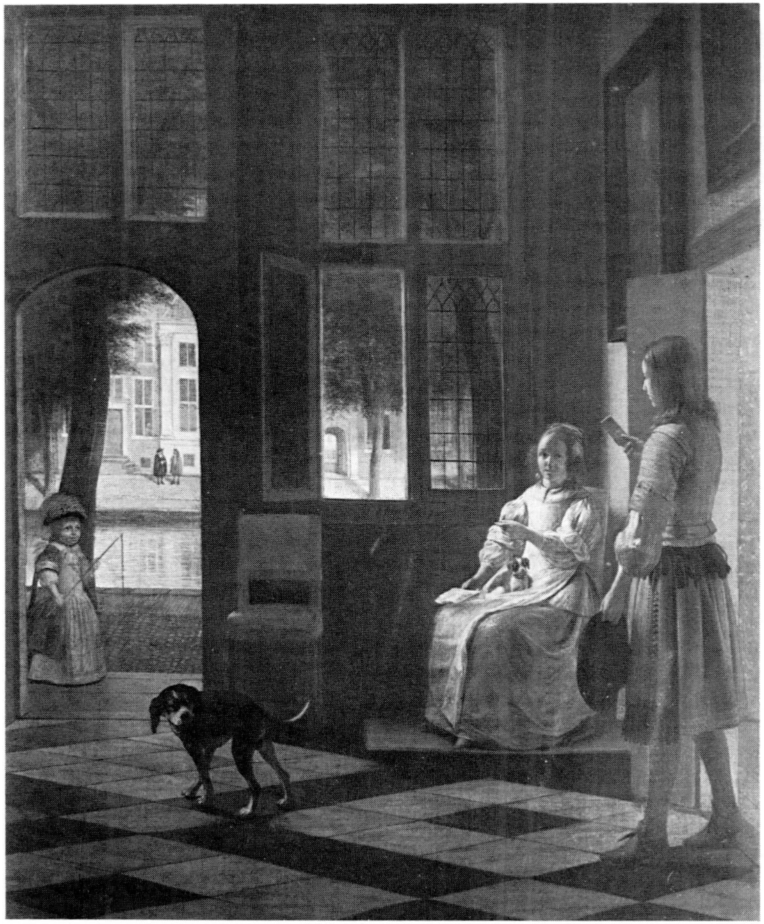

89. Pieter de Hooch, *A Woman and a Young Man with a Letter*, signed and dated 1670. Canvas, 68 x 59 cm. Amsterdam, Rijksmuseum

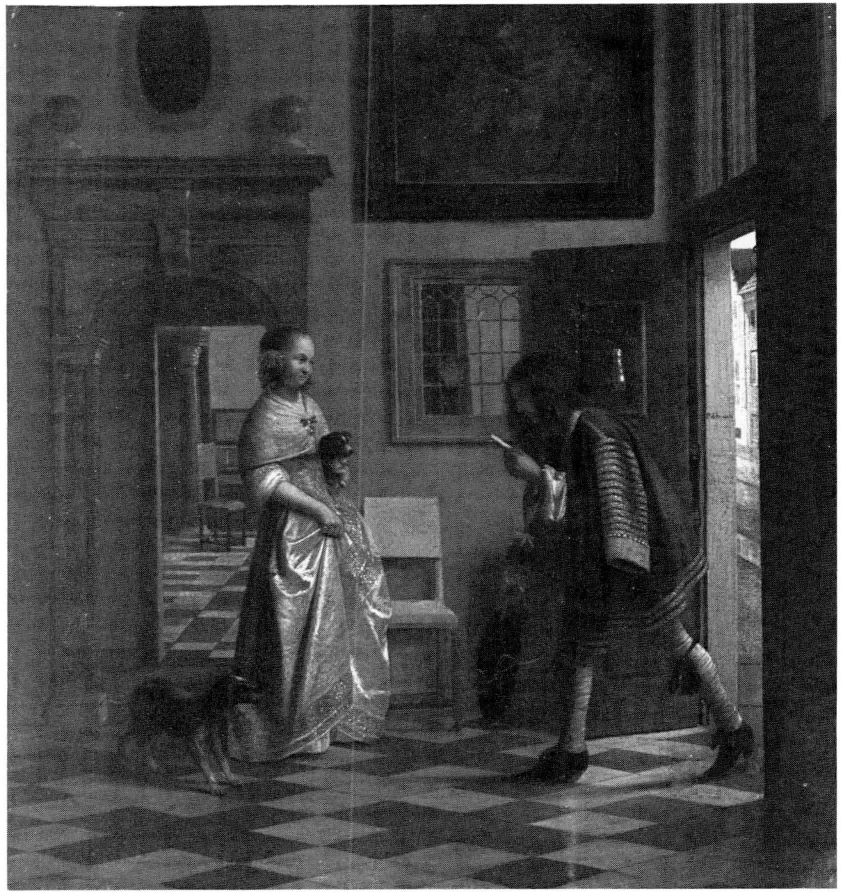

90. Pieter de Hooch, *The Love Letter*. c. 1668-70. Canvas on panel, 57 x 53 cm. Hamburger Kunsthalle

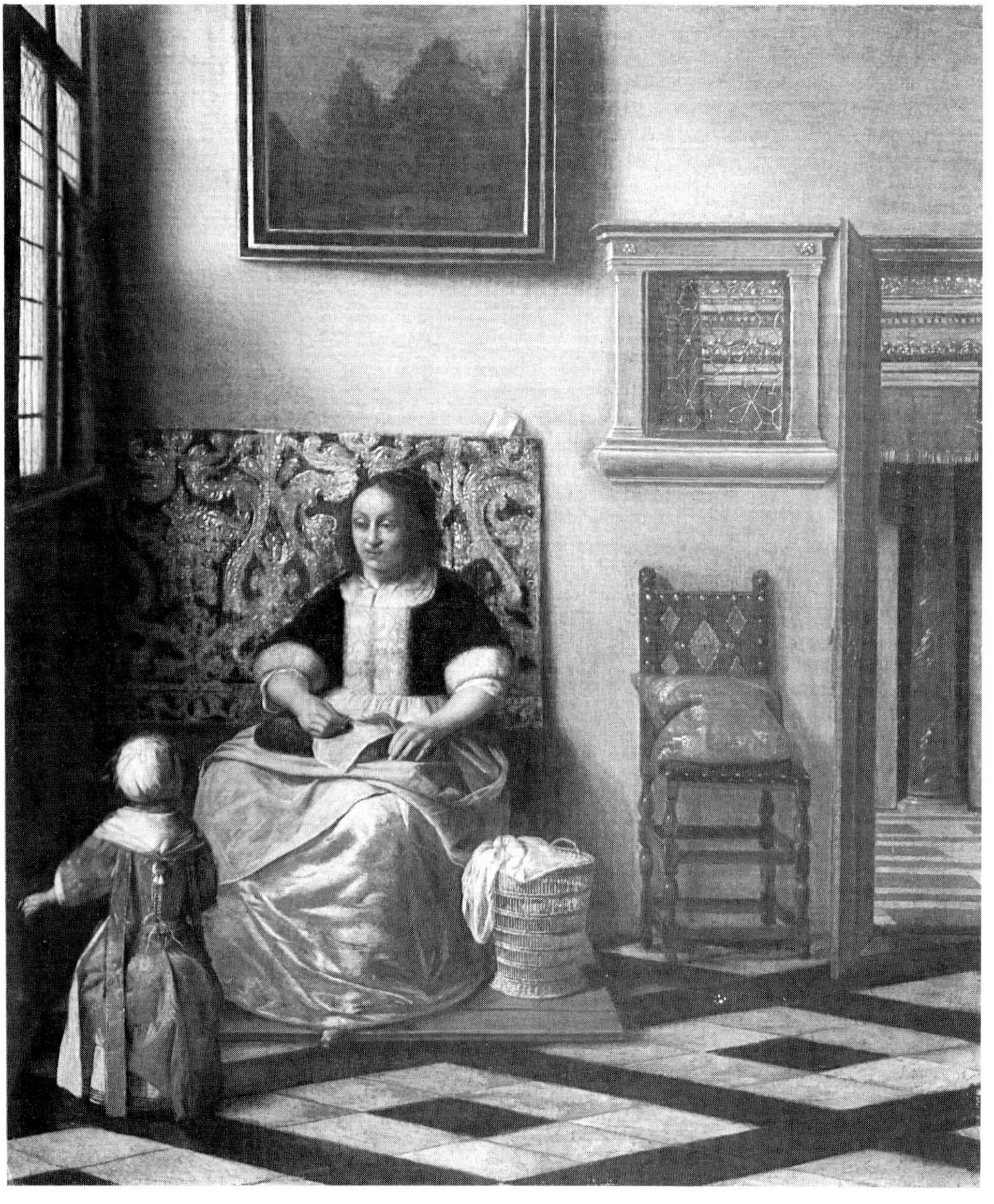

91. Pieter de Hooch, *Lady with Needlework and Child*. c. 1668. Canvas, 55 x 45 cm. Lugano, Thyssen-Bornemisza Collection

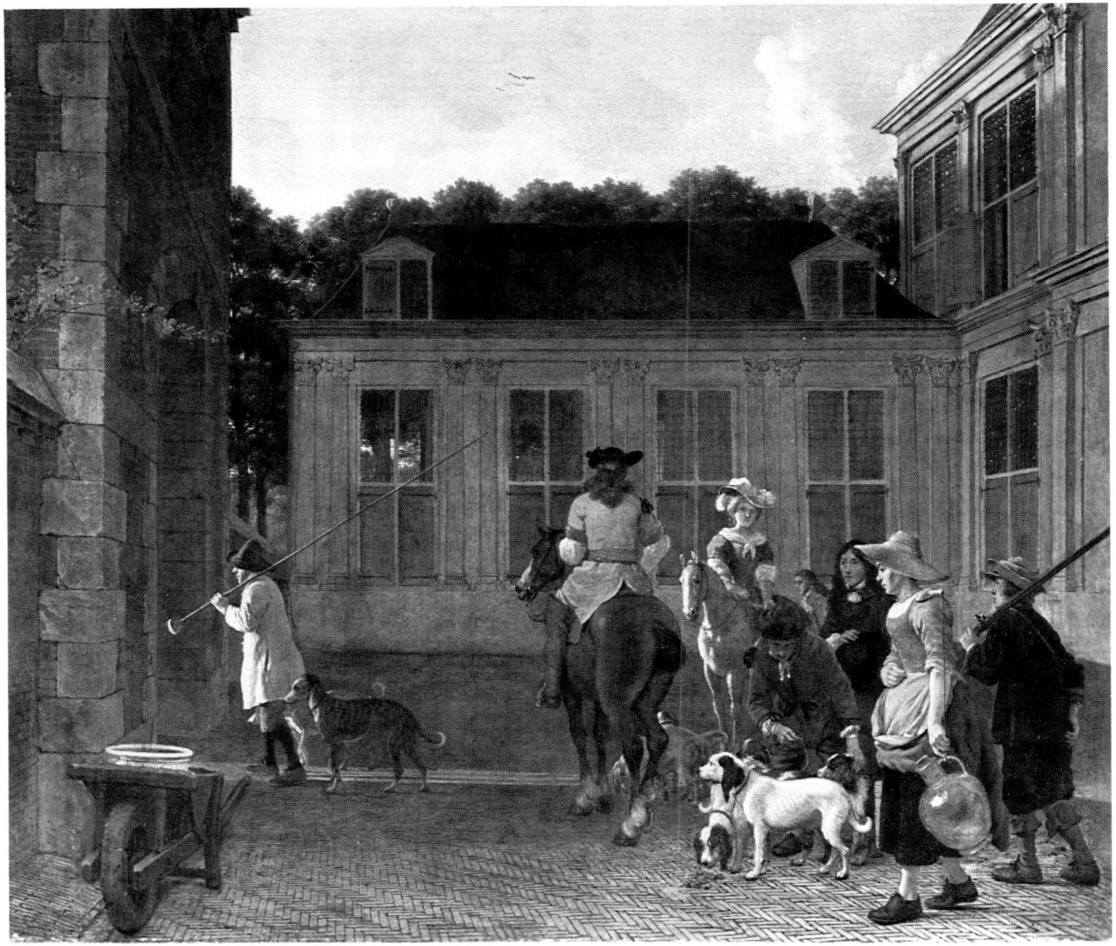

92. *Hunting Party in the Courtyard of a Country House*. 1665-70. Canvas, 68 · 6 x 81 · 3 cm.
The Detroit Institute of Arts, Gift of Mr. and Mrs. James S. Whitcomb, no. 58.169

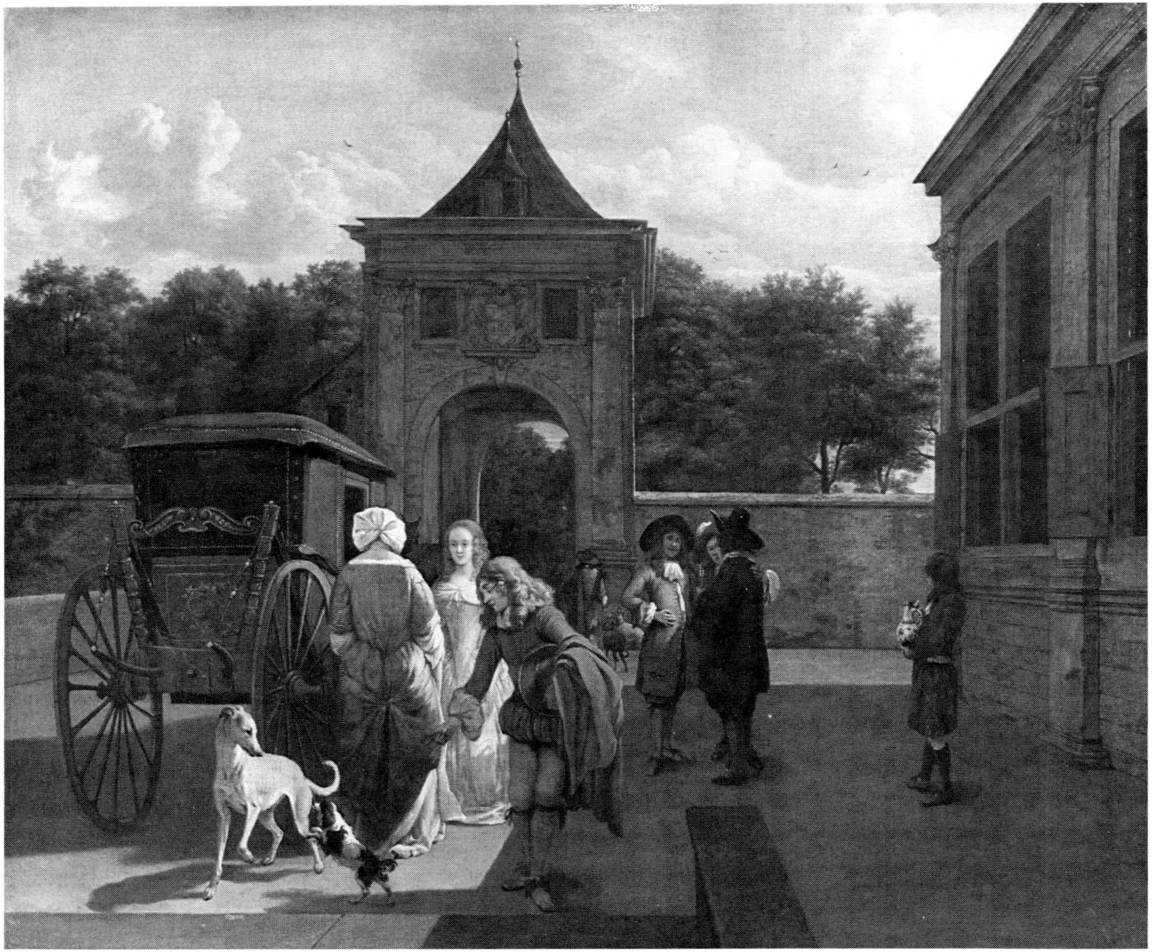

93. *Figures with Coach in a Courtyard*. 1665-70. Canvas, 67 · 5 x 82 cm. Present location unknown

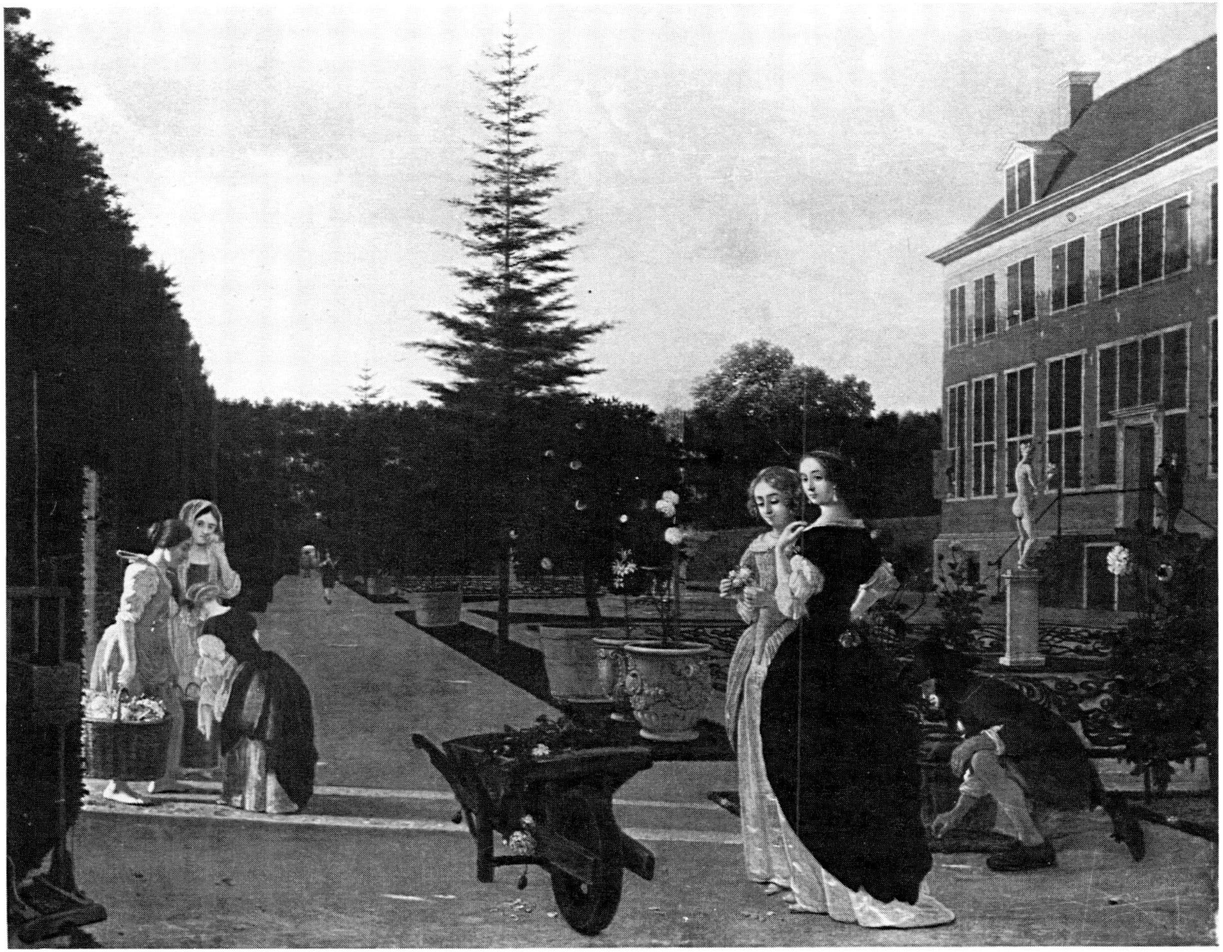

94. *Women in a Garden*, signed "P D Houghe," apparently changed from "L D Jonghe" and dated 1676. Canvas, 82 x 107 cm. Cape Town, Count Labia collection

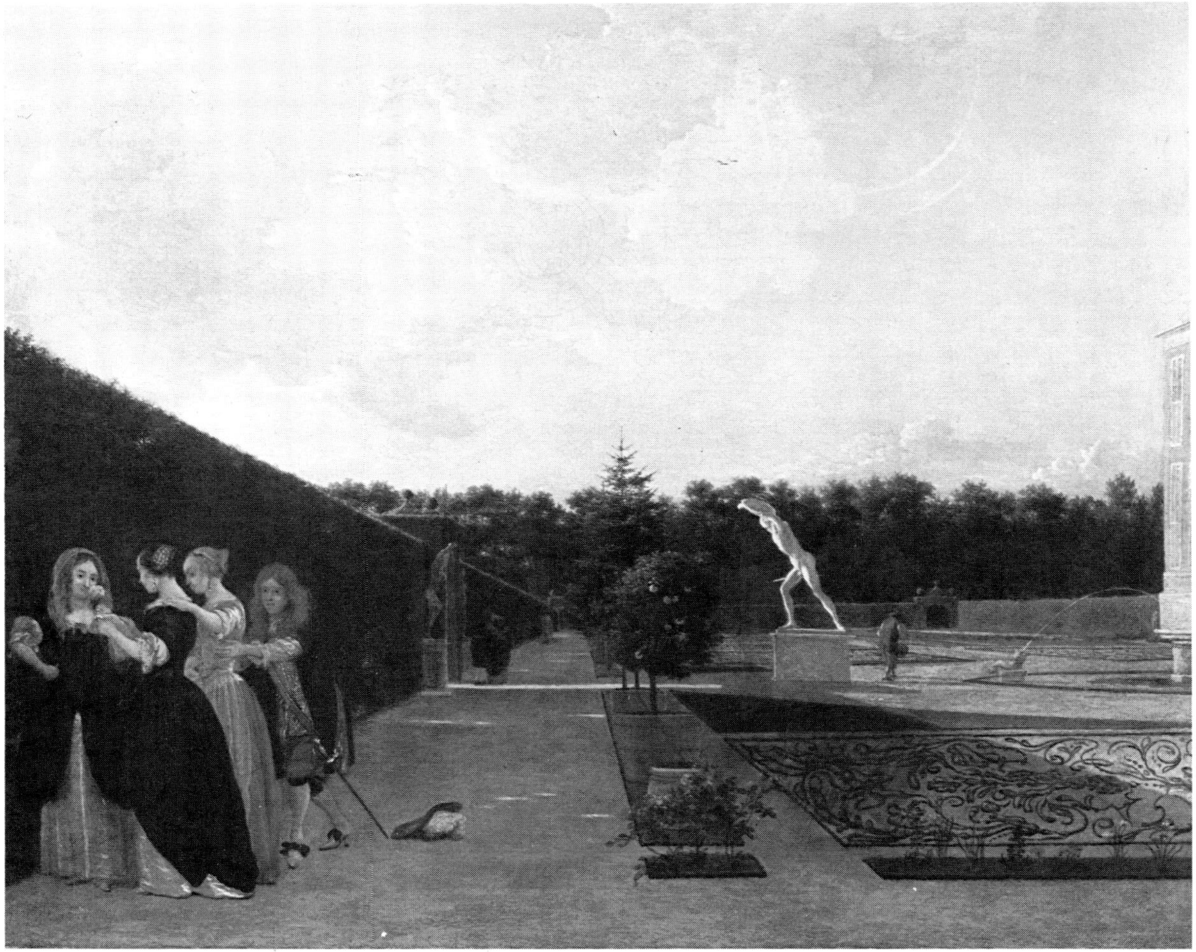

95. *A Formal Garden*. c. 1675. Canvas, 60 · 3 x 74 · 9 cm.
Windsor Castle. Reproduced by gracious permission of Her Majesty Queen Elizabeth II

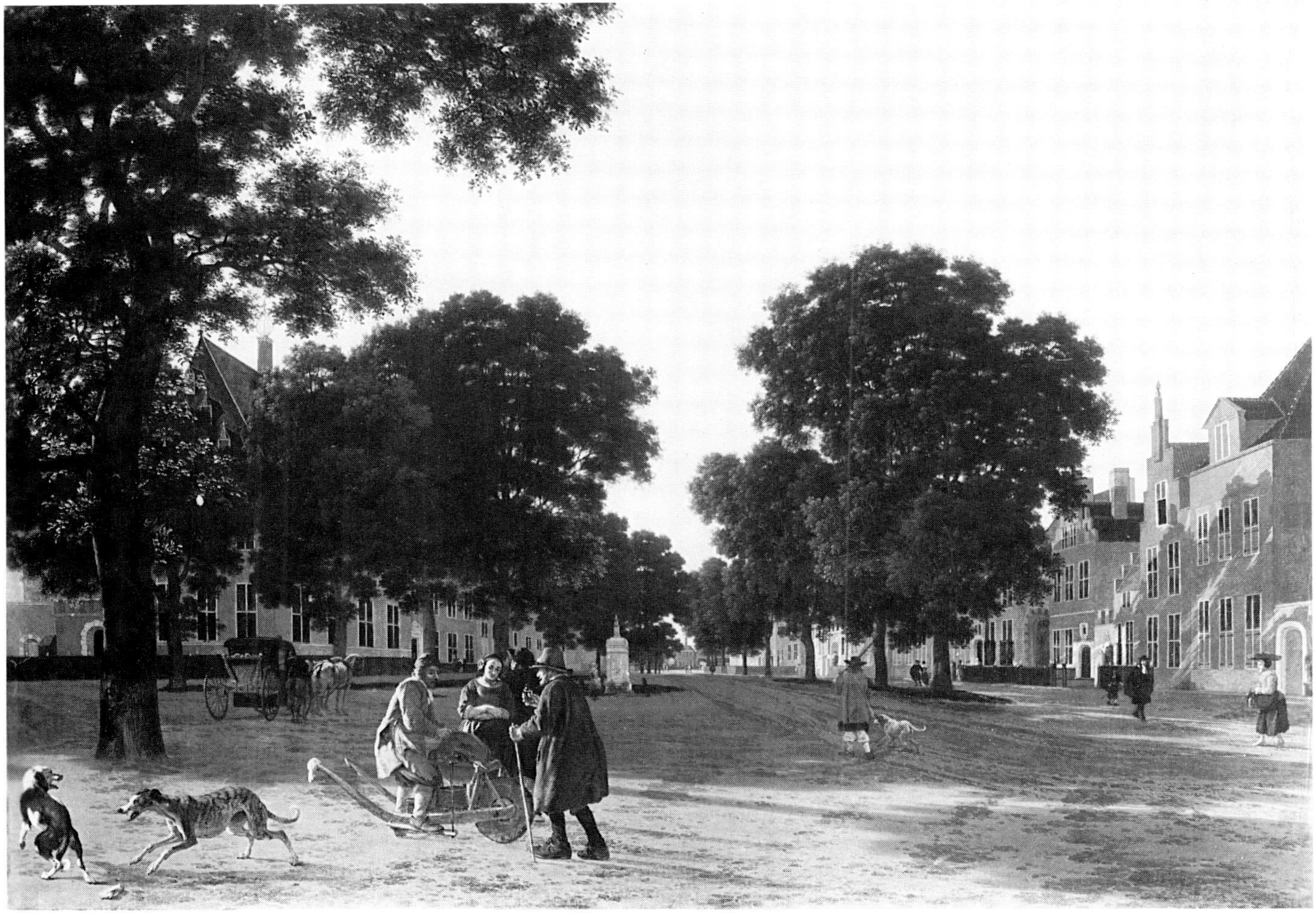

96. *Kneuterdijk in The Hague*. 1665-70. Canvas, 130 x 193 cm. Vienna, Kunsthistorisches Museum

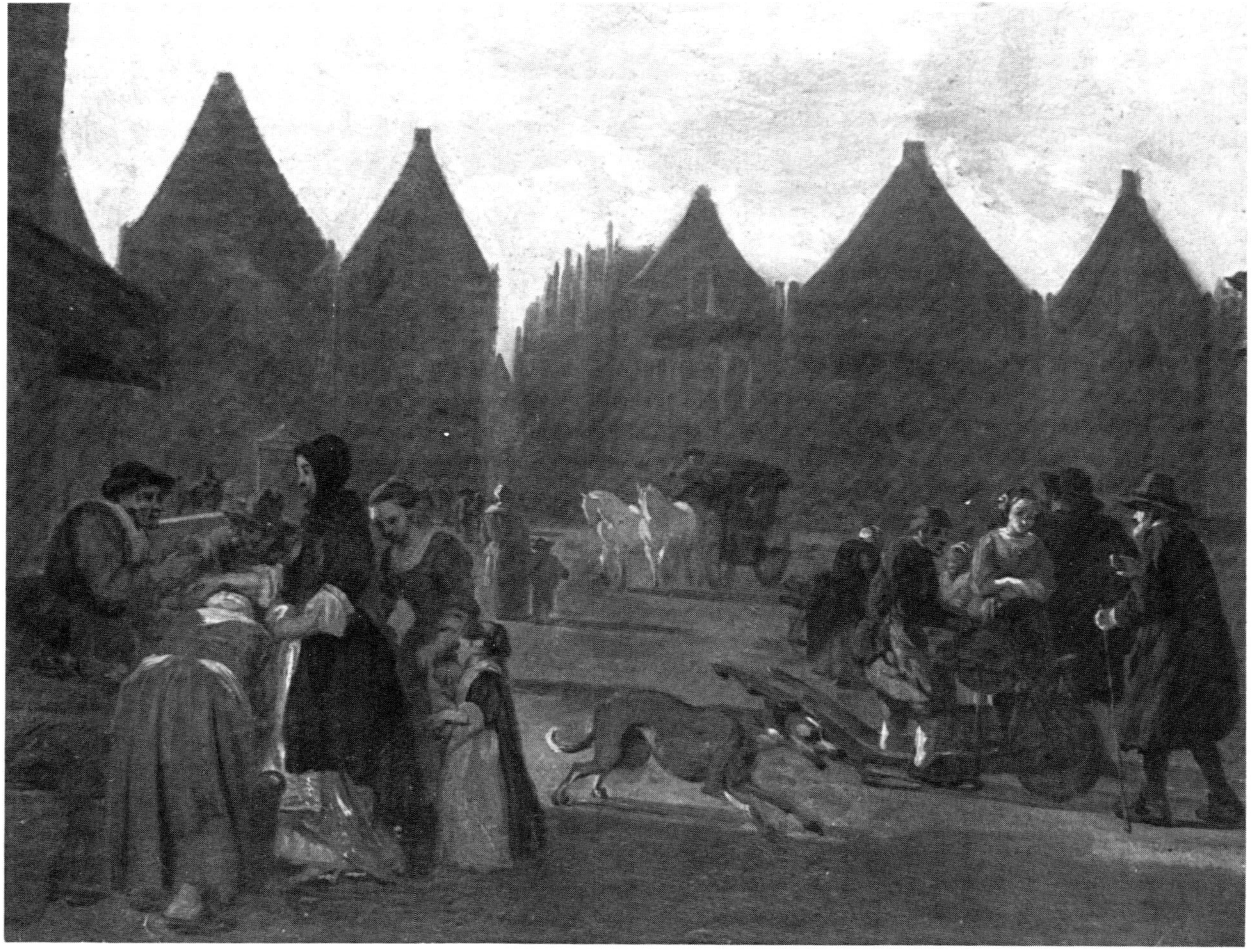

97. *A Market Place*. 1665-70. Oil on paper, 19 · 7 x 26 cm. London, British Museum.
Reproduced by permission of the Trustees of the British Museum

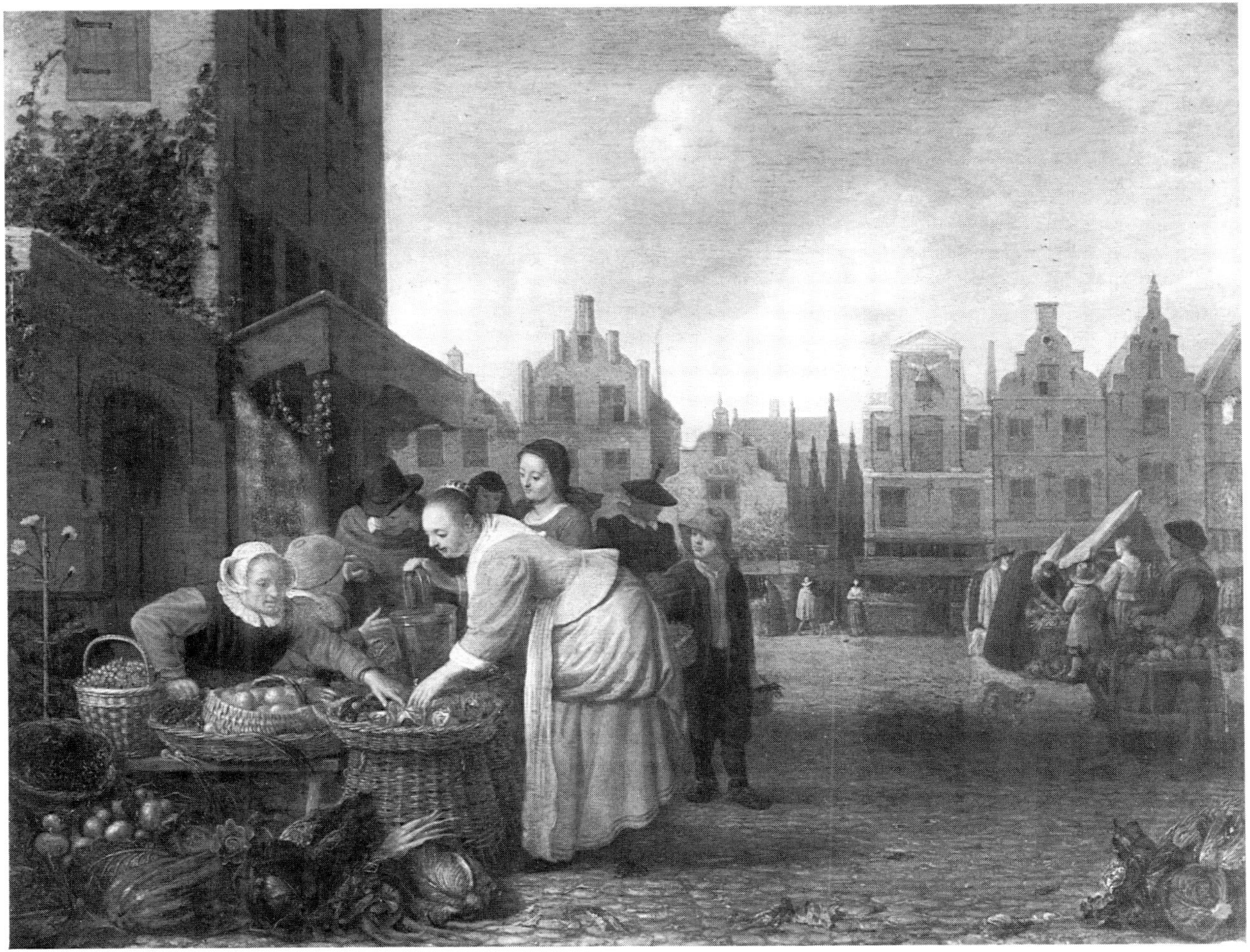

98. Hendrick Sorgh, *The Groote Markt at Rotterdam*, signed and dated 1654. Panel, 30 · 5 x 40 cm. Rotterdam, Museum Boymans-van Beuningen

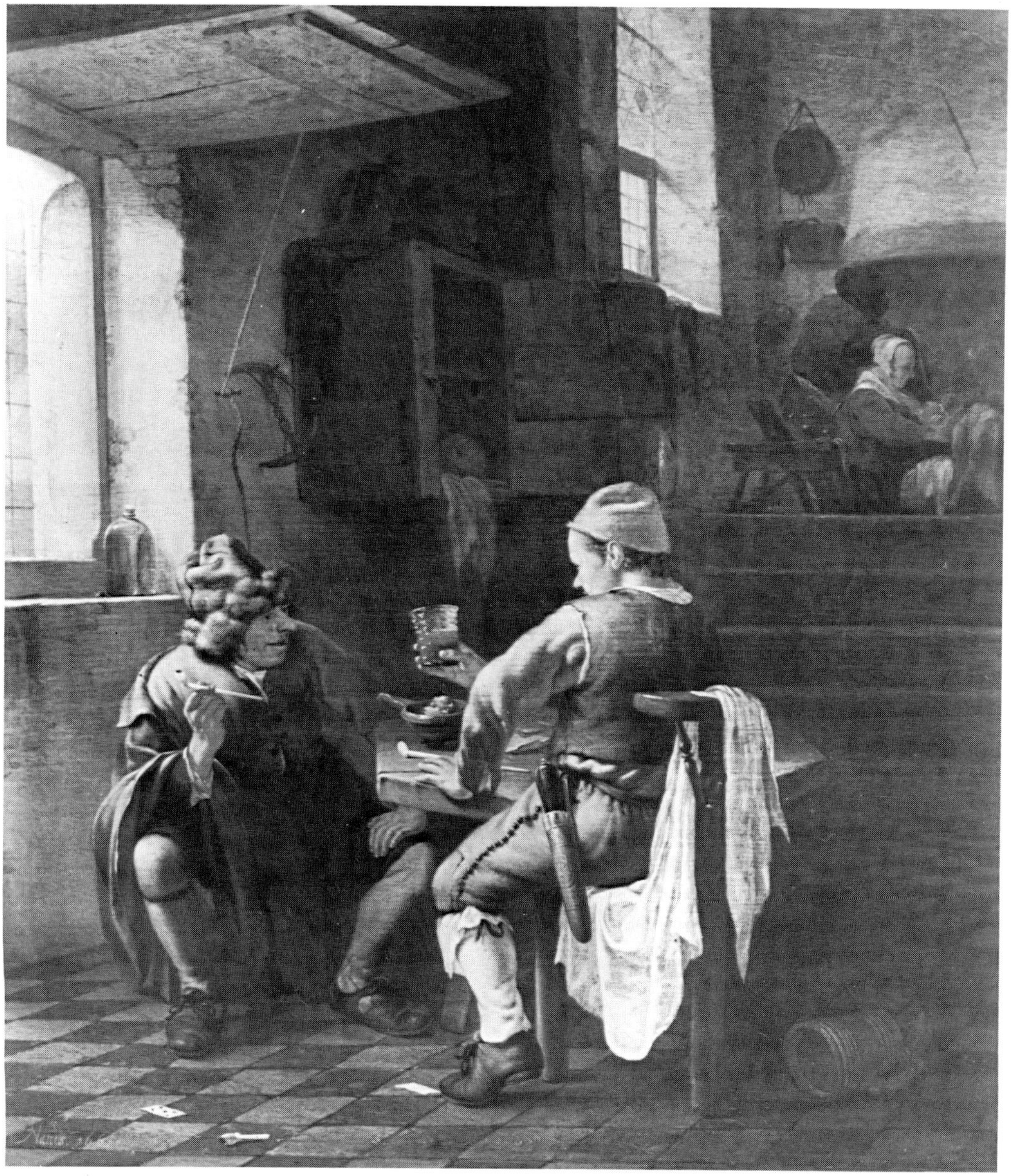

99. Jan Natus, *Interior with Smoker and Drinker*, signed and dated 1661. Panel, 52 x 41 cm. Berlin, Private Collection

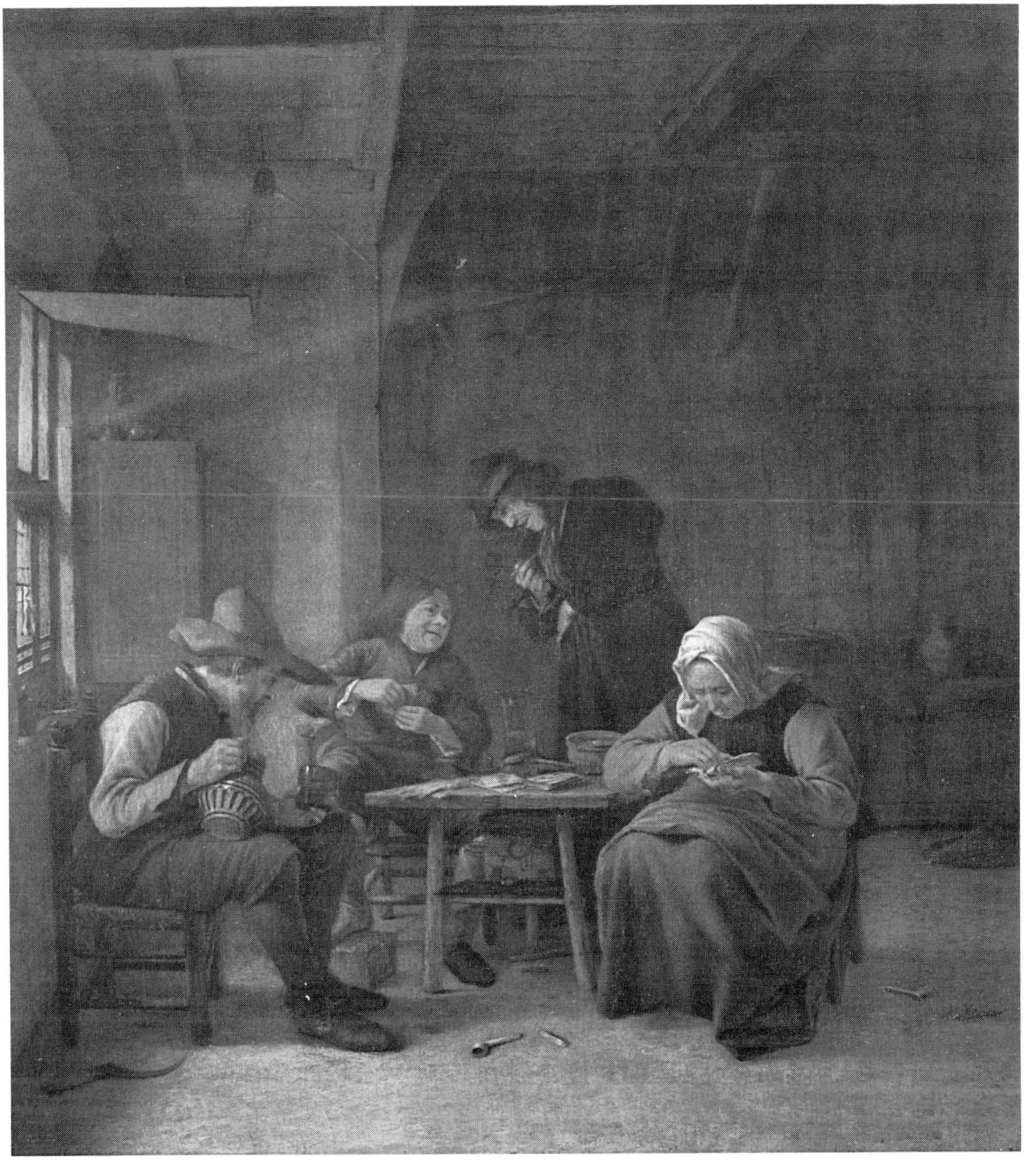

100. Jacob Andries Schaeck, *Interior with Peasants,* signed and dated 166(?). Panel, 34 x 30 cm. Present location unknown. Photograph courtesy of the Rijksbureau voor Kunsthistorische Documentatie, The Hague

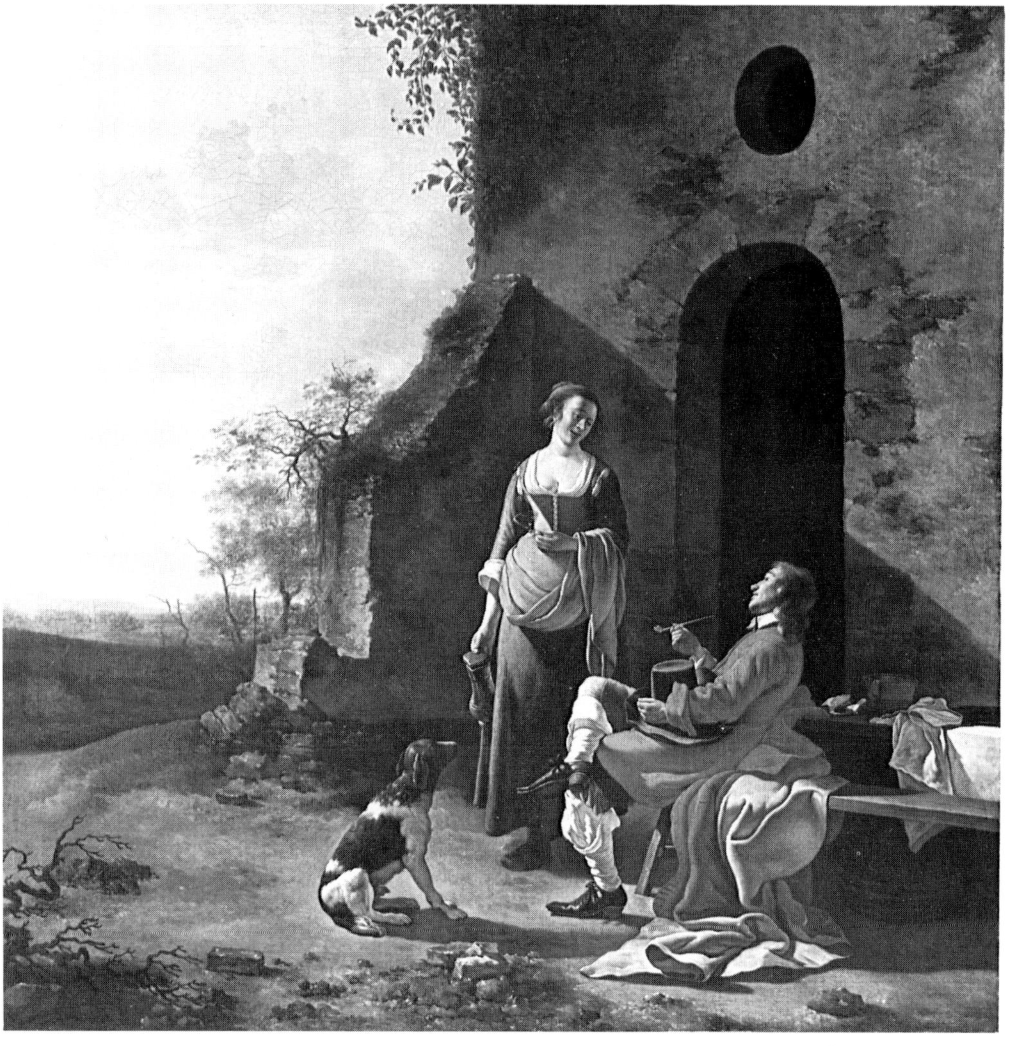

101. Jan van der Meer of Utrecht, *The Entrance of a Tavern,* signed and dated 1653. Canvas, 70 x 66 cm. Paris, Louvre